Key Resources on Teaching, Learning, Curriculum, and Faculty Development

Robert J. Menges
B. Claude Mathis

Key Resources on Teaching, Learning, Curriculum, and Faculty Development

*A Guide to
the Higher Education Literature*

 Jossey-Bass Publishers

San Francisco   •   London   •   1988

KEY RESOURCES ON TEACHING, LEARNING, CURRICULUM,
AND FACULTY DEVELOPMENT
A Guide to the Higher Education Literature
by Robert J. Menges and B. Claude Mathis

Copyright © 1988 by: Jossey-Bass Inc., Publishers
350 Sansome Street
San Francisco, California 94104

&

Jossey-Bass Limited
28 Banner Street
London EC1Y 8QE

Library of Congress Cataloging-in-Publication Data

Menges, Robert J.
  Key resources on teaching, learning, curriculum,
and faculty development.

  (The Jossey-Bass higher education series)
  Includes indexes.
  1. Education, Higher—Bibliography.   2. College
teaching—Bibliography.   3. Universities and colleges—
Curricula—Bibliography.   I. Mathis, B. Claude.
II. Title.   III. Series.
Z5814.U7M45   1988   [LB2322]   016.378   88-42794
ISBN 1-55542-118-0

Manufactured in the United States of America

The paper in this book meets the guidelines for
permanence and durability of the Committee on
Production Guidelines for Book Longevity of the
Council on Library Resources.

JACKET DESIGN BY WILLI BAUM

FIRST EDITION

Code 8838

The Jossey-Bass
Higher Education Series

Consulting Editor
Teaching and Learning

Kenneth E. Eble
University of Utah

Contents

Preface

Compiling this volume of key resources provided a welcome opportunity to explore the higher education literatures that deal with teaching, learning, curriculum, and faculty development. Like scholarship in other academic fields, these literatures can be described as quite diverse in content, highly variable in quality, and sometimes deplorable in style. Unlike work in many other fields, however, most of this scholarship is relatively recent, and much of it is scattered throughout older disciplines. We have attempted to reach back in time to include older, seminal works and to reach widely across disciplines in order to include publications from a variety of fields.

After the initial search, we confronted difficult choices about what should be included. The project had to be less exhaustive than we wished, since publisher's guidelines limited us to approximately 600 annotated items. We excluded works that logically belonged in other compilations of key resources, but we avoided imposing a limit based on recentness of publication date. In our judgment, what may otherwise seem somewhat odd choices are actually anchor points for understanding some aspects of the topics we cover.

Bibliographers are collectors, and collecting is a special kind of scholarship. To collect comprehensively, as bibliographers do, means reviewing much more than the best. "To be a first-rate scholar, you must have a taste for all that is second-rate, third-rate, nth-rate. For a scholar's collection is always comprehensive. Where practicalities limit comprehensiveness, the other great scholastic principle—whimsy—comes into play" (Eisenberg, 1987, p. 22). If some of our choices strike readers as a bit whimsical, we trust that further consideration will reveal how those items fit into the large bibliographic puzzle we have assembled.

Criteria for Inclusion

Omission of a work from this bibliography should not be construed as a criticism. At times the decision not to include a reference was difficult to make. In general, our criteria for including a work in this compilation, and thereby labeling it a key resource, emphasize its frequency of citation or its integrative function as a stepping-stone toward new understanding.

Specifically, our selections include:

1. Major reference works, such as bibliographies, indexes, data bases, and periodicals. We have cited these publications not only for the information they contain but also because they help the reader go beyond primary sources. They become keys to literature and data not described in this book.
2. Works of general usefulness to researchers and practitioners. Works that merely reiterate viewpoints were omitted. Publications included are those we feel point the way most effectively to additional resources.
3. Works that clearly advance the boundaries of the field of higher education and are themselves theoretical contributions to the organization of the field. These touchstones provide the frames of reference for shaping opinion and research.
4. Works that contain ample and comprehensive reference lists rather than less well documented publications. Despite some notable exceptions, we sought to include sources that provide the reader with sufficient documentation to continue pursuing a topic beyond the information provided by this book.
5. Books and articles in which works are cited that might have been included in this volume if not for the constraints of manuscript length. Rather than include articles that represent condensations of data and opinion contained in a larger book, we usually cite the more complete source.
6. Highly visible works and works that a student or scholar would probably need to investigate a specific field.

7. Very few sources such as speeches, dissertations, and project reports, although subsequent publications based on these sources may be included. Many reports of institutional research contain much that is worthwhile and are available through the ERIC system. Including this body of information would have taken space better filled with volumes from the published literature.

8. Works that are generally available at libraries or through information retrieval systems such as ERIC.

9. Works published or in production by mid 1987.

Using This Book

We have selected from the literature about four-year colleges and universities in compiling this book. Several literatures are excluded because they are the subject of other volumes in the Jossey-Bass key resources series. These are works that deal primarily with community colleges, with the administration and organization of higher education, and with student personnel services. We have included a few works on graduate and professional education because they make more general contributions to knowledge about college and university teaching. Each of these is annotated in the chapter and subsection of the book most appropriate to its content and listed under the entry "Graduate and Professional Education" in the subject index at the back of the book.

The table of contents displays our organizational scheme. Chapters in this volume address the following topics: the origin of the field of higher education; teaching; learning; curriculum; faculty and staff development; periodicals, bibliographies, and other helpful resources; and the future evolution of the field. The book concludes with a name index and a subject index. The name index includes the authors of works annotated in this volume—including authors of chapters in edited collections—and other authors mentioned in the annotations.

We do not consider teaching, learning, curriculum, and faculty development generic categories that stand alone, independent of each other. We view them as interdependent in their effects on the process of college and university education. For that reason, many works could have been placed in more than one chapter; however, we chose to annotate each work in only one and to cross-list it in other chapters to which it is relevant.

In each chapter the annotations are organized into subsections and alphabetized by author. Annotations vary in length: in each, we attempt to provide readers with an understanding of the work's content while using the fewest possible words. Readers should not assume that the quality or importance of a work is signaled by the annotation's length. About 10 percent of the entries are marked by stars, which indicate that we consider these works to be seminal contributions to the literature on higher education. We accept full responsibility for these designations and are aware that awarding stars is, at best, a matter of informed judgment.

This book is meant to be used primarily by readers who seek some idea of the dimensions of the field of higher education. Many users will browse; the organization of the annotations, together with the introductory statements, is meant to encourage this type of inquiry. Other readers may wish to use the book as a reference. The indexes and cross-references should expedite this type of use. Readers may approach this book in several different ways: some may begin by skimming annotations in sections of special interest to them, others may use the name and subject indexes to locate relevant entries, and those who wish to start with a small but representative selection of the entries may review the starred annotations or the even more selective list included in Chapter One.

We take full responsibility for the selection and annotation of each work included in this volume as well as the introductory comments that begin each chapter. We are fully aware that condensing another person's work into an abstract of moderate length is a game rarely won. If there is praise for doing this right, we welcome it. If there is blame for missing the point, we accept it and welcome the correction of our mistakes.

Acknowledgments

We acknowledge the able and dedicated assistance of our colleague Patricia Terando. Without her skill in using the word processor and bibliography software to compile the manuscript, this book might never have reached its readers.

We also acknowledge with gratitude the many people working at the Northwestern University library and other major academic libraries who quietly and efficiently found materials we were unable to locate ourselves. The reference and interlibrary loan staff at Northwestern University handled our requests with patience and reliability. During the time we spent working at several other campuses, we especially appreciated the assistance of staff members at Cubberly Library, Stanford University; Gutman Library, Harvard University; and Milbank Memorial Library, Teachers College, Columbia University. Finally, reviewers engaged by Jossey-Bass offered constructive suggestions that improved our work.

Evanston, Illinois Robert J. Menges
September 1988 B. Claude Mathis

Reference

Eisenberg, E. *The Recording Angel.* New York: McGraw-Hill, 1987.

The Authors

Robert J. Menges is professor of education and social policy at Northwestern University, program director of Northwestern's Center for the Teaching Professions, and a fellow of the American Psychological Association. He received his B.A. degree (1960) in psychology from Gettysburg College, his M.A. degree (1963) in psychology from Boston University, and his Ed.D. degree (1967) in the college teaching of psychology from Teachers College, Columbia University. Previously Menges was a member of the faculty at the University of Illinois, Urbana-Champaign, and an instructor at Teachers College, Columbia University.

Menges's scholarly work deals with teaching and learning in postsecondary education. Currently he is investigating the effects of feedback to teachers and studying ways of increasing the involvement and responsibility of students in their learning. His publications include *Psychological Studies of Clergymen* (1965, with J. E. Dittes), *The Intentional Teacher* (1977), a chapter entitled "Instructional Methods" in *The Modern American College* (1981, edited by A. W. Chickering), and "Barriers to the Progress of Women and Minority Faculty," in the *Journal of Higher Education* (1983, with W. J. Exum). Menges also has produced a series of videotapes, "College Classroom Vignettes," which have been widely used in teaching improvement programs.

B. Claude Mathis is professor of education and social policy and of psychology at Northwestern University. He is also currently director of Northwestern's Center for the Teaching Professions, an appointment he has held since the founding of the center in 1969. He received his B.A. (1949) and M.A. (1950) degrees in psychology from Texas Christian University and his Ph.D. degree (1956) in educational psychology from the University of Texas. Mathis was associate dean of the Graduate School at Northwestern University from 1964 to 1969 and associate dean of the School of Education from 1970 to 1978. From 1983 to 1986 he was director of Northwestern's Lilly Endowment Post-Doctoral Teaching Awards Program. He is a fellow of the American Psychological Association.

Mathis's major research and scholarly interests have been in the areas of teaching and learning, faculty development, academic careers, and adult development. His experience includes extensive consultation with colleges and universities in the areas of faculty development and the improvement of teaching. His publications include *Psychological Foundations of Education: Learning and Teaching* (1970, with J. Cotton and L. Sechrest), *Profiles in College Teaching* (1972, with W. McGaghie), and *Teaching: A Force for Change in Higher Education* (1974, with S. Holbrook).

Key Resources on Teaching, Learning, Curriculum, and Faculty Development

1

Overview of Four Literatures: Teaching, Learning, Curriculum, and Faculty Development

Higher education in the United States has been nurtured, developed, described, evaluated, and otherwise reported in a literature that has grown exponentially during the past thirty years. Contributions occur in many disciplines and often appear in obscure sources. The task of determining key resources about students, faculty, teaching, and the curriculum that can be generally agreed upon by a majority of readers places an impossible burden on the literature and those who judge it. Citations selected for this volume are those that we think are important because of the issues they present and the ideas they contain. Our selection criteria are enumerated in the preface.

Higher Education as a Field of Study

The richness and variety of scholarship contained in this representative collection should help dispel the notion that higher education is a derivative field of study, existing only as a subspecialty of the social science disciplines. While our field's scholarly methods may be those of history, sociology, psychology, anthropology, political science, or economics, the ideas and rhetoric belong to an energetic group of scholars who have helped define an independent field of study. The emerging independence of the field

1

is indicated by the increasing number of doctoral programs available nationally to prepare specialists in higher education. This growth has paralleled the development of centers for research on higher education at research universities. Specialists are being prepared whose training combines the best that the disciplines have to offer with the unique problems and perspectives of higher education as a distinct field of concentration for research.

One might expect breadth in the literature surveyed here, if only because these topics are so diverse. Even by limiting the resources in this book to four-year colleges and universities, the scope of problems and issues, and the diversity of institutional cultures, remains immense. Our topics should not be regarded as independent domains of discourse, each existing in its own mutually exclusive universe. We view teaching, learning, curriculum, and faculty development as elements in a universe that might be described as educational processes in higher education. These elements are multiplicative rather than additive in the equation of education. Without each of them, that is, without teaching, learning, a curriculum, and a faculty, the education that students receive in colleges and universities would revolve largely around incidental experience. Because of the interdependence of these topics, many of the references could be classified under several rubrics in the table of contents. Thus, we list the more far-reaching items in more than one section.

The items in each category represent a considerable span of time. A simple solution would have been to place a limit on the number of years to be covered by selecting only resources for the past ten, or even twenty, years. Assuring contemporary relevance would have permitted more extensive coverage of the available literature from that time period, and one might argue that worthwhile ideas would be replicated in one form or another in the most recent publications. We think that scholarship in higher education is left the poorer, however, by omitting items that anchor a particular concept. Undergraduate study is one example. The inclusion of Eliot's inaugural address as president of Harvard in 1869 (no. 402) sets the stage for an approach to undergraduate education that endures to this day. What better way to start the journey of understanding than to begin with an authentic historical precedent?

Another example is Cardinal Newman's *The Idea of a University* (no. 418). While his thoughts about academe were first advanced in the 1850s, the ideal he expressed then remains a strong force anchoring much of the debate about liberal education and general studies.

Some citations may appear to relate only tangentially to their categories. For example, the works by Bok (nos. 387, 388) at first seem to be relevant only to a collection about administration and administrators in higher education. On further thought, however, these books present distinctive views about the contemporary world of universities. His call for reform at the classroom level and his support for the involvement of higher education in the solution of social problems are but two ideas that point the way for change in teaching and curricula. The fact that the president of Harvard University supports these ideas lends them special credibility. Another example is the book by Schrecker (no. 608) detailing events in academe during the 1950s when the late Senator McCarthy and his investigations invaded the ivory tower. The legacy of this episode in the history of the academic professions still makes academicians uneasy in the face of congressional investigations. It also heightens sensitivity to issues of academic freedom and faculty accountability. Her book is not a study of the academic professions, but it delineates a time of trouble and soul-searching for both faculty and the organizations that represented them. Similarly, the book by Daniels, Kahn-Hut, and Associates (no. 494) presents multiple perspectives about the student-faculty strike at San Francisco State College in 1968. The content has implications for faculty and student rights, curriculum, and teaching; yet its central theme is about none of these. Readers will find other examples of items that seem to fit nowhere, yet are relevant everywhere.

Publication Patterns

Publication patterns vary for the major topics of this volume. Most articles about teaching are published in journals about college teaching and learning. The same applies to the curriculum. Articles and books about faculty development are distributed among journals in a much more eclectic manner and reflect the specific emphasis of faculty development programs. Publications in higher education are also separated by the divisions of study in doctoral programs for higher education. Labels of specialization defining professional associations in higher education reinforce the boundaries that separate published efforts.

To view higher education as having fixed boundaries between its intellectual subsystems is, of course, an arbitrary although convenient way to divide the study of higher education. We all recognize that to write about the curriculum is by implication also to write about teaching and about faculty.

Development of higher education as a field of study parallels the great growth of the higher education enterprise in the United States since 1945 when World War II ended. Specializations in fields of knowledge often emerge from social needs and from the confluence of social forces that create a market for knowledge about specific institutions. This growth and its resulting focus on higher education as an independent field of study can be traced by the creation of publications devoted specifically to some aspect of higher education. Before 1945, the major journal for articles about higher education was the *Journal of Higher Education,* which introduced its first volume in 1930. *Sociology of Education* (1927) was another early source. Until 1945, the literature of higher education, for the most part, was found in journals containing articles about education in general. Of course, books about higher education were published, but they were often commentaries on personal experiences or analyses of events without the benefit of primary research data. Beginning in 1946 with the first volume of the *Journal of General Education,* the field of higher education began to establish its identity through publications focusing on specific aspects of higher education. *College Teaching* was introduced in 1953 as *Improving College and University Teaching.* In 1959, the Association of American Colleges began publishing its *Bulletin* as the journal entitled *Liberal Education.* Federal support for research in higher education led to the establishment of the ERIC Clearinghouse on Higher Education in 1968. Its research reports series started in 1972 with the cooperation, first, of the American Association for Higher Education and, more recently, of the Association for the Study of Higher Education. The reports reveal how the field of higher education began to solidify research boundaries and more finely hone specializations for researchers. These developments were accompanied by the establishment in 1967 of Jossey-Bass Publishers and its subsequent emergence as the major publishing house devoted to works about higher education.

The *Chronicle of Higher Education* appeared in 1966, giving higher education its own newspaper. In 1969, *Change: The Magazine of Higher Learning* was created for general commentary about higher education. Other specialized journals that began publication during the decade of the 1970s include *Higher Education* (1971), *Instructional Science* (1972), *Teaching Sociology* (1973), *Research in Higher Education* (1973), *Teaching of Psychology* (1974), and *Studies in Higher Education* (1976). The series of volumes sponsored by the Carnegie Commission on Higher Education helped to disseminate research about specific issues in higher education during the post–World War II period. The Carnegie Council on Policy Studies in Higher Education has also sponsored a number of books and reports that extend the work of the Carnegie Commission.

Master Key Resources

Although institutional growth in higher education has diminished, the growth of the literature continues unabated. Much of this literature constitutes worthwhile contributions, although an increasingly large amount displays the redundancy typical of social sciences as they move toward professional adulthood.

The number of the accumulated publications, even since 1960, together with their breadth of coverage, makes it difficult to recommend how a reader should approach the literature covered in this volume. One might begin with the starred key resources because we judge them to be of particular importance. For readers wishing an even more economical way to sample the items covered by this volume, we have prepared the following shorter list. These twenty-one items might be thought of as "master key" resources. Each of them opens to readers not only its own contents but also leads beyond itself to many other resources. Some of these items are collections, and each has an extensive bibliography. Readers will not go wrong by using them as introductions to the topics of teaching, learning, curriculum, and faculty development in higher education. For more complete descriptions of these master keys, see the complete numbered entry.

> Bergquist, William H., and Phillips, Steven R. "Components of an Effective Faculty Development Program." (1975) (no. 476)
> This approach to faculty development, highly influential during the 1970s, differentiates three dimensions: organizational development, instructional development, and personal development.
> Bowen, Howard R. *Investment in Learning: The Individual and Social Value of American Higher Education.* (1977) (no. 257)
> According to this economist's ambitious synthesis of research, higher education is generally well worth its substantial costs.
> Bowen, Howard R., and Schuster, Jack H. *American Professors: A National Resource Imperiled.* (1986) (no. 550)
> Demographic, economic, and interview data lead to concerns that the academic profession is likely to suffer a significant loss of talent unless its quality becomes a matter of national priority.
> Boyer, Ernest L. *College: The Undergraduate Experience in America.* (1987) (no. 258)
> Most publicized of the mid 1980s critiques of postsecondary education, this study's visibility was further enhanced by its support from The Carnegie Foundation for the Advancement of Teaching.
> Braskamp, Larry A.; Brandenburg, Dale C.; and Ory, John C. *Evaluating Teaching Effectiveness: A Practical Guide.* (1984) (no. 150)
> This guidebook discusses varieties of information for evaluating college teaching and gives advice about how each kind of information is best used.
> Chickering, Arthur W., and Associates. *The Modern Amer-*

ican College: Responding to the New Realities of Diverse Students and a Changing Society. (1981) (no. 263)
In forty-two chapters, students, faculty, curriculum, and other topics are viewed through a life cycle developmental perspective.

Conrad, Clifton F. (ed.). *ASHE Reader on Academic Programs in Colleges and Universities.* (1985) (no. 398)
These twenty-one selections whet the intellectual appetite for further investigation of the sources from which they are drawn.

Dunkin, Michael J. "Research on Teaching in Higher Education." (1986) (no. 224)
This excellent review covers what is known from contemporary research on college teaching and identifies issues that deserve further research.

Eble, Kenneth E. *The Craft of Teaching: A Guide to Mastering the Professor's Art.* (2nd ed.) (1988) (no. 14)
This engaging, humanistic view of teaching provides realistic and specific advice for any college teacher.

Epstein, Joseph (ed.). *Masters: Portraits of Great Teachers.* (1981) (no. 52)
Sixteen eminent persons provide elegant descriptions of the teachers who most influenced them.

Finkelstein, Martin J. (ed.). *ASHE Reader on Faculty Issues in Colleges and Universities.* (1985) (no. 497)
These twenty-five reprinted selections provide a convenient overview of writings about the work and the career patterns of faculty.

Fuhrmann, Barbara S., and Grasha, Anthony F. *A Practical Handbook for College Teachers.* (1983) (no. 18)
Research-based advice is combined with practice-based exercises in this treatment of the day-to-day realities of college teaching.

Knefelkamp, Lee; Widick, Carole; and Parker, Clyde A. (eds.). *Applying New Developmental Findings.* (1978) (no. 289)
Seminal theories of social, cognitive, and moral development are summarized and applied to college students.

Levine, Arthur. *Handbook on Undergraduate Curriculum.* (1978) (no. 412)

This readable reference volume is basic to understanding current and historical curricular trends.

McKeachie, Wilbert J. *Teaching Tips: A Guide for the Beginning College Teacher.* (8th ed.) (1986) (no. 36)

Blending scholarship and practicality, these tips are of value to teachers in higher education regardless of level of experience.

Mathis, B. Claude. "Faculty Development." (1982) (no. 522)

Theory and research are synthesized in the first *Encyclopedia of Educational Research* article about faculty development.

Milton, Ohmer; Pollio, Howard R.; and Eison, James A. *Making Sense of College Grades: Why the Grading System Does Not Work and What Can Be Done About It.* (1986) (no. 368)

Suggestions for reforming grading practices are offered in light of the authors' conclusions that grades determine what and how students learn.

Parker, Clyde A., and Schmidt, Janet A. "Effects of College Experience." (1982) (no. 299)

This review of studies of the impact of college summarizes findings and critiques the prevailing metaphors underlying much of the research.

Riesman, David. *On Higher Education: The Academic Enterprise in an Era of Rising Student Consumerism.* (1981) (no. 423)

The author describes the decline of faculty influence and documents the rising influence of students; greater consumer influence brings on an accompanying threat to academic standards.

Rudolph, Frederick. *Curriculum: A History of the American Undergraduate Course of Study Since 1636.* (1977) (no. 424)

A lucid and critical history of the curriculum ranging from the founding of Harvard into the 1970s.

Sanford, Nevitt (ed.). *The American College: A Psychological and Social Interpretation of the Higher Learning.* (1962) (no. 310)
The twenty-nine chapters in this psychological and social view of students and institutions were highly influential and set the tone for much subsequent scholarship.

Keeping Current

It is possible to keep reasonably up-to-date with the literature in these fields by regular examination of about a dozen items. We recommend the following diversified journals, research reports, and annuals.

For carefully reviewed scholarship, see the *Journal of Higher Education, Research in Higher Education,* and the *Review of Higher Education.* For reviews and syntheses of research, see the annual *Higher Education: Handbook of Theory and Research* and the periodic *ASHE-ERIC Reports.* Annual annotated listings of significant articles and books are promised by the *Higher Education Bibliography Yearbook* (no. 662).

For writings more applied in emphasis, see the monthlies *American Association for Higher Education Bulletin (AAHE Bulletin)* and *Change: The Magazine of Higher Learning;* the quarterly *College Teaching;* and the annual *To Improve the Academy,* sponsored by the Professional and Organizational Development Network in Higher Education. The Cooperative Institutional Research Program's freshman survey (no. 250) provides a yearly report of attitudes and demographics of students new to higher education. Finally, the Jossey-Bass annual catalogue is a good single source for representative new publications.

2

Teaching and
Teaching Effectiveness

The effects of teachers on students have been characterized in many ways. Teachers may inspire and motivate. They may direct and indoctrinate, coach and demonstrate, guide and facilitate. Inescapably, teachers serve as models. Sometimes they are also powerful agents of socialization. Teachers are always perceived as authority figures, and they may choose to allocate that authority almost exclusively to themselves or to share it in some measure with learners.

One reason the study of teaching is so complex and so difficult is that each of these apparently contradictory characterizations is potentially consistent with "good" teaching. Effectiveness in teaching depends not on a single characteristic but on the appropriate fit among many variables. These variables include the purposes of the teaching-learning encounter, characteristics and preferences of teachers and learners, circumstances of the teaching-learning activities and of the larger environment in which those activities occur, and methods used for determining success of the teaching and of the learning. Effective teachers monitor and manage all of these variables, ensure their consistency, and fashion them into a pleasing whole. The result of this complex process is the creation of circumstances in which appropriate learning is increasingly likely to occur (Menges, 1981).

This notion of teaching is very broad. It encompasses both mediated, distance education and face-to-face classroom instruction. It includes many outcomes beyond acquisition of subject matter knowledge, such as competence in communication, facility with problem finding and problem solving, ability to manage time efficiently, and skills of effective studying.

The key resources in this chapter can help teachers and researchers think more creatively and systematically about teaching-learning processes in higher education. These resources discuss what successful teachers do and how they view what they do, propose various activities intended to bring about particular learning outcomes, and describe techniques for evaluating those activities and outcomes.

This chapter has five sections. The first section includes items that address teaching, broadly defined. In these resources, teachers at all levels of experience can find research-based advice about the responsibilities and roles typical of contemporary college and university teaching, and researchers will find many unsolved problems that are amenable to further investigation. The second section contains anecdotal descriptions by successful teachers, some quite prominent, of how they teach and how they think about teaching. The third section offers guidance for planning instruction along with descriptions and evaluations of particular instructional techniques. The fourth section covers procedures for assessing the success of instruction, such as course and teacher evaluation systems, and resources about other activities and programs for improving teaching. Research on college teaching is voluminous, and we devote the final section to articles that review existing research and discuss issues about conducting research on teaching.

Guidelines for Teaching

From time to time, all teachers need advice about the problems and challenges of their work. Research-based advice about teaching has a venerable history. It was in 1899, for example, that William James published his *Talks to Teachers*. Like those lectures, much of the subsequent literature on teaching centers on precollege education. The extensive and provocative *Models of Teaching* (Joyce and Weil, 1986, no. 30) is a convenient introduction to precollege work. The third edition of the *Handbook of Research on Teaching* is a massive research compendium, but only one of the thirty-five chapters is devoted to postsecondary education (Dunkin, 1986, no. 224).

Early research on college teaching drew mostly from the psychology of the time. Eaton (1932, no. 11) derives teaching principles from the work of prominent psychologists, and the report by Seashore (1910, no. 44) presents a critique by psychologists of teaching in their own discipline. In 1920, Klapper (no. 31) noted that "the field of college pedagogy is still virgin soil" (p. 43) but nevertheless managed to fill nearly 600 pages with comments about it. A few years later, Good (1929, no. 22) set forth his survey of research covering the period since World War I, and soon thereafter Payne and Spieth (1935, no. 43) synthesized more than 400 sources in an attempt to spare teachers from having to read them in order to determine which were of value. As a final reference for this early period, Hangartner's (1955, no. 26) dissertation-based volume is an invaluable study of pedagogic practices in eighteenth- and nineteenth-century colleges.

Guides to scholarly work from World War II to the early 1960s include Buxton (1956, no. 5), the essays collected by Cooper (1958, no. 7) and by Estrin and Goode (1964, no. 16), papers sponsored by the U.S. Office of Education (Hatch, 1966, no. 27), and the volume edited by Lee (1967, no. 33) under sponsorship of the American Council on Education. Other reviews and critical assessments of research are included in the last section of this chapter.

Several guides for college teachers build on this research tradition: eight editions of McKeachie's *Teaching Tips* (1986, no. 36), which first appeared in 1951, and the British volume by Beard and Hartley (1984, no. 2), now in its fourth edition. Other items that are international in scope include a commission report from Great Britain (Hale, 1964, no. 25) and two UNESCO publications (MacKenzie, Eraut, and Jones, 1976, no. 37; Bligh, 1980, no. 3).

Among books based less on research and more on their authors' personal observations and experiences are Highet's two classics (1950, no. 28; 1976, no. 29) and the collections from Harvard University edited by Cronkhite (1950, no. 8) and by Gullette (1982, no. 24).

This literature has given us no grand theory of instruction for higher education. As is clear from the annotations below, however, we have more than intuitive advice or cookbook-style recipes. Several of these publications present concepts significant for both research and practice. These include the notions of "evocative" teaching (Axelrod, 1973, no. 1), the dimensions of "intellectual excitement" and "interpersonal rapport" around which Lowman's (1984, no. 34) approach to teaching is organized, and taxonomies such as Umstattd's (1964, no. 47) classification of teaching techniques according to the relative amounts of control they give to the teacher and to learners. As a final concept of interest, consider the fundamental notion of "involvement" put forth by the Study Group on the Conditions of Excellence in American Higher Education (1984, no. 45) and further explored by Cross (1987, no. 9).

Chickering and Gamson (1987, no. 6) have derived principles of good practice for college teachers. These principles are more subtle than they may first seem, as any faculty discussion of their article quickly demonstrates. The literature on guidelines for teaching deserves more attention from those who seek generalizable, research-based principles.

Personal Accounts of Teaching

Most of the authors represented in the previous section are concerned with principles of teaching that they believe have general applicability, and many of them write from an impressive conceptual and empirical base. This section includes firsthand accounts of teaching by innovative or otherwise successful teachers. Most publications are descriptions of how the authors practice their craft and their art. Compared with the previous section, these accounts are less likely to be based on research or to spring from extensive theory, but they have the strengths of concreteness, immediacy, and often passion.

In some cases, these teachers are persons with considerable visibility and accomplishment even beyond teaching, as in the collections by Peterson (1946, no. 57) and by Epstein (1981, no. 52). A few items deal with particular settings, such as Wright and Burden (1986, no. 62) on the small college, or with a specific topic, such as open admissions (Shor, 1980, no. 60). Many essays, such as those by the "new teachers" who contributed to the volume by Flournoy and Associates (1972, no. 54), are concerned with innovative teaching. In the collection by Runkel, Harrison, and Runkel (1969, no. 58), each author describes an attempt to alter teacher-student relationships in his or her classroom. Extensive auto-biographical discussions are provided by Fairfield (1977, no. 53) on the subject of graduate education and by Macrorie (1970, no. 55) and Elbow (1986, no. 51) on the teaching of writing.

Planning and Providing Instruction

Most teaching in postsecondary education is course-centered. Planning usually begins by identifying who is likely to take the course; when, where, and for how long class meetings will occur; and what expectations about the course are held by colleagues and others in the sponsoring institution. In light of this information, the teacher plans the course according to a content coverage approach: deciding topics to be covered; identifying texts, lecture subjects, and other materials appropriate for those topics; and determining activities that, when graded, reveal how well students have learned the designated material.

This course-centered and content-centered approach is criticized by those who favor a more learner-centered orientation. The first step in planning for teaching, according to the latter view, is to focus on the learners and to define how they are expected to change as a result of the teaching-learning encounter. Teaching activities and evaluation methods congruent with these learner-centered goals are then selected.

The centrality of students may be stated explicitly, as in the title of a recent volume, *Teaching as Though Students Mattered* (Katz, 1985, no. 109). Or a comprehensive systems framework may be used (Kemp, 1985, no. 112), which begins with explicit learner characteristics and takes great pains to define subject matter clearly (Gilbert, 1976, no. 96) and to express instructional objectives unambiguously (Mager, 1975, no. 120).

Other approaches to planning and providing instruction have been derived from information-processing research (Bjork,

1979, no. 68), literary theory (Scholes, 1985, no. 130), and experiential learning (for example, Chickering, 1977, no. 80; Bowen, 1987, no. 73). The coherent "models for teaching," derived by Joyce and Weil (1986, no. 30) from work in precollege settings, offer still other ideas for planning.

Many items in the first section of this chapter differentiate among various levels and types of learning outcomes. We include resources that conceptualize as outcomes the skills of learning and the processes of learning. For example, instruction might be intended to enhance communication skills (Civikly, 1986, no. 82), the ability to make judgments (Abercrombie, 1960, no. 63), or the capacities for thinking, defined either as critical thinking (Meyers, 1986, no. 121) or in other ways (Bligh, 1986, no. 69). Dressel and Thompson (1973, no. 86) suggest that independent study can also be thought of as an outcome of instruction; they describe independent study not only as an activity to be completed but as a "capability" to be developed through education.

The large number of items on lecturing and on small group instruction can be located through the index, as can specialized publications on such topics as introductory courses, team teaching, and collaborative learning. When a publication ranges across several instructional procedures, it is indexed under "teaching methods." Items specific to a particular method are indexed under the name of that method. These include simulations, contracts, role playing, self-instruction, the case method, the personalized system of instruction, and so on. Weston and Cranton (1986, no. 140) describe a helpful procedure for selecting instructional techniques appropriate for particular circumstances.

To note the slow rate at which teaching practices change in colleges and universities is to note the obvious. Many decades ago, Coe (1929, no. 83) identified some negative "by-products of the college classroom" (p. 5), all of which are still with us. They include inadequate training of college teachers, dominance of the professor in the teaching-learning process, and a grading system with such undesirable side effects as fostering in students "a desire to appear to know" (p. 7). Most teaching methods perpetuate these by-products, although two significant exceptions should be noted. The Personalized System of Instruction (PSI) is intended to increase student responsibility for learning and to reduce the prominence of teachers and tests. A great deal of research supports PSI's effectiveness (see Ruskin, 1974, no. 129; Robin, 1976, no. 126; and other indexed items). Nevertheless, its use has declined, apparently because it violates the role expectations and values held by faculty and because it must be introduced carefully and gradually into the institution (Friedman, Hirsch, Parlett, and Taylor, 1976, no. 94). The second exception is computer-assisted learning. Research with even fairly primitive hardware and software typically finds some advantages for computer-mediated learning. Given advances in miniaturization, memory power, processing speed, and user convenience along with pressures of the marketplace, a dramatic increase in the extent and variety of learning via computers seems inevitable. Some contend that the characteristics of university organizations (Rossini, 1984, no. 127) and the preconceptions of faculty (Baron, 1985, no. 65) make it unlikely that formal higher education will be hospitable to electronically mediated learning activities; others (Bok, 1985, no. 70; Jackson, 1986, no. 107) are more optimistic. We are only beginning to see major effects of the microcomputer revolution on teaching and learning. Although the "great books" on this subject have yet to appear, several provocative items are indexed under "technology and teaching."

Evaluating and Improving Instruction

This section covers evaluation of teaching competence for the purposes of personnel review and improvement of teaching. Although most professionals feel ambivalent about performance evaluations, at least when applied to themselves, evaluations are nevertheless accepted as inevitable for organizational accountability. Even for self-improvement, some systematic evaluative information is essential. Ambivalent feelings about evaluation may be responsible for the enormous literature on course and teacher evaluation, as some seek to defend particular practices and others to discredit them.

End-of-course evaluations provided by students have been studied in nearly overwhelming detail and variety. This "student ratings" research, as it has come to be known, goes back many years.

Remmers (1929, no. 205), for example, completed well-regarded early investigations at Purdue University in the 1920s. The practice grew during higher education's years of expansion and during the rise of student consumerism. By the early 1970s, there was sufficient research for a major review (Costin, Greenough, and Menges, 1971, no. 157).

Recent comprehensive reviews can serve as guides through this vast body of work. In 1976, Feldman published the first of what became a series of meticulous reviews on the relationships between student ratings and a number of variables, including grades, class size, faculty experience and research productivity, and so on (nos. 163 to 171). Marsh (1984, no. 189) deals with some of these issues as well as with the multidimensional nature of teaching as reflected in evaluation instruments. Studies of the criterion validity of student ratings are reviewed by Benton (1982, no. 147). Much research on student ratings is atheoretical, although Hind, Dornbusch, and Scott (1974, no. 178) offer a theory of evaluation with applications to faculty members at one university.

Two research questions in the student ratings literature deserve special notice. One asks about the relationship between student evaluations of teachers and student learning. This topic attracted considerable attention after Rodin and Rodin (1972, no. 207) contended that the most positive evaluations went to teachers from whom students learned least. Subsequent research has firmly reversed that finding, documenting a relationship between ratings and learning that is at least moderately positive and that varies in sensible ways depending on what teaching dimension is being rated (Cohen, 1981, no. 156; Benton, 1982, no. 147). The second research question of interest asks if students can be seduced into rating highly expressive (entertaining) teachers positively, even when there is little educational content being communicated. Researchers have found that this "Doctor Fox" effect (Naftulin, Ware, and Donnelly, 1973, no. 198) does not appear to threaten the validity of properly constructed evaluation forms (Abrami, Leventhal, and Perry, 1982, no. 143; Marsh and Ware, 1982, no. 190).

Several books offer guidelines for systems of faculty evaluation that go beyond student ratings, and some of these systems go beyond teaching into other areas of faculty work. Among them are Centra (1979, no. 153), Seldin (1984, no. 208), Braskamp, Brandenburg, and Ory (1984, no. 150), and Miller (1987, no. 195). Other references can be located through the index under "teaching evaluation systems," as can writings about "posttenure faculty evaluation."

This mass of scholarship does converge on a positive conclusion: Well-designed programs for evaluating courses and teachers, when used for personnel review, are much more beneficial than they are harmful. Further, programs of student ratings can contribute to significant improvements in teaching, at least when faculty can consult with someone about their evaluations (Menges and Brinko, 1986, no. 192).

This section also contains items on the improvement of teaching. Despite widespread occurrence of teaching improvement activities, it is not evident how faculty participation in those activities should be related to faculty reward systems (O'Connell, 1983, no. 199). Teaching improvement activities take different forms and are evaluated differently depending on the assumptions guiding them, and there are disagreements about what underlying presuppositions are most appropriate for teaching improvement approaches (Lindquist, 1978, no. 186; Tiberius, 1986, no. 215). Nevertheless, many programs have been conducted, and some have been evaluated (O'Connell and Meeth, 1978, no. 200).

Among evaluations of campus-level teaching improvement programs are Eble and McKeachie's (1985, no. 162) report about projects funded by the Bush Foundation and Lacey's (1983, no. 183) study of the Lilly Endowment Post-Doctoral Teaching Awards Program. Briefer documents discuss particular techniques intended to improve teaching. These include grants of money (Lowry and Taeusch, 1953, no. 187), faculty teams (Sweeney and Grasha, 1979, no. 214), teaching consultants (Boud and McDonald, 1981, no. 148), deliberate applications of research findings (Donald and Sullivan, 1985, no. 159), theory-based workshops (Heller, 1982, no. 175), and such curricular change projects as competence-based courses (Grant and others, 1979, no. 173; Mentkowski and Doherty, 1984, no. 193). A review of research about such techniques found positive results for most of them, although the quality of individual studies leaves much to be desired (Levinson-Rose and Menges, 1981, no. 184).

We also include in this section several key resources on the subject of innovation. Davis (1979, no. 158) and Kozma (1985, no. 181) offer models and theories about developing and adopting teaching innovations. Snapshots of innovations in use at particular times are provided by Brick and McGrath (1969, no. 151) and by Heiss (1973, no. 174). McPherron (1982, no. 188) reports an interesting five-year follow-up of innovative practices in the teaching of sociology.

Research on Instruction

Key resources in this section are of two kinds: reviews of research about teaching in higher education and discussions of research methods. The latter are either primary sources that exemplify a particular research approach or discussions of research issues pertinent to that approach.

The most comprehensive recent reviews of research on instruction are by Dunkin (1986, no. 224) and McKeachie, Pintrich, Lin, and Smith (1986, no. 237). McKeachie and his colleagues give considerable attention to studies of both learning and teaching. More specialized review topics include electronic media for instruction (for example, Clark, 1983, no. 219), conventional classroom teaching methods (Dubin and Taveggia, 1968, no. 223), and the science laboratory (Hofstein and Lunetta, 1982, no. 229).

Early studies of college-level teaching applied methods of experimental psychology to the classroom. These methods had been appropriated from the physical sciences, and the optimistic expectation was that tightly controlled experiments would yield a body of reliable knowledge about teaching through "hundreds and thousands of tiny but reliable accretions" (Douglass, 1929, p. 273, no. 222). Descriptions of such studies can be found in Jones (1923, no. 231) and Douglass (1929, no. 222) as well as in several items annotated in the first section of this chapter. Pressey and Associates (1927, no. 240) report eighteen studies under the title of *Research Adventures in University Teaching;* they call for investigations by teachers in all fields to shed light on the very practical problems of instruction. Subsequent reviews, however, show that such research became the province of specialists and that it was published almost exclusively in psychology and education journals (Good, 1941, no. 228; McKeachie, 1963, no. 234). During the growth years of the 1960s and 1970s, the diversity of research increased as did the number of disciplines with their own publications about research on teaching (see the list of periodicals in Chapter Six).

A serious difficulty for research on teaching, frequently pointed out by reviewers, is the problem of identifying appropriate criterion measures. No one disputes that changes in learners comprise the proper evidence for effective teaching. But it is not always clear what form those changes should take, what evidence is adequate for establishing that they have occurred, and what procedures should be used to gather that evidence. Too often researchers and reviewers settle for the convenient criterion, namely, acquisition of knowledge as measured by course examinations, even when examinations are of unknown reliability and validity (Hudelson, 1928, no. 230; Dubin and Taveggia, 1968, no. 223; Schramm, 1962, no. 241).

More complex research designs have emerged, partly because of the availability of multivariate research techniques (see, for example, Siegel and Siegel, 1967, no. 242). Research has also benefited from the convenience that computers bring to data analysis. Some studies ask how differences in student characteristics interact with particular instructional methods, not only for acquiring course content but also with regard to student attitude and motivational outcomes. Although trait-treatment research does not always find clear results (for example, Goldberg, 1972, no. 227), its effectiveness may improve when more sensitive measures are used.

Including detailed data about classroom events, as was done by Solomon, Rosenberg, and Bezdek (1964, no. 243) and by Mann and others (1970, no. 238), adds considerable richness to information about student characteristics and student outcomes. Other promising areas for further research, some of which have been noted by reviewers, include observational studies of teaching in particular settings, ethnographic documentation of exemplary teaching practices, investigations of professors' values and beliefs and how they relate to teaching, inquiries into how students cognitively process course content, and research on students' study habits and practices.

Despite many inadequacies in our knowledge base, it would be a mistake to conclude that one method of teaching is as good as another or that research provides no guidelines for instructional practice. Here are examples of three carefully researched areas from which practical implications can fairly easily be drawn. First, it is well established that the amount of interaction in college class-rooms is typically very low and that most classroom discourse is at the lowest cognitive level (Karp and Yoels, 1976, no. 108; Ellner, Barnes, and Associates, 1983, no. 226). Thus typical classroom events may inhibit rather than facilitate complex learning. Second, it was determined long ago (Jones, 1923, no. 231) that the content of a classroom presentation is better remembered when it is followed by a test. Finally, the Personalized System of Instruction has known benefits for learning and increases the student's responsibility for learning (for example, see Dunkin, 1986, no. 224).

Yet even casual observation of college teaching reveals that such findings are not widely known, even less widely accepted, and rarely implemented. Resistance to improving teaching and learning is endemic to higher education. Regardless of the relevant knowl-edge base, faculty members appear to be unable to agree about what are desirable improvements, much less about the particular form they should take. Better understanding of the processes of change and innovation and of the resistances to them constitute yet another challenge for researchers.

References

Coe, G. A. "Byproducts of the College Classroom." In S. Eddy (ed.), *Am I Getting an Education?* Garden City, N.Y.: Doubleday, Doran, 1929.

Douglass, H. R. "Controlled Experimentation in the Study of Methods of College Teaching." *University of Oregon Education Series*, 1929, *1*, 265–316.

Dressel, P. L., and Thompson, M. M. *Independent Study.* San Francisco: Jossey-Bass, 1973.

Klapper, P. (ed.). *College Teaching: Studies in Methods of Teaching in the College.* Yonkers-on-Hudson, N.Y.: World Book, 1920.

Menges, R. J. "Instructional Methods." In A. W. Chickering and Associates, *The Modern American College: Responding to the New*

Realities of Diverse Students and a Changing Society. San Francisco: Jossey-Bass, 1981.

Payne, F., and Spieth, E. W. *An Open Letter to College Teachers.* Bloomington, Ind.: Principia Press, 1935.

Pressey, S. L., and Associates. *Research Adventures in University Teaching: Eighteen Investigations Regarding College and University Problems.* Bloomington, Ill.: Public School Publishing, 1927.

Guidelines for Teaching

★1   Axelrod, Joseph. *The University Teacher as Artist.* San Francisco: Jossey-Bass, 1973. 246 pages.

The art, as opposed to the science, of university teaching is a neglected topic in the literature of college teaching. This book, the result of a research project directed by the author at the Center for Research and Development in Higher Education at the University of California, Berkeley, adds significantly to an understanding of this art. Data from interviews with professors and visitations in classes provide the focus for the themes developed by the author, who states that "the hero of the book is the professor of humanities who attempts to escape the labyrinth of academic life, who seeks the freedom he needs in order to be an effective university teacher. The thesis of the book is that there is only one way: he must become an artist in the classroom. He must turn his mind toward unknown arts. . . . Every professor of humanities is reliving the Daedalus myth." Part One presents four models of "evocative" teaching, illustrated in Part Two with transcripts of class meetings. Part Three, with the use of systems analysis, describes the setting in which the professor must practice his or her art. Part Four discusses educational reform. Scholars in the humanities will find the book especially sympathetic to their perceptions of teaching.

★This symbol signifies classic works throughout this volume.

2   Beard, Ruth M., and Hartley, James. *Teaching and Learning in Higher Education.* (4th ed.) London: Harper & Row, 1984. 253 pages.

This textbook for teachers in higher education nicely balances references to research with practical advice. The broad literature referred to has its greatest depth in work done in Great Britain. The book provides detailed coverage of teaching aims, goals, and objectives; the psychology of learning (including personality variables); student issues (adjustment and study skills); teaching methods (including lecture, discussion, practical and laboratory work, and methods where the teacher is less prominent, such as the Personalized System of Instruction and computers); and evaluation. Throughout the book there is careful attention to the learner's perspective, that is, to the needs and characteristics of learners. This volume is an excellent introduction to what is known about college and university instruction. It is potentially useful for teachers at all levels of experience and from a variety of fields.

3   Bligh, Donald A. *Methods and Techniques in Postsecondary Education.* Paris: UNESCO, 1980. 138 pages.

Literature reviews, field visits, and a worldwide mail survey contribute to this discussion of higher education "teaching methods currently in use in various parts of the world." Chapters provide discussion of precise objectives for teaching, selection of colleges by students and selection of students by colleges, design of courses using a sequential model, methods of teaching, methods of student assessment, models of department organization, and evaluation of courses and teaching. There is a bibliography of 1,285 items.

4   Bridges, Charles W. (ed.). *Training the New Teacher of College Composition.* Urbana, Ill.: National Council of Teachers of English, 1986. 149 pages.

The contributors contend that all new instructors of composition, including graduate teaching assistants as well as part-time and adjunct faculty, should be given substantive support for their teaching. Yet few directors of composition programs are aware of efforts to accomplish this purpose beyond their own departments. More than a dozen chapters solicited from teachers of writing deal with peer critiques and grading; a sourcebook of classroom activities; technical writing; inventive and spontaneous writing; and training programs, workshops, and seminars on the teaching of writing. Although the book lacks a unifying basis in theory or research, practitioners will likely profit from the clearly described and tested suggestions.

5   Buxton, Claude. *College Teaching: A Psychologist's View.* San Diego, Calif.: Harcourt Brace Jovanovich, 1956. 404 pages.

This book, along with McKeachie's *Teaching Tips*, was for many years the major source of information for psychologists, and academics in general, who sought reliable advice about college teaching. The author devotes four chapters to an overview of higher education and to the place of psychology in the curriculum. He then introduces chapters on such specific teaching issues as planning the introductory course, lecturing, discussion, case analysis, examinations, grading, classroom morale, advising, and knowing the students we teach. Not much has changed about the daily details of teaching methods in higher education since this book was written. It deserves to be read by anyone interested in the traditional advice that the discipline of psychology has to offer, both to beginning professors and their more experienced colleagues.

6   Chickering, Arthur W., and Gamson, Zelda F. "Seven Principles for Good Practice in Undergraduate Education." *American Association for Higher Education Bulletin,* 1987, *39* (7), 3-7.

Growing out of a research review and conference, this brief essay offers "seven principles based on research on good teaching and learning in colleges and universities." In undergraduate education, good practice (1) encourages contact between students and faculty, (2) develops reciprocity and cooperation among students, (3) uses active learning techniques, (4) gives prompt feedback, (5) emphasizes time on task, (6) communicates high expectations, and (7) respects diverse talents and ways of learning. The importance of the content being taught is acknowledged but not directly addressed in this discussion. There is a section on the qualities an institutional environment should have if it is to favor these practices, and a page of selected research citations closes the article. While few faculty members would dissent from these statements as important values, there is considerable controversy about how they are best implemented. Consequently, the article can be the first step toward productive analysis and planning.

7   Cooper, Russell M. *The Two Ends of the Log: Learning and Teaching in Today's College.* Minneapolis: University of Minnesota Press, 1958. 317 pages.

Concern about anticipated increases in numbers of college students during the 1960s prompted the Association of Minnesota Colleges to organize a conference in 1958 for a representative group of faculty from that state's colleges and universities. This volume includes conference addresses and summaries of discussion groups. Noteworthy chapters, which effectively convey knowledge available and views prevailing at that time, are included on students (N. Sanford), on student learning (W. J. McKeachie), on examinations to promote learning (R. L. Ebel), and on particular instructional techniques and media. W. H. Cowley also provides an excellent history of college teaching during the previous century. This volume provides a very accessible snapshot of the higher education teaching and learning landscape as the 1950s drew to a close.

8   Cronkhite, Bernice. *A Handbook for College Teachers: An Informal Guide.* Cambridge, Mass.: Harvard University Press, 1950. 272 pages.

Recognizing that "in a sense teaching cannot be taught, since essentially it must be a flaming and an outgoing of the spirit," the Radcliffe Graduate School arranged a series of evening lectures where experiences of successful teachers could be shared with graduate students considering college teaching careers. These chapters are based on those lectures and deal with student-teacher relationships, teaching methods in the major families of disciplines, "mechanics" of speech, and various issues of the academic profession. Of particular relevance to teaching and learning are chapters on the teaching process (I. Richards), conflicts in the learning process (W. Perry), evaluation of teaching (G. Allport), and values in teaching (W. Westin). There is much more art than science in these chapters; they may be seen as embodying and conveying the state of the art of university teaching at the end of the first half of the century, at least as viewed by scholars at Harvard.

9   Cross, K. Patricia. "Teaching for Learning." *AAHE Bulletin*, 1987, *39* (8), 3-7.

In this brief article the author discusses the central themes of the reform movement in higher education and points out that little attention has been given in reform literature to the role of individual teachers in improving learning in college classrooms. Three general principles for supporting effective student learning are presented for teachers to follow: actively involving students in the learning task, providing practice with feedback, and setting high but attainable goals for learners. The article continues with a discussion of the role of assessment in improving learning in higher education. The author concludes her critique by asserting that classroom teaching in higher education should be taken much more seriously than it has been in the past.

10   Dressel, Paul L., and Marcus, Dora. *On Teaching and Learning in College: Reemphasizing the Roles of Learners and the Disciplines in Liberal Education.* San Francisco: Jossey-Bass, 1982. 241 pages.

This book presents much of Paul Dressel's thinking about teaching and learning in higher education. The authors divide their work into three parts, each of which can be read independently. Part One is organized around four prototypes of teaching: discipline-centered, instructor-centered, student-centered cognitive, and student-centered affective. Part Two focuses on the characteristics of the disciplines and their relationship to effective teaching and learning. Part Three offers material that bridges the disciplines in order to adapt courses and programs to a transdisciplinary context.

This book is essential reading for anyone interested in the point of view of the senior author about teaching and learning in college.

11   Eaton, T. H. *College Teaching: Its Rationale*. New York: Wiley, 1932. 264 pages.

The author draws implications for college teaching from the then current psychological views of E. L. Thorndike, William James, R. S. Woodworth, and John Dewey. Thirty principles are presented from their work, each with examples and rationale, covering a broad range of teaching goals and methods. While the psychology is somewhat dated, the book contains a great deal of sensible pedagogical advice, probably ahead of its time.

★12   Eble, Kenneth E. *Professors as Teachers*. San Francisco: Jossey-Bass, 1972. 202 pages.

This book is a report of the Project to Improve College Teaching, sponsored from 1969 to 1971 by the American Association of University Professors and the Association of American Colleges and funded by the Carnegie Corporation. The author, who also directed the project, includes in this report gleanings from the wide range of project activities and his own perceptive insights about the state of the art of college teaching at the time of the study. The first section, on college teaching, presents chapters about professors in the classroom, attitudes toward teaching, and teaching effectively. The second section, on discussion and proposals, includes evaluating teaching, what students want, learning to teach, faculty development, rewards of teaching, and the teaching environment. The final chapter asks the question "Is teaching obsolete?" The author notes in the epilogue that "if college teaching is to be improved, diverse forces must change both attitudes and practices." This book provides a scholarly, insightful inquiry into those diverse forces.

13   Eble, Kenneth E. *The Aims of College Teaching*. San Francisco: Jossey-Bass, 1983. 187 pages.

The author discusses college and university teaching in a context that goes far beyond techniques of teaching and subject matter competencies. According to his preface, the book focuses on what one is as a teacher and what one becomes as a result of adhering to high ideals for teaching and working to attain these goals. The first two chapters deal with developing a teaching style and with the importance of character in expressing that style. Chapter Three continues the discussion of the person in teaching. Chapter Four pursues answers to the question of whether teaching is an art, a science, or a craft. Chapters Five and Six confront the problem of conflicts between scholarship, research, and teaching. In Chapter Seven the author presents his seven deadly sins of teaching. Chapter Eight discusses how teachers learn to teach. Chapter Nine presents the author's view of the aims of education, and the final chapter compares his assessment of higher education in the 1960s with the early 1980s. The book is a delightful excursion into many domains associated with college and university teaching but not covered in standard treatments of the topic.

★14   Eble, Kenneth E. *The Craft of Teaching: A Guide to Mastering the Professor's Art.* (2nd ed.) San Francisco: Jossey-Bass, 1988. 250 pages.

In this literate and practical discussion of teaching, the author's approach is that of a humanist with a personalistic frame of reference. Realistic suggestions and abundant specific advice are included for improving the teaching of any instructor in higher education. The chapters cover such topics as the lecture as discourse, discussion in the classroom, the classroom as a place for teaching, the use of seminars and tutorials, advising students, and teaching outside the classroom. Several chapters on "grubby stuff and dirty work" include useful advice about testing, assignments, using texts, grading, cheating, the bad class, and other problems that teachers commonly encounter. The author discusses the preparation of college teachers as well as his perception of the mythology of college teaching. This second edition contains added material on critical thinking and motivation. This book belongs to that group of useful, practical books about college teaching represented by McKeachie's *Teaching Tips* and Highet's *The Art of*

Teaching. College teachers, from teaching assistants to seasoned veterans, will find something of value in this unique volume.

15   Ericksen, Stanford C. *The Essence of Good Teaching: Helping Students Learn and Remember What They Learn.* San Francisco: Jossey-Bass, 1984. 180 pages.

From his research-based knowledge in psychology and his experience as a professor, the author aims "to give the teacher a conceptual base for making decisions about how to do a better job in managing the classroom hour." In making decisions about what to teach, teachers should remember that meaningful materials are better retained than rote materials. Appropriate techniques are outlined for learning information that is memorized and concepts that must be understood. Other chapters discuss lecturing and motivation; the teacher as evaluator, counselor, and mentor; and how to assess and sustain the quality of teaching over time. This volume would be an excellent text for workshops or study groups on the analysis and improvement of teaching.

16   Estrin, Herman A., and Goode, Delmer M. (eds.). *College and University Teaching.* Dubuque, Iowa: Brown, 1964. 628 pages.

Beginning in 1953, the journal *Improving College and University Teaching* has published articles about college teaching by those who practice it. This volume collects 122 of those articles by eighty-nine authors from seventy-seven campuses, presenting them in three major sections: the professor's professional role, college students, and curriculum and method in college teaching. Informed more by the writers' personal experiences than by systematic data, these selections present the professor as a "bringer of light rather than a mere repository of knowledge in a particular field."

17   Foley, Richard P., and Smilansky, Jonathan. *Teaching Techniques: A Handbook for Health Professionals.* New York: McGraw-Hill, 1980. 180 pages.

Out of their own teaching and workshop experiences, the authors present "an integrated and systematic approach for improving instruction in the health professions." Chapters cover lecturing, use of questions, group discussion, clinical problem solving, lessons aimed at skill development, and instructional design. The text is concise, and the book includes many useful checklists and self-diagnostic instruments. Although the examples are drawn from the health professions, the principles they illustrate apply to most other fields as well.

★18   Fuhrmann, Barbara S., and Grasha, Anthony F. *A Practical Handbook for College Teachers*. Boston: Little, Brown, 1983. 315 pages.

The title of this text suggests that it might be a "cookbook" for college teachers. While the content is practical, the authors provide solid scholarship for their message. They start with an overview of college teaching that looks at the past, present, and future of this essential element of postsecondary education. A chapter on personal values in teaching disavows any notion of the one best way to success. Subsequent chapters cover theories of learning and teaching by presenting cognitive, behaviorist, and humanistic perspectives. The recognition of learning styles and teaching styles is discussed as an antecedent to designing classroom experiences. Getting students involved in the classroom, evaluating student learning, assessing teaching for instructional improvement, using media in the classroom, and considering alternative course designs are representative of the range of topics covered by the authors. The book concludes with a perceptive chapter on defining effective teaching. Anyone planning to teach at a level above the high school will find this handbook a useful, informative, and provocative source to guide the development of an individual frame of reference for teaching and learning.

19   Gardiner, John J. (ed.). *ASHE Handbook on Teaching and Instructional Resources: An Instructional Resource Handbook for Courses in the Field of Higher Education.* Washington, D.C.: Association for the Study of Higher Education, 1987. 164 pages.

Persons teaching courses about curricula, instruction, and staff development as well as other areas of higher education will find this handbook useful. Chapters include sample course syllabi, discussion of instructional use of games and simulations (R. Birnbaum), case material (D. Dill), data bases and electronic communications (J. Ratcliff), annotated bibliographies on college teaching (R. Menges) and on higher education as a field of study (J. Grace), and descriptions of higher education associations (J. Gardiner) and of the National Center for Research on Improving Postsecondary Teaching and Learning (J. Stark).

20   Glaser, Robert. "Ten Untenable Assumptions of College Instruction." *Educational Record,* 1968, *49,* 154–159.

As college teachers plan and conduct their courses, they appear to act according to ten assumptions that Glaser contends are contradicted by educational theory and research. Some of those doubtful assumptions discussed by Glaser are as follows: the specific knowledge acquired by students is related to the long-range educational goals in the minds of instructors; all people learn in the same way and in approximately the same amount of time; listening to lectures and reading books are powerful means for changing student behavior; a college professor is, by virtue of that title, a good professor of knowledge; teaching is an art requiring no tools and no underlying technology; and the structure imposed upon knowledge by a discipline is the best structure for transmitting that knowledge to students. Each assumption is elaborated in a few paragraphs of discussion. Although not documented with research citations, the assertions are sound and remain timely; their implications deserve consideration by teachers and researchers alike.

21   Goldsmid, Charles A., and Wilson, Everett K. *Passing on Sociology: The Teaching of a Discipline.* Belmont, Calif.: Wadsworth, 1980. 432 pages.

Citing Durkheim that "pedagogy depends on sociology more closely than any other science," the authors proceed to write good sociology about teaching across the disciplines as well as in sociology. They make clear their own presuppositions and their preferred teaching goals, namely, (1) critical (or reflective) thinking, (2) extension of ideas (or propositions or insights) to new populations or situations, and (3) skills in inquiry. After chapters about each of these goals, a section of six chapters is devoted to "means," the methods and tools for reaching the teaching goals. Two final chapters discuss evaluation of student achievement and instructor competence.

★**22**   Good, Carter V. *Teaching in College and University: A Survey of the Problems and Literature in Higher Education.* Baltimore, Md.: Warwick and York, 1929. 557 pages.

Previous research and writings on education have been consolidated in this substantial volume and their contents extrapolated to higher education. Hundreds of sources are noted in the text and in an eighty-page bibliography; many of them are quoted at length or summarized in some detail. The volume provides an extraordinary amount of information about work through the 1920s and especially the decade following World War I, using a psychological perspective with a focus on education. Major chapters deal with objectives and standards in higher education, curriculum, psychology of learning, teaching methods, and measurement.

23   Goodman, Paul. *Compulsory Mis-Education and The Community of Scholars.* New York: Vintage Books, 1964. 339 pages.

These two extended essays recount the author's views applied to all levels of education. To reduce the negative effects on students who feel compelled to pursue higher education, he proposes (1) having several experimental colleges require a two-year "maturing activity" after high school and prior to matriculation and (2) having some prestigious universities "abolish grading, and use testing only and entirely for pedagogical purposes as teachers see fit." He sees the problem of community as the young meeting "academics who interpose the administrative framework of instruction to prevent personal contact, and an impersonal morality not different from that of the world outside." Implications are explored of a proposal "for bands of scholars to secede and set up where they can teach and learn on their own simple conditions."

★24   Gullette, Margaret M. (ed.). *The Art and Craft of Teaching.* Cambridge, Mass.: Harvard-Danforth Center for Teaching and Learning, 1982. 130 pages.

The Harvard-Danforth Center for Teaching and Learning assists faculty and students interested in improving the quality of teaching at Harvard University. These essays are by individuals who are active teachers and who take seriously their teaching responsibilities. The nine chapters discuss such topics as varieties of teaching, the first day of class, the theory and practice of lectures, questioning, the role of the section leader, the rhythms of the semester, suggestions for beginning teachers, teaching essay writing, and grading and evaluation. The writing is personalistic, but each author communicates his or her own enthusiasms for the classroom. Teaching assistants would find the book especially useful as a brief introduction to managing the problems of entering college teaching.

25   Hale, Sir Edward (chair). *Report of the Committee on University Teaching Methods.* London: Her Majesty's Stationery Office, 1964. 173 pages.

Beginning in 1961, Sir Edward chaired a committee of university educators "to make a comparative study of undergraduate teaching methods and practices current in the universities and colleges of Great Britain in the fields of arts and pure and applied sciences." This committee solicited information from a variety of sources, including surveys of students and teachers. Much of the report is devoted to discussing structure, of both degree courses and the academic year; how students use their time; effectiveness of lecture, discussion, and practical classes; and examinations. In addition to the value of the data presented, the report is of interest because of its point in history (at a time when rapid growth of enrollments was anticipated) and because of the reserve with which conclusions and recommendations are stated—for example, "We give reasons for not accepting without qualification the view of the Commission on Higher Education that there is little virtue in formal lectures given to small audiences."

26 Hangartner, Carl A. *Movements to Change American College Teaching, 1700-1830.* New Haven, Conn.: Yale University Press, 1955. 389 pages.

From 1700 to 1830, as Harvard lost its monopoly in higher education and as the influence of German universities grew, the basic instructional traditions in American colleges became firmly established. This historical study is based on student diaries, textbooks, institutional records, and educational writings of the period. It documents five movements that affected formal relationships among teachers, students, and the classroom: (1) replacing the nonspecialized tutor with the specialized professor, (2) increasing time devoted to lecturing relative to recitation, (3) the introduction and spread of lectures illustrated by experiments in the physical sciences, (4) changing the language of the classroom from Latin to English, and (5) greater use of the logical synthetic method in teaching most subject matter, as illustrated by the Lockean and Cartesian logic texts. The overarching theme during this historical period is the general tendency toward specialization, a tendency that can be found in each of these five movements.

27 Hatch, Winslow R. (comp.). *Student Involvement and the University.* Corvallis: Oregon State University Press, 1966. 538 pages.

As a specialist in higher education with the U.S. Department of Health, Education, and Welfare during the early 1960s, the author oversaw production of a series of booklets called "New Dimensions in Higher Education," originally published by the U.S. Government Printing Office. Fourteen of these essays are gathered in this volume with a new introduction by the editor. In the introduction he captures a theme that ran through many of the booklets, especially those he authored or coauthored, six of which are reprinted here. That theme is active learning, learning in which the student is involved, "learning that is characterized by discovery or guided discovery, enquiry or inquiry, or in somewhat more prosaic language, teaching that is problem-oriented." The author describes the teacher's role in active learning as a director of student learning. Essays by other authors touch on related issues and programs—for example, study abroad, advance standing, and the impact of college. Given the government origins of the series, it is an important statement of 1960s thinking about higher education practice as deliberately informed by social science and education research.

28   Highet, Gilbert. *The Art of Teaching*. New York: Vintage Books, 1950. 259 pages.

This spirited book presents a literate defense of the premise that teaching is an art and not a science. As one might anticipate, this humanist author with both scholarly and educational credentials emphasizes intuitive judgments about what contributes to effective teaching. Relying on personal observations as evidence, he presents a lively and challenging discourse on teaching in general and on the specific application of teaching methods to the college classroom. A companion volume, *The Immortal Profession: The Joys of Teaching and Learning*, published by the author some twenty-six years after this one, should be read in order to appreciate the continuity of his interest in teaching and learning throughout his academic career.

29   Highet, Gilbert. *The Immortal Profession: The Joys of Teaching and Learning*. New York: Weybright and Talley, 1976. 223 pages.

The author, a noted critic and classical scholar, has brought together in this volume a collection of essay chapters on teaching, ranging from his comments about the illusion of human progress to his views regarding teaching college teachers how to teach. After pointing out in the preface that the art of teaching is an inexhaustible theme, he provides a rich and varied journey for the scholar interested in pursuing the phenomenon of teaching. This book follows by twenty-six years the popular best-seller by Highet, *The Art of Teaching*. They should be read together.

30   Joyce, Bruce, and Weil, Marsha. *Models of Teaching.* (3rd ed.) Englewood Cliffs, N.J.: Prentice-Hall, 1986. 518 pages.

This volume presents more than twenty approaches to teaching, each based on extensive theory and research and described in terms of classroom use. The four families of models are information processing (inquiry training, advance organizers, and so on), personal (nondirective teaching, synectics, and so on), social (role playing, jurisprudential inquiry, and so on), and behavioral systems (mastery learning, assertive training, and so on). Other chapters discuss educational outcomes that can be expected from each model and how teachers might use the models proficiently. This book addresses teachers in precollege settings, but many of the approaches have been or can be adapted to college instruction. Because of its uniquely comprehensive and integrative character and its explicit classroom applications, the volume illustrates quite vividly the range of approaches available to college teachers interested in experimenting with different models of teaching.

31   Klapper, Paul (ed.). *College Teaching: Studies in Methods of Teaching in the College.* Yonkers-on-Hudson, N.Y.: World Book, 1920. 583 pages.

In his own chapter, "General Principles of College Teaching," the editor asserts, "The field of college pedagogics is still virgin soil and no significant or extensive program for improved methods of teaching has yet been advanced." He contends that good teaching is controlled by clearly conceived aims, begins at the point of contact between subject matter and student life, and is well organized and thorough. Of the twenty-eight chapters, twenty-five deal with particular subject matter: sciences (six chapters), social sciences (eight), languages and literature (five), arts (two), and vocational education (four). Most chapters follow a uniform outline that places the subject within the curriculum, describes methods appropriate for teaching it, and discusses how to determine "whether the subject has been of worth to the student." Several chapters include bibliographies valuable for tracing early writings on college pedagogy in that field.

32 Lancaster, Otis E. *Effective Teaching and Learning.* New York: Gordon and Breach, 1974. 358 pages.

From his years of offering seminars on college teaching for engineering teachers, the author offers this "fundamental treatise for institutes on teaching." Its chapters cover setting objectives; modes of communication; such teaching strategies as case studies, guided design, and homework; and evaluation of learning. Advice is practical and the suggested exercises are likely to be helpful. Although examples are drawn from engineering subjects, the principles they illustrate are generalizable to other fields.

33 Lee, Calvin B. T. (ed.). *Improving College Teaching.* Washington, D.C.: American Council on Education, 1967. 407 pages.

An outgrowth of the American Council on Education's 1965 annual meeting, these essays are directed toward academic administrators as well as classroom teachers. The nearly fifty contributions include several commissioned papers and commentaries on them by other writers. The commissioned papers are "Conflicting Academic Loyalties" (R. A. Nisbet); "Who Teaches the Teachers?" (W. M. Wise); "Future Faculty" (A. M. Cartter); "Innovations in College Teaching" (S. Baskin); "Research in Teaching" (W. J. McKeachie); "Evaluation of Teaching Performance" (J. W. Gustad); and "Reforming General Education" (D. Bell). These selections nicely represent the breadth of scholarship on college teaching in the middle 1960s.

★34 Lowman, Joseph. *Mastering the Techniques of Teaching.* San Francisco: Jossey-Bass, 1984. 245 pages.

The recent attention given to college teaching has produced reports on such diverse topics as the support of technology as the one best way to improve teaching and effective teaching as a therapeutic encounter. Lowman's approach is essentially conservative and aims at helping the college teacher "excel at traditional college teaching using group meetings in the lecture/discussion format." The author's background in clinical psychology is useful in his analysis of the dynamics of the classroom. The classic study of Mann and his colleagues at the University of Michigan, *The College Classroom: Conflict, Change, and Learning,* now out of print, forms the basis for Lowman's discussion of teaching and learning in the college classroom. This book is a useful guide for embryonic academicians just beginning to practice their craft as well as for those more experienced who are in need of reexamining their concepts of teaching.

35   McGuire, Christine H.; Foley, Richard P.; Gorr, Alan; Richards, Ronald W.; and Associates. *Handbook of Health Professions Education: Responding to New Realities in Medicine, Dentistry, Pharmacy, Nursing, Allied Health, and Public Health.* San Francisco: Jossey-Bass, 1983. 569 pages.

Broad in scope, this volume describes the major health-related fields, how they have evolved, and the forces that will shape their development in the future. Of the twenty-five chapters, all based on research, most pertinent to this key resources volume are the chapters on instructional media and methods (R. P. Foley), student and practitioner evaluation (C. H. McGuire), and faculty evaluation and development (F. T. Stritter). These chapters, in particular, have considerable value for fields other than the health professions.

★36   McKeachie, Wilbert J. *Teaching Tips: A Guide for the Beginning College Teacher.* (8th ed.) Lexington, Mass.: Heath, 1986. 353 pages.

Teaching Tips, now in its eighth edition, has guided more beginning college teachers than any other resource. The author states that the book "was written to answer the questions posed by new college teachers, to place them at ease in their jobs, and to get them started effectively in the classroom." The writing is not complex, the content is relevant and brought up-to-date in each succeeding edition, and the coverage is directed at those practical matters that lead to effectiveness as a teacher. Part One covers getting started and deals with teaching in the college or university culture, managing time in preparing for a course, and meeting a class for the first time. Part Two includes chapters that provide useful information about organizing effective discussions, using student-centered discussion methods, and roles for the teacher. Lecturing, testing, and grading are discussed in Part Three, and Part Four contains chapters devoted to teaching techniques, tools, and methods. This includes material on teaching writing, one-on-one counseling, independent study, programmed learning, the use of computers in teaching, audiovisual techniques, laboratory teaching, games and simulations, and microteaching. Part Five consists of chapters on teaching the large class. Part Six presents perspectives on teaching and the teaching environment and covers such topics as motivating students, ethical standards in teaching, and student ratings of faculty. *Teaching Tips* will continue to influence the beginning college teacher. It replaces the mythology surrounding the college classroom and the act of teaching with a creative blend of research findings and practical advice.

37   MacKenzie, Norman I.; Eraut, Michael; and Jones, Hywel C. *Teaching and Learning: An Introduction to New Methods and Resources in Higher Education.* (2nd ed.) Paris: UNESCO, 1976. 224 pages.

This revision of a much discussed 1970 UNESCO publication includes a new annotated bibliography. The discussion moves from a conventional instructor-based framework about teaching and learning to a learner-based framework. This approach is elaborated through discussions of "new media" and their uses, the approaches to teaching and learning usually called systematic, and ways of developing new materials and support services congruent with the systematic approach.

38   Milton, Ohmer. *Alternatives to the Traditional*. San Francisco: Jossey-Bass, 1972. 156 pages.

In this book about how professors teach and how students learn, the author presents research evidence that challenges traditional teaching practices. He contends that the real issues of reform in higher education are related to misconceptions we have about how students learn rather than to issues about a better way to teach. The book covers such topics as research about learning, grading, nontraditional learning approaches, and interdisciplinary learning. Many of the traditions of higher education are challenged. The author ends by stating the principal thesis of the book: "Efficient teaching by the faculty does not necessarily promote sufficient learning by the students." The reader will find the exploration of this thesis a provocative and interesting excursion.

39   Milton, Ohmer, and Associates. *On College Teaching*. San Francisco: Jossey-Bass, 1978. 404 pages.

This guide to contemporary practice in college teaching "seeks to improve college teaching by encouraging everyone involved in undergraduate instruction to consider some new approaches as well as to improve old approaches to teaching." The book consists of chapters by the senior author and colleagues in academic institutions throughout the United States. The topics covered include approaches to teaching, clarifying objectives, leading discussions, lecturing, classroom testing and feedback for learning, computers in the classroom and individualized instruction, contract learning, specifying and achieving competencies, case studies, simulation and gaming, field experience learning, older students, and the evaluation of teaching. The wide range of topics covered and the sound advice provided by the authors make this volume worth reading for those interested in seeking ways to break old habits and trying new approaches to college teaching.

40   Milton, Ohmer, and Shoben, Edward J., Jr. (eds.). *Learning and the Professors*. Athens: Ohio University Press, 1968. 216 pages.

These essays about the need to change instructional practices in colleges and universities are addressed to those capable of making a reappraisal of college teaching and initiating action to carry it out. Ohmer Milton writes about the state of the establishment, John Gardner discusses the flight from teaching, Logan Wilson presents his views on setting institutional priorities, and William Hutchinson argues that effective teaching still exists in spite of the flight from teaching. Howard Gruber discusses negative results in studies of teaching, Sidney Pressey presents two basically neglected psychological problems, and Ruth Eckert and Daniel Neil offer their observations about studies of teachers and teaching. Robert Pace discusses his research on college environments; Paul Dressel and Irvin Lehmann present their views on the impact of college on student attitudes, values, and critical thinking abilities. The criterion problem in higher education is the subject of an essay by Donald Hoyt, and Laurence Siegel discusses research about improving teaching and learning. Essays by Henry Johnson, Ross Mooney, and Edward Shoben deal with the role of universities as schools, the problem of leadership, and change and relevance in higher education. Although written twenty years ago, these essays address issues and problems very much alive today. This book would be useful as a supplementary reader for an introductory course on higher education.

41   Morrill, Paul H., and Spees, Emil R. *The Academic Profession: Teaching in Higher Education*. New York: Human Science Press, 1982. 363 pages.

This book grew out of a class on college teaching taught by the authors. The contents, however, are broader than most how-to approaches to teaching at the college level. The authors are concerned with the professional roles played by faculty and the major tasks that make up academic work, but the major attention is given to the teaching process and the relationship between teachers and students in higher education. The contents cover such topics as learning theories, planning to teach and classroom methods, teacher characteristics, the innovative instructor, creativity and motivation, a general teaching model, techniques for learning, educational technologies, and course designs. There are chapters on related topics, such as faculty development, academic freedom, and evaluation. The writing is not complex and is directed toward the beginning college teacher with no previous exposure to the topics covered. The book may be a useful introduction for persons outside the field of higher education who are motivated to learn about college teaching.

42   Nelson, Cary (ed.). *Theory in the Classroom.* Urbana: University of Illinois Press, 1986. 272 pages.

These nine original essays deal with interpretative theory from a variety of perspectives and with its implications for pedagogical practices. The editor notes questions pertinent to many of the essays: Are some theoretical positions (on interpretation) at odds with conventional teaching practices? What role do students have in articulating theory? What happens to an interpretative practice in making it teachable? In addition to interpretative theory itself, the authors deal with several areas of content, including feminist theory, radical theory, popular culture, and technical writing. The book is mainly theoretical, giving most attention to content to be taught and assumptions about how one teaches. The authors cite a few illustrations from syllabi and course projects, but there is little attention to classroom activities and procedures.

43   Payne, Fernandus, and Spieth, Evelyn W. *An Open Letter to College Teachers.* Bloomington, Ind.: Principia Press, 1935. 380 pages.

The intent of this "open letter" is to summarize significant developments in higher education so that every teacher need not "wade through the enormous mass of educational literature, only a small portion of which is of value." Ten extensive chapters with more than 400 references note criticisms and handicaps to college teaching, experiments in curriculum and teaching methods, case descriptions of a number of exemplary teachers, and methods for measuring student abilities and achievements. This is an excellent, comprehensive survey of opinions and practices through the mid 1930s, growing out of the authors' bibliographic work for a project sponsored by the American Association of University Professors.

44   Seashore, Carl E. "Report of the Committee of the American Psychological Association on the Teaching of Psychology." *Psychological Monographs,* 1910, *12,* 1–93.

The committee circulated a "questionary" to normal schools and institutions both with and without psychological laboratories. Replies from each are reported in detail, followed by recommendations from the committee. First among them is to "teach psychology," since much of the content reported as being taught was "sense physiology, moralizing, loose pedagogy, or logical quibble." Recommendations regarding teaching method include "keep the students doing things, instead of merely listening, reading, or seeing them done. . . . Cramming is bad only when it is not done often enough." The committee asserted that the lecture method, which they termed much abused, may be used in such legitimate forms as the organizing lecture, the demonstrating lecture, and the special topics lecture. The report is of interest primarily because most of its practical suggestions are relevant even today.

45   Study Group on the Conditions of Excellence in American Higher Education. *Involvement in Learning: Realizing the Potential of American Higher Education.* Washington, D.C.: National Institute of Education, 1984. 99 pages.

This monograph consists of the final report of a study group appointed by the director of the National Institute of Education to "suggest ways in which policy analysis, research, and recommendations for improvement in higher education could be developed and implemented." The group was chaired by Kenneth Mortimer, and the members were Alexander Astin, Zelda Gamson, J. Herman Blake, Harold Hodgkinson, Howard Bowen, and Barbara Lee. The report calls attention to both the successes and the signs of difficulty for higher education. Recommendations, grounded in behavioral science and education research, are offered in the areas of increasing student involvement, realizing high expectations, and assessment and providing feedback. A section on implications of the conditions of excellence is included with recommendations for graduate schools, external agencies, and the research community. This report presents a comprehensive portrait of the strengths and weaknesses of higher education in the United States. The recommendations chart a logical and necessary course for American higher education if entry into the next century is to be accomplished with today's aspirations of a commitment to excellence and equity.

46   Tead, Ordway. *College Teaching and College Learning: A Plea for Improvement.* New Haven, Conn.: Yale University Press, 1949. 56 pages.

The Spalding Lecture for 1947–48 at Yale permitted Tead to emphasize "the need for indirect learning." Indirect learning is a by-product of direct teaching and includes social skills, character assets, standards of excellence, effective communication, and a sense of wonder. Indirect learning can be attained through a greater variety of classroom activity and through supervised nonclassroom activity but should not be left to the extracurriculum. Chapters are devoted to discussions of the teacher and to suggestions for improving teaching and learning. This is a nontechnical essay by the then chairman of the New York City Board of Higher Education.

47   Umstattd, J. G. *College Teaching: Background, Theory, Practice.* Washington, D.C.: University Press, 1964. 355 pages.

For this extensive text, the author draws on both his own courses on college teaching and previous surveys. Chapters deal with the purposes of higher education in general and of particular types of institutions, the characteristics of students (especially motivational variables), evaluation and counseling procedures, and instructional techniques. The chapters on instruction are particularly thorough in defining and analyzing twenty-four different techniques classified primarily by the amount of control they relegate to students or teachers.

Personal Accounts of Teaching

48 Beidler, Peter G. (ed.). *Distinguished Teachers on Effective Teaching: Observations on Teaching by College Professors Recognized by the Council for Advancement and Support of Education.* New Directions for Teaching and Learning, no. 28. San Francisco: Jossey-Bass, 1986. 96 pages.

In 1981, the Council for Advancement and Support of Education (CASE) initiated its annual Professor of the Year selection. The reports in this volume are drawn from a selection of finalists for this award who agreed to respond to a wide range of questions about their views on teaching and the profession of teaching. Questions cover the connection between teaching and research, teaching and the "real world," student learning, and the influence of mentors. The eight chapters begin with a discussion of the sample of CASE professors and the teachers who influenced them. The remaining chapters present responses to seven other questions. The report provides interesting, useful information about the attitudes and values of professors who are regarded by their peers as exceptional teachers.

49 Buxton, Thomas H., and Prichard, Keith W. (eds.). *Excellence in University Teaching.* Columbia: University of South Carolina Press, 1975. 291 pages.

The editors have assembled essays about university teaching intended "to provide some documentary evidence of the problems and possibilities of teaching at the college level." Chancellors and presidents of colleges and universities were asked to provide the names of teachers on their faculties who have been recognized in some way for the excellence of their efforts. The book is composed of essays written by these nominees. Part One addresses attitudinal and methodological perspectives in college teaching with essays by Kenneth Reckford, Philip Phenix, Robert Sherwin, Richard Mann, Alton Oviatt, Ralph Bienfang, W. D. Keller, Irwin Marcus, Keith Prichard, Conwell Strickland, Kenneth Cooper, Joseph Panuska, Thomas Jones, Robert Brasted, Thomas Buxton, Stuart Rice, J. Allen, Glenn Frank, and Thomas Langford. Part Two includes essays on the prognosis for the future by Peter Bien, Francis Hart, Huston Smith, S. N. Postlethwait, William Driscoll, and Duane Manning. A selected bibliography on college teaching is included. While many of the essays are personalistic, they offer insights about college teaching not always available in the more didactic textbooks, especially those advocating a "one best way" approach.

50   Cahn, Steven M. (ed.). *Scholars Who Teach*. Chicago: Nelson-Hall, 1978. 246 pages.

This book consists of seven essays about teaching by practicing scholars in a variety of disciplines. Rather than reminiscences about the careers of the authors, the essays are practical statements that reflect what outstanding teachers have to say about their teaching, written to encourage beginning college teachers to think through their own approaches. An appendix contains a useful statement about the uses and abuses of grades and examinations. The book should appeal to those who eschew a prescriptive approach to instruction but nevertheless find advice from veteran teachers useful.

51   Elbow, Peter. *Embracing Contraries: Explorations in Teaching and Learning*. New York: Oxford University Press, 1986. 314 pages.

A noted teacher of writing here collects his works on teaching and learning published over a twenty-year period. These twelve essays reach far beyond the particular field of writing as he seeks principles that produce good learning and teaching despite the "contraries" they raise. His search for "coherence and fruitfulness in processes we often see as messy or useless" is revealed in essays about thinking, where the contraries are logical thinking and intuitive thinking; about teaching, where one deals with students who must both submit to their teachers and resist them; about evaluation of learning and teaching, which embodies the contrary pulls of objectivity and subjectivity; and about inquiry, which can proceed both by alternating between contraries and by blending or merging contraries. For illustration he draws on "nondisciplinary" and interdisciplinary courses. He also discusses his reactions to Freire's writings, competency-based education, and collaborative faculty peer evaluation. Lucidly written, this is a highly provocative resource for teachers in any field.

★**52**   Epstein, Joseph (ed.). *Masters: Portraits of Great Teachers.* New York: Basic Books, 1981. 265 pages.

The editor carried the germ of the idea for this book in his mind for some time after reading an essay by Edmund Wilson entitled "Christian Gauss as a Teacher of Literature." When Epstein became editor of *The American Scholar,* he persuaded the editorial board to initiate a series of essays on great teachers. The sixteen essays reprinted here represent the fruits of that venture. They range across a spectrum of disciplines. Many of the authors are great teachers themselves writing about teachers who have influenced them. The essays meet a high standard of excellence, both in style and in substance.

53   Fairfield, Roy P. *Person-Centered Graduate Education.* Buffalo, N.Y.: Prometheus, 1977. 269 pages.

Graduate education has not easily welcomed the humanistic reforms of nontraditional, self-directed, experiential, person-centered learning. This book discusses external degree programs that during the 1960s and 1970s attempted to include those reforms. There is special reference to the Antioch Graduate School of Education and the Union Graduate School, which at its high point had thirty-two institutional members, and to the author's role as coordinator/director in those programs. The book is part institutional history, part program description, and part poetic journal. The style is personal, catching the style of the humanistic movement of the times.

54   Flournoy, Don M., and Associates. *The New Teachers.* San Francisco: Jossey-Bass, 1972. 206 pages.

Seventeen "new teachers" describe what they do in their courses. Though teaching in a variety of disciplines, they share four characteristics: They "teach with their lives," they aim for deep and personal learning, their work goes beyond the physical classroom, and they serve as the counterculture at their institutions. They are also on the move; eleven of the seventeen relocated or made plans to relocate during the time this book was in process. These essays are neither expositions of theory nor reports of research. They are descriptions of experimental teaching practices and statements of strongly held personal values.

55   Macrorie, Ken. *Uptaught*. New York: Hayden, 1970. 187 pages.

A teacher of college writing shares his developmental journey toward what he calls the Third Way of teaching. Along the way, he and his students found it necessary, if they were to continue their development, to kill "engfish, a language in which fresh truth is almost impossible to express." The resulting approach to teaching involves considerably more mutual respect and dialogue with students than do conventional approaches. Here it is engagingly documented through classroom anecdotes and student writing.

56   Martin, Warren Bryan (ed.). *New Perspectives on Teaching and Learning*. New Directions for Teaching and Learning, no. 7. San Francisco: Jossey-Bass, 1981. 157 pages.

This volume contains essays by holders of fellowships from the Danforth Foundation who were invited to write "short reports on positive or negative incidents in their teaching careers." About a dozen reports are organized in each of three sections: "Through teaching, the teachers learn," "Through teaching, the students learn," and "Through teaching, learning to handle controversial issues." The reports are informal in style, usually a page or two in length, and convey a sense of immediacy and sincerity. As cases from the real world of college teaching, they are unique stimuli for reflection and discussion.

57   Peterson, Houston (ed.). *Great Teachers, Portrayed by Those Who Studied Under Them*. New York: Vintage Books, 1946. 351 pages.

This collection of essays by students of outstanding teachers throughout history contains many worthwhile portraits. They range from James Russell Lowell's observations about Ralph Waldo Emerson as a lecturer to Helen Keller's tribute to her teacher, Ann Mansfield Sullivan. Many of the writers are respected teachers in their own right; their essays provide a wealth of insights about the human element in teaching. Tributes to Woodrow Wilson, Frederick Jackson Turner, George Lyman Kittredge, Sigmund Freud, and Mark Hopkins are included, among others. The essays are as much recognitions of the distinctiveness of the persons involved as they are descriptions of specific teaching approaches. Anyone interested in a humanistic approach to the art of teaching will find this book a worthwhile source for viewing effective teaching as the expression of a powerful personality.

58   Runkel, Philip; Harrison, Roger; and Runkel, Margaret (eds.). *The Changing College Classroom*. San Francisco: Jossey-Bass, 1969. 359 pages.

Prepared during a time of increasing ferment in American higher education, these essays are first-person accounts of classroom innovations written by the teachers who developed them. The cirtical characteristic of these approaches is that they made "some change in the traditional student-teacher relationship in the college classroom." Of the sixteen chapters, four are devoted to educational theory or principles of innovation. The remainder describe "new practices," for freshman writing, programmed learning, teaching outside of one's field, engineering, business, and outreach projects. The practices are varied both in content and in method. Many of the essays convey a good deal of passion, and they comprise an interesting snapshot of a major growth period of postsecondary education. They are distinctive because of their focus on teacher-student relationships.

59   Sheffield, Edward F. (ed.). *Teaching in the University: No One Way.* Montreal: McGill-Queen's University Press, 1974. 252 pages.

This collection consists of twenty-three essays by teachers identified as excellent in a survey of 7,000 alumni of Canadian universities. Each describes personal beliefs about teaching and some favorite procedures. A fine arts professor says teaching is giving; an English professor says a teacher must thoroughly know and live his field; a lecturer shares techniques for a dramatic presentation; a biologist "sells" his subject. Teaching is viewed as honesty, creativity, involvement, and sensitivity. A chemistry teacher gives a "live exhibit" of how a chemist thinks; geology is related to the teaching of the arts and literature. Other topics discussed are authority, teaching, and education; teaching as relationships; phases of moving from the known to the unknown; and balancing research and teaching. A home economics professor discusses uses of student-centered teaching, and a professor of pharmaceutical education describes how he uses situation problems. The editor analyzes and summarizes these essays about college teaching. A major accomplishment of the book is to give evidence that shows that effective teaching has many faces, all of them attractive.

60   Shor, Ira. *Critical Teaching and Everyday Life.* Boston: South End Press, 1980. 270 pages.

Drawing on his experience with experimental teaching approaches during the open admissions years at City University of New York and on Freire's writings, Shor presents the story of the working class in college. His "empowering" theory of knowledge results in a critical or liberatory classroom that "pushes against the conditional boundaries of consciousness." This is a vividly written account with detailed examples from several of his literature and composition courses.

61 Taylor, Harold (ed.). *Essays in Teaching*. New York: Harper & Row, 1950. 239 pages.

The authors of these essays were professors at Sarah Lawrence College at the time that the editor was president. They write about their individual subjects and about the idea of a college, in order to tell how they stimulate and hold student interest. The subjects covered are literature, philosophy, psychology, poetry, history, art, music, and biology. Additional essays deal with teacher and student relationships, education and the family, Western values and the individual, and individual students. Some of the content shows its age, but the writers were all recognized for their scholarship at the time the collection was assembled, and many of the articles present refreshing insights about the interactions between teachers, students, and subject matter.

62 Wright, Richard A., and Burden, John A. *Teaching in the Small College: Issues and Applications*. Westport, Conn.: Greenwood Press, 1986. 188 pages.

Teachers in small colleges suffer from a dearth of empirical research about their work setting and particularly about teaching and learning in that setting. This book is aimed at providing some of the needed knowledge. It grew out of a 1984 conference, "Teaching in the Small College," which drew participants from Kansas, Nebraska, and Oklahoma. Five of the thirteen chapters are based on papers from that conference. Many chapters are first-person accounts of how the authors practice their profession, and many of them effectively evoke details of small college life—for example, instructions to new faculty on one campus to "greet anything that moves." Chapter topics include the one-person department, working with a teaching improvement committee, implementing a computer planning committee, teaching outside one's area, teaching liberal arts and religion, and teaching through local history. This is an excellent resource for a college professional development committee as well as for individual faculty at small colleges.

Planning and Providing Instruction

63 Abercrombie, M.L.J. *The Anatomy of Judgment: An Investigation into the Processes of Perception and Reasoning.* London: Hutchinson, 1960. 156 pages.

This research was conducted in a course designed to improve the diagnostic judgments of medical students. The course gave more attention to the processes of observing and thinking than to the results of those processes. Free group discussion was the primary vehicle for learning, as a recognition of the essentially social nature of learning diagnostic judgment. Students who learned in this way, compared with control students, discriminated better between facts and conclusions, drew fewer false conclusions, considered more than one solution, and were less adversely influenced by their experience with problems confronted earlier. The author's broad-ranging discussion of the topic of judgment, as well as the results of the experiment, have made this book an importance influence on later efforts toward collaborative or cooperative learning. The implications are as sound for undergraduate learners as they are for graduate or professional students.

64 Armstrong, R.H.R., and Taylor, J. L. (eds.). *Instructional Simulation Systems in Higher Education.* Cambridge, England: Cambridge Institute of Education, 1970. 216 pages.

Simulations are used as instructional tools in a variety of disciplines but are difficult to describe and evaluate. This volume begins with an overview chapter on college teaching research by Ruth Beard. Then thirteen contributors present case studies of particular simulations in military science, international relations, urban studies, and management, or they discuss more general topics, such as the effectiveness of simulations for instruction. The extensive details about what the simulations contain and how they are administered make the book particularly useful.

65   Baron, Naomi S. "Priesthood and Pedagogy: Examining
       Presuppositions." *EDUCOM Bulletin,* 1985, *20* (4), 13–16.

After a brief review of the evolution of computers in higher
education, Baron contrasts presuppositions about teaching held by
the "computer priesthood" (for example, software designers and
professors of computer science) with those held by the "pedagogical
priesthood" (professors in traditional disciplines). Presuppositions
of the latter group lead them to resist incorporating computers into
their teaching since they believe that, for example, "liberal arts
education is essentially nonvisual, that most teaching is a one-to-
many relationship exemplified by the lecture, and that academics
specialize in one narrow area." Suggestions are made about how the
presuppositions of both groups might be questioned and modified.

66   Berte, Neal R. (ed.). *Individualizing Education by Learning
       Contracts.* New Directions for Higher Education, no. 10.
       San Francisco: Jossey-Bass, 1975. 103 pages.

Learning contracts are written agreements between students and
teachers outlining the amount of work to be done and the credit that
the work will earn. Contracts are a means to individualize instruction within courses or for the student's entire program. Authors of
these sourcebook chapters present details about implementing
learning contracts in five institutions. They also discuss how
contracts affect the advising process and how evaluation of the use
of contracts might be conducted. Learning contracts can be costly,
particularly in faculty time, and may require reorientation of
faculty attitudes; on the other hand, the authors find that contracts
increase student choice and feelings of responsibility.

67   Billson, Janet M. "The College Classroom as a Small
       Group: Some Implications for Teaching and Learning."
       Teaching Sociology, 1986, *14,* 143–151.

From the considerable body of theory and research on small groups
in laboratory and training settings, the author has derived information applicable to college teaching and learning. She presents
fifteen principles of small group interaction, such as: "Every

participant in a group is responsible for the outcome of the group interaction. . . . Small groups function in two fundamental areas, task and socio-emotional. Morale, cohesion, solidarity, and effective problem-solving rest on the achievement of balance between them. . . . A group will set its own norms of behavior and will expect conformity to them. These norms may extend to the professor." Many of these principles are familiar, but each of them, as elaborated by the author, takes on new meanings and implications in the context of the college classroom. As a study document, this article may enhance faculty sensitivity and skill regarding group process.

68   Bjork, Robert A. "Information Processing Analysis of College Teaching." *Educational Psychologist*, 1979, *14*, 15–23.

Recent research on information processing can significantly improve college instruction because, according to the author, it better reflects the capabilities of college students than do stimulus-response or reinforcement theories. He discusses several research-based principles including the spacing effect, variable encoding, levels of processing, and the need for structure. Each principle is applied to such practical topics as how to study, course design, and lecturing.

69   Bligh, Donald (ed.). *Teaching Thinking by Discussion.* Philadelphia: Taylor & Francis, 1986. 246 pages.

Varieties of discussion techniques are described and illustrated in this collection of mostly British articles. Emphasis is on the kind of thinking each technique requires and promotes. Approaches termed tutorless or task-centered include (1) strategies for introducing group work (buzz groups, paired learning, horseshoe groups), (2) creative thinking groups (brainstorming, synectics), (3) project groups (group discussion, syndicates), and (4) case discussion. Approaches that use tutors include subject-centered tutorials and student-centered tutorials. Other chapters deal with issues that cut across approaches, such as developing skills necessary for leading groups, evaluating the effectiveness of groups, and trust. Included in the book are a glossary and a bibliography, with some annotations.

70 Bok, Derek. "Looking into Education's High-Tech Future." *EDUCOM Bulletin*, 1985, *20* (3), 2-10, 17.

In a broad-ranging essay, Harvard's president discusses "the power to transform the university" that new technologies possess, at least in theory. "At the very least, universities should manage to use technology to engage students in a more active process of thinking and problem solving that will help them learn more effectively." He gives examples showing that technology can reduce some of the drudgery involved in the tasks of writing, calculating, and administration; more efficiently teach facts and routines; and more effectively develop higher levels of thinking through tutoring, simulations, and expert systems. Cautions and objections about new technologies are also raised and discussed.

71 Boud, David (ed.). *Developing Student Autonomy in Learning*. New York: Nichols, 1981. 222 pages.

Contributors to this book write from their own experience about ways teachers can go beyond transmitting knowledge to helping students "take increasing responsibility for their own learning." Three chapters discuss student-peer-teacher relationships, the notion of power, and other conceptual issues. Seven case studies are drawn from several countries and range across history, engineering, medicine, psychology, architecture, and nursing. They illustrate such formats as independent study, tutoring, and contracts. The final two chapters deal with resistance to these approaches and discuss how they might be implemented successfully.

72 Boud, David; Keogh, Rosemary; and Walker, David. *Reflection: Turning Experience into Learning*. New York: Nichols, 1985. 170 pages.

From their work in continuing professional education, the authors have struggled toward a model for integrating learners' prior experience with their current learning and for ensuring that current learning is active. What turns experience into learning, they contend, is reflection; they conceive of reflection as a cycle of identifying what occurred, acknowledging the feelings the experience produced, and analyzing its meaning. This book deals with a variety of approaches to reflection and with applications to numerous areas: autobiographies and other kinds of writing, debriefing techniques and skills of attentive listening, skills of learning and organization, and collaborative inquiry and cooperative research. In a particularly provocative chapter, S. Kemmis argues that critical reflection is always a social and political activity shaped by ideology, although it may not always be regarded as such. The collection is a useful contribution to the literature on experiential learning.

73   Bowen, Donald D. "Developing a Personal Theory of Experiential Learning: A Dispatch from the Trenches." *Simulation & Games,* 1987, *18,* 192–206.

After he was exposed to experiential learning through T-groups, the author became dissatisfied with his customary use of lecture-discussion methods. From theory, research, and his subsequent experience, he has derived "a collection of working principles and hypotheses" that teachers in any field will find useful as guidelines for implementing experiential learning. He differentiates four types of experiential exercises: the illustrative exercise, the practice-feedback exercise, the vicarious learning exercise, and the self-assessment exercise. A summary table presents the nineteen principles discussed in the article, covering the design, selection, and use of experiential techniques. These principles should assist teachers who want to move toward more experiential teaching to think systematically about the new approach.

74   Bramley, W. *Group Tutoring: Concepts and Case Studies.* New York: Nichols, 1979. 221 pages.

This discussion of work with small groups of students has an especially strong theoretical underpinning, primarily from systems theory. Studies of tutoring groups identify significant characteristics of both group processes and effective leadership. Although the book is demanding for the nonspecialist, it could be a useful text for professional development workshops led by a specialist in group work.

75 Brewer, I. M. *Learning More and Teaching Less: A Decade of Innovation in Self-Instruction and Small Group Learning*. Guildford, Surrey, England: Society for Research into Higher Education and NFER-NELSON, 1985. 176 pages.

The author describes her distinctive approach to teaching plant anatomy, which incorporates self-pacing, audio/visual/print modules, and a good deal of peer interaction, including small group discussions of projected slides. The approach is termed SIMIG (Self-Instruction by Modules followed by Interaction among Groups). During ten years of use of the method, students have achieved greater mastery of facts and greater ability to solve problems, while reporting greater satisfaction. The relationship of this method to student learning styles and its application to other fields of study are also discussed at a nontechnical level.

★76 Brown, George. *Lecturing and Explaining*. London: Methuen, 1978. 134 pages.

This book analyzes the common professorial activities of lecturing and explaining. Two chapters deal with explaining (defined as "giving understanding to someone else"), three with delivering lectures, and one with helping students learn from lectures. Each chapter contains research-based expositions and eminently practical activities designed for practice. The forty-five activities include explaining a comparison or thesis, analyzing structure in lectures, improving diction and expressiveness, observing a lecture, and using students' reactions. The book is indispensable for teachers wishing to improve their explanations and lectures. It can be read alone or as part of a group experience, with as much time as desirable spent pursuing the suggested activities.

77   Brown, George, and Tomlinson, David. "How to Improve Handouts." *Medical Teacher*, 1980, *2*, 215-220.

This is one of a series of brief and extremely helpful how-to articles from a British journal written for medical educators. Handouts for use both during class and during private study are discussed and illustrated from medical courses. Issues of handout design, timing of distribution, and completeness of information are discussed from the authors' practical and research experience. The most important advice, applicable to all levels and fields of education, is to prepare handouts with particular learning objectives in mind and to use them to structure student participation rather than for passive reading.

78   Carnegie Commission on Higher Education. *The Fourth Revolution: Instructional Technology in Higher Education.* New York: McGraw-Hill, 1972. 102 pages.

The "fourth revolution" refers to the role in instruction of electronic communication technologies and data processing. This revolution is "adding to rather than replacing older approaches [the previous revolutions] as the teacher once added to what the family could offer, as writing then added to oral instruction, as the book later added to the hand-written manuscript." By the year 2000, the author predicts, perhaps 80 percent or more instruction off campus and 10 to 20 percent of instruction on campus is likely to involve these technologies. Implications are discussed for faculty, students, and such campus agencies as libraries. "Reasonable goals" for instructional technology are targeted for 1980, 1990, and 2000. While this report to the Carnegie Commission on Higher Education did not anticipate certain developments—for example, optical discs for data storage and retrieval—it contains helpful observations regarding adaptations, both internal and external, that people and institutions must make to these new modes of teaching and learning.

79   Carroll, David W. "Use of the Jigsaw Technique in Laboratory and Discussion Classes." *Teaching of Psychology,* 1986, *13*, 205-210.

In the jigsaw technique, each student in a small group is given a task essential to that group's project. The technique increases interaction and reduces competition among class members. This article describes use of the technique in a research methods class, where each student contributes one part of a research project (preparing instructions, running subjects, analyzing data, and so on). Students evaluate the technique favorably; since its introduction in the course, fewer students drop the course and grades are higher. Although this description is limited to one course, readers interested in using more cooperative activities in their classes will find that the jigsaw technique is easily modified for other courses and other disciplines.

★80   Chickering, Arthur W. *Experience and Learning: An Introduction to Experiential Learning.* New Rochelle, N.Y.: *Change* Magazine, 1977. 89 pages.

Experiential learning is contrasted with the university's traditional emphasis on theoretical, analytic, and reflective studies. Problems of awarding credit for experiential learning and providing appropriate staff and institutional support are discussed, and potentials for both student development and faculty development are explored. Examples of course plans and individual learning contracts provide practical illustrations. This book is a readable, balanced presentation of an often controversial topic.

81   Christensen, C. Roland. *Teaching and the Case Method: Texts, Cases, and Readings.* Boston, Mass.: Harvard Business School, 1987. 290 pages.

This book is used in the author's interdisciplinary seminar on teaching offered for Harvard faculty and graduate students. It is intended to disseminate to a wider audience the tradition and tools of case study methodology, which originated at the Harvard Business School. Included are a course outline, illustrative cases used in the seminar, and readings about teaching and learning reprinted from other sources. At meetings of the seminar, participants focus on teacher and student classroom roles, using such cases as "The Day the Heat Went On" and "The Case of the Dethroned Section Leader." Other issues central to the course and illustrated by cases include questioning, listening, student apathy, disruptions, and cheating. Most of the cases are set in business schools, but the readings are not focused quite so narrowly; all in all, the issues raised are easily generalized to other fields. The individual selections provide fascinating reading, and the book is an invaluable stimulus for faculty discussion and study.

82   Civikly, Jean M. (ed.). *Communicating in College Classrooms*. New Directions for Teaching and Learning, no. 26. San Francisco: Jossey-Bass, 1986. 103 pages.

"The unquestioning ease with which we approach our communication experiences may be our biggest obstacle to effective interaction in the classroom and elsewhere." These ten chapters address classroom communication issues and always keep the concern with effectiveness prominent. Of special interest are summaries of research and practice on communication apprehension (J. A. Daly) and on stages of developing interpersonal relationships (J. A. DeVita). Topics of other chapters include cultural diversity, communication style, humor, and confrontation.

83   Coe, George A. "Byproducts of the College Classroom." In Sherwood Eddy (ed.), *Am I Getting an Education?* Garden City, N.Y.: Doubleday, Doran, 1929, pp. 5–13.

The author has observed considerable student antagonism toward faculty, and he attributes it not to the strong disciplinary measures by which professors previously controlled students but rather to more recent conditions that prevent honesty between them. Among these factors, he cites the failure to train teachers "to understand their own minds and the minds about them," a marking system that fosters in students "a desire to appear to know," and the "overwhelming prominence" of the professor in the classroom. This essay has interest that is more than just historical since Coe's insights apply almost uncannily to many student-faculty relationships today.

84   Cross, K. Patricia. "A Proposal to Improve Teaching." *AAHE Bulletin*, 1986, *39* (1), 9–14.

In this perceptive essay the author calls attention to the fact that teaching in the college classroom has progressed little since its beginnings in the twelfth century. "Teaching as telling" still dominates classroom instruction. The author identifies external forces for change, such as the students themselves, the availability of technology, the growing interest in assessment and program evaluation, and the growing concern with alterable variables in educational research. The author believes that higher education is about to take college teaching seriously, and the major portion of the article is devoted to discussing what that means. The article is rich in content, and the author's points about the readiness of institutions for change combine effective scholarship with a pragmatic, attainable set of suggestions.

85   Diamond, Robert M.; Eickmann, Paul E.; Kelly, Edward F.; Holloway, Robert E.; Vickery, Tom R.; and Pascarella, Ernest T. *Instructional Development for Individualized Learning in Higher Education.* Englewood Cliffs, N.J.: Educational Technology Publications, 1975. 189 pages.

Individualized instruction, according to the systematic approach presented here, has six elements: flexible time schedules; diagnosis, remedial sequences, and unit exemptions; content options; student evaluations with alternate forms; a choice of locations; and alternate forms of instruction. The processes of instructional design, production, implementation, and evaluation are described and illustrated from projects of the Center for Instructional Development at Syracuse University. Costs of this approach are discussed, and an appendix deals with facilities needed to support the independent learning activities sometimes required.

86 Dressel, Paul L., and Thompson, Mary M. *Independent Study.* San Francisco: Jossey-Bass, 1973. 162 pages.

Independent study is usually treated only as a learning experience sometimes made available to students. These authors argue that it should be treated as "a capability to be developed." They discuss activities that increase students' academic autonomy at different points during undergraduate education, and they describe typical approaches, including several foundation-funded projects. Such obstacles as student passivity, which such programs must overcome, are noted and suggestions are made for developing approaches that view independent study more as a curriculum than as unrelated, discrete experiences.

87 Duchastel, Philippe. "Toward the Ideal Study Guide: An Exploration of the Functions and Components of Study Guides." *British Journal of Educational Technology,* 1983, *14,* 216-231.

Study guides give students maps for particular course assignments. Each of five components of a prototype study guide is described and illustrated: purpose, significance, and goals; text references; outline of subject matter; questions on subject matter; key words and phrases. Study guides are most useful when instruction departs from single texts and when content from diverse sources must be coordinated and integrated. Until we have more research-based information about student study practices, the advice in this article makes good practical sense.

88 Epstein, Herman T. *A Strategy for Education.* New York: Oxford University Press, 1970. 122 pages.

Students at Brandeis University pressed for changes in a biology course for nonscientists, and those changes led to the approach described in this book. The author attempted to design a course to teach "what a biologist does when he is doing biology." Students in the course "recreate" the research on a particular problem by reading through a set of papers under faculty guidance. In effect, faculty teach their own current research fields, and there are as many "courses" as there are teachers. Each meeting of the course is described, and an appendix reprints the first paper read along with an account of how the instructor used the paper in class to prompt student questions. Applications of the approach to other fields such as economics are also given, as are applications to other types of institutions. The method seems to work well with 80 to 90 percent of students who are selected according to the author's guidelines.

89   Feasley, Charles E. *Serving Learners at a Distance: A Guide to Program Practices.* ASHE-ERIC Higher Education Research Report no. 5. Washington, D.C.: Association for the Study of Higher Education, 1983. 69 pages. (ED 238 350)

The availability of educational programs beyond the bounds of the traditional college and university campus has a long history in higher education, with agricultural extension agents sponsored by land-grant colleges as an early model. This monograph discusses distance education and presents the dimensions of this rapidly growing phenomenon in higher education. After a brief summary of the attributes of distance learners, the author describes the faculty who serve these students. He then discusses how distance learning is provided, with an emphasis on the range of media used for extension instruction. Serving learners at a distance has progressed far beyond helping farmers with problems of agricultural management. This monograph is a useful and informative introduction to off-campus instruction.

90   Ferster, C. B. "Individualized Instruction in a Large Introductory Psychology College Course." *Psychological Record*, 1968, *18*, 521–532.

This approach, based on behavioral psychology, aims at "creating and maintaining new verbal behaviors in the classroom." During the self-paced course, a student schedules an interview with another student after both of them have read a particular section of the text (about 3,000 words). After one student presents the content of the reading assignment, "the listener comments on how the speaker covered the topic of the text, mentions important omissions, corrects inaccuracies of concept or language, or converses on some aspect of the subject matter." After three to five interviews on separate sections, the student takes a mastery quiz. Except for the interviews, the approach is much like the Personalized System of Instruction. In addition to documenting that students developed "a fluent active speaking repertoire," research showed that the course led to high achievement and to the instructor taking a role as an "ally who helps the student to master the content and concepts needed to certify him."

91 Finkel, Donald L., and Monk, G. Stephen. "Teachers and Learning Groups: Dissolution of the Atlas Complex." In C. Bouton and R. Y. Garth (eds.), *Learning in Groups*. New Directions for Teaching and Learning, no. 14. San Francisco: Jossey-Bass, 1983, pp. 83–97.

Some teachers shoulder the responsibility for providing students with "motivation, enlightenment, and a sense of purpose. Like Atlas, such teachers support the entire enterprise." Rather than holding on to all teaching functions, the teacher can learn to differentiate them and then distribute some of them appropriately to individual students or groups of students. The authors suggest how this can be done through an analysis of the course as a social system. Descriptions of several professors at work illustrate class activities before and after dissolution of the Atlas complex.

★92 Frederick, Peter. "The Dreaded Discussion: Ten Ways to Start." *Improving College and University Teaching*, 1981, *29*, 109–114.

The author believes that the key to retaining course material is "to own the discovery of a new learning insight or connection and to express that discovery to others." While classroom discussion seems to make such learning more likely, actually leading discussions prompts considerable fear and frustration for faculty. Ten specific ways of starting a discussion are described in detail, under the assumption that good planning is essential for a good discussion. They include testing goals and values, using concrete images, finding illustrative quotations, breaking into smaller groups, generating truth statements, forcing debate, and setting nonstructured scenes. The article contains practical wisdom and stimulating ideas from which systematic research might be generated.

93   Frederick, Peter J. "The Lively Lecture—Eight Variations." *College Teaching*, 1986, *34*, 43-50.

Lectures can and should provide interactive student participation, according to this author. Eight approaches to the lively lecture are described: the exquisite oral essay; the participatory lecture; problem solving (demonstrations, proofs, and stories); energy shifts (alternating mini-lectures and discussions); textual exegesis (modeling analytical skills); cutting large classes in half without losing control (debates); smaller groups in large classes (simulations and role playing); "bells and whistles" (the affective, emotional media lecture). Choice of an approach depends on the teacher's goals for students at a particular class meeting. These suggestions are practical and intuitively appealing. They deserve systematic investigation and articulation with theories of teaching and learning.

94   Friedman, Charles P.; Hirsch, Stanley; Parlett, Malcolm; and Taylor, Edwin F. "The Rise and Fall of PSI at MIT." *American Journal of Physics*, 1976, *44*, 204-211.

Following several small-scale trials, the Personalized System of Instruction was adopted for MIT's introductory physics course, which then enrolled more than 600 students. After four semesters the method was discontinued, and this article is a "postmortem" about what happened and why. The fall of PSI was due less to any shortcoming in bringing about student learning than to some initial organizational problems and especially to differences in perceptions about the innovation by those involved with it. Some of the issues about which perceptions differed in critical ways were what constituted success or failure of such an innovation, whether PSI could accommodate the "richness" of physics, what kind of course organization students really wanted, and what role was appropriate for faculty who led sections. The contribution of educational research and development specialists to such an effort is also discussed.

95   Fuller, Robert G. (ed.). *Piagetian Programs in Higher Education.* (7th printing) Lincoln, Nebr.: ADAPT Program, University of Nebraska, 1987. 175 pages.

In 1975, development of special college courses along Piagetian lines was begun at Nebraska under ADAPT, "Accent on Developing Abstract Processes of Thought." Impetus for the approach came from an observed inconsistency between what college students are expected to and what they are able to do. That is, although much college work presupposes that students can reason at Piaget's level of "formal operations," research shows that most college freshmen have great difficulty doing so. The contributors to this volume trace the roots of ADAPT in Piagetian theory; describe applications in science, social science, and humanities courses at Nebraska; and list similar programs on about a dozen other campuses.

96   Gilbert, Thomas F. "Saying What a Subject Matter Is." *Instructional Science*, 1976, 5, 29-53.

Defining subject matter is "the foremost unresolved issue in education." Gilbert's approach is to define subject matter as one does in the world of work, by deciding what one who has mastered the subject would accomplish, rather than how one can behave. History, for example, might then be defined as "mastery of predictions about social events." A curriculum map is developed and illustrated with reference to the social sciences. Among the "accomplishment objectives," which are used to derive learning and teaching activities for social science instruction, are the following: observing events, isolating variables, classifying variables, ordering causal relationships, seeking and selecting information, and making predictions. Gilbert's approach is a significant curriculum and course development tool, considerably broader than the behavioral objectives approach, and readers can profitably generalize it to other disciplines.

97   Goffman, Erving. "The Lecture." In *Forms of Talk.*
Philadelphia: University of Pennsylvania Press, 1981,
pp. 162–195.

In this beautifully composed piece, originally delivered as a lecture,
the prize-winning sociologist/author discusses lecturing in general
as well as with reference to college classrooms. There are illuminating discussions about purpose: "A lecture, then, purports to take the
audience right past the auditorium, the occasion, and the speaker
into the subject matter upon which the lecturer comments." About
technique: "Lecturers mark a natural turning point in the
acquisition of fresh-talk competence when they feel they can come
close to finishing a segment without knowing yet what in the world
the next will be, and yet be confident of being able to come up with
(and on time) something that is grammatically and thematically
acceptable, and all this without making it evident that a production
crisis has been going on." About the multiple self-projections of the
speaker: "Sensing that time is running short, a speaker may change
voice and let the hearers in on the fact that the pages he is now
turning over are ones he has now decided to summarize in fresh talk
or even skip, projecting the rather touching plea that he be given
credit for what he could have imparted." This is an essay with many
layers of meaning, rewarding both for its eloquent style and for its
provocative content.

98   Griffin, C. Williams (ed.). *Teaching Writing in All
Disciplines.* New Directions for Teaching and Learning,
no. 12. San Francisco: Jossey-Bass, 1982. 93 pages.

The movement called "writing across the curriculum" proclaims
(1) that writing is a process that can be taught, and (2) that writing
is a cognitive act, assisting learning in a variety of fields. Research
pertinent to those assertions is summarized by B. F. Walword, H. L.
Smith, and T. Fulwiler. Other authors describe class activities,
assignments, and grading practices involving writing in a variety of
fields, including mathematics and finance. A number of administrative arrangements characteristic of effective programs are also
described.

99   Gross, Francis L., Jr. "Teaching Cognitive-Moral Development in College (A Generalist Approach)." *Journal of General Education,* 1981, *32,* 287–308.

A course is described that aims at teaching cognitive-moral development. Students learn several cognitive development theories and are guided through exercises that elicit discussion of moral problems posed in literature and film. Details of course topics, exercises, and assignments provided here are useful for anyone interested in how this approach might be implemented.

100 Harrison, Shelley A., and Stolurow, L. M. *Improving Instructional Productivity in Higher Education.* Englewood Cliffs, N.J.: Educational Technology Publications, 1975. 272 pages.

These papers from a 1973 government-sponsored conference discuss technologically based instructional innovations. Descriptions and some evaluative information are provided about innovations classified into three categories: group and bounded learning environments (audio-tutorial, interactive lectures, and so forth); individualized and bounded learning environments (PLATO, Personalized System of Instruction, and so forth); and personal, open learning environments (home study, cultural activities, and so forth). Although technology has progressed enormously since 1973, these categories remain helpful.

101 Hayes-Roth, Frederick. "The Machine as Partner of the New Professional." *IEEE Spectrum: Journal of the Institute of Electrical and Electronics Engineers,* 1984, *21,* 28–31.

Like other professionals, academics must store and sort the sometimes overwhelming amounts of information and data made available through electronic technology. This article discusses ways electronic devices will supplant some human professionals by automating their work. The same devices will also stimulate growth of new professions that deal with human problems that machines cannot solve. Professionals who depend on intellectual skills alone may not survive. The author states, "In the future I expect knowledge systems to reduce the time a professional will need to spend in memorization, gathering, analysis, and reasoning to reach useful judgments. However, intuition and perception, two distinctively human skills, will become more and more important, especially in proportion to other skills."

102 Henderson, Euan S., and Nathenson, Michael B. (eds.). *Independent Learning in Higher Education.* Englewood Cliffs, N.J.: Educational Technology, 1984. 336 pages.

The extraordinary accomplishments of the first twelve years of Great Britain's Open University are presented with an emphasis on the topic of course development. Contributors describe their theoretical framework, which draws on theories of adult development, and give examples of the following: preliminary organizers, self-assessment and self-remediation strategies, activity-based learning, use of case studies and project-based learning, and developing study skills. Illustrations from course materials range across many disciplines and include many ingenious and motivating devices. This is an excellent resource for course developers and for those working in distance education or in other settings that require learner independence.

103 Hill, William F. *Learning Through Discussion: Guide for Leaders and Members of Discussion Groups.* Beverly Hills, Calif.: Sage, 1969. 64 pages.

This manual for discussion groups in both classroom and nonclassroom settings elaborates a nine-step "group cognitive map." Discussion is governed by these steps rather than by the arbitrary authority of the leader. Once a text to be discussed has been selected, the map prescribes these steps: definition of terms and concepts, general statement of author's message, identification of major themes or subtopics, allocation of time, discussion of major themes and subtopics, integration of material with other knowledge, application of the material, evaluation of the author's presentation, and evaluation of group and individual performance. The book also describes appropriate skills and roles for both members and the group as a whole. Criteria of a good group are listed.

104 Horn, Robert E., and Cleaves, Anne (eds.). *Guide to Simulations/Games for Education and Training.* Beverly Hills, Calif.: Sage, 1980. 692 pages.

Hundreds of games and simulations for all levels of education are listed. Annotations describe how each is structured and played, and sometimes include evaluative comments. About half the book is devoted to essays that evaluate simulations/games by type or by field—for example, computer simulation games, frame games, history games and simulations, sex role games and simulations. The book includes an author index, a game index, and a producer index. Although somewhat dated, this remains the most comprehensive compendium of its kind.

105 Hursh, Barbara A., and Borzak, Lenore. "Toward Cognitive Development Through Field Studies." *Journal of Higher Education,* 1979, *50,* 63–78.

Field study programs include both full-time work experiences and combinations of part-time work with part-time study. Students in this research worked full time in community service agencies, and their experiences appear to have enhanced their cognitive development. Numerous changes reported by students or inferred from student papers are interpreted in terms of role theory. Role discontinuity, the abrupt change from the student role to the intern role, and role ambiguity, the initially unclear role of the intern, apparently produced a readiness for learning by making students more open to new perspectives. Alternative ways to reduce role conflicts are discussed.

106 Hyman, Ronald T. *Improving Discussion Leadership.* New York: Teachers College Press, 1980. 154 pages.

Discussion can be improved, says the author, if people are trained in the skills of discussion leadership. Readers of this book can use its evaluation forms and study its six chapters on basic discussion skills: contributing, crystalizing, focusing, introducing/closing, questioning, and supporting. Suggestions for practicing the skills are also given. Other chapters deal with disruptive behaviors in discussions and with giving and receiving feedback during discussion. The book is a readable and very practical resource for group leaders at all educational levels.

107 Jackson, Gregory A. "Technology and Pedagogy: Making the Right Match Is Vital." *Change,* 1986, *18* (3), 52-57.

Diverse applications of technology to higher education instruction are illustrated through brief case reports: tutoring in basic science, discovery learning in a science laboratory, problem solving in composition, simulation in a finance course. Some approaches are highly directive and others are open; some are group-based and others are individualized. The author discusses the complexities of matching instructional software with the professor's pedagogical preferences, skills, and objectives. This article can stimulate productive discussion in institutions beginning to define ways technology might enhance teaching.

108 Karp, David A., and Yoels, William C. "The College Classroom: Some Observations on the Meanings of Student Participation." *Sociology and Social Research,* 1976, *60,* 421-439.

What determines students' decisions about whether or not to speak during discussion? Ten college classes, ranging from twelve to sixty-five students, were studied, using questionnaires and direct observation. Regardless of the size of the class, about the same number of students participated—nine to ten. Early in the life of the class, norms emerged about which students were likely to participate, a "consolidation of responsibility" phenomenon that relieved other students from the responsibility of participation. Differences in how students and teachers define "intellectual work" are also discussed. The compromises students make between these views result in a kind of civil attention in which "they must appear committed enough not to alienate the teacher without at the same time showing so much involvement that the situation becomes risky for them." This study is a provocative contribution to understanding the dynamics of discussion, especially dynamics peculiar to postsecondary education.

109 Katz, Joseph (ed.). *Teaching as Though Students Mattered.* New Directions for Teaching and Learning, no. 21. San Francisco: Jossey-Bass, 1985. 112 pages.

The editor believes that students should become an object for study by the teacher and that students should be more active participants in their own learning. These essays illustrate that point of view in a variety of fields across the curriculum. The volume grew out of a project supported by the Fund for the Improvement of Postsecondary Education.

★**110** Keller, Fred S. "Good-Bye, Teacher . . .'." *Journal of Applied Behavioral Analysis,* 1968, *1*, 79–89.

This address to the American Psychological Association is an early description of the Personalized System of Instruction by the founder of that approach. It evolved from work in the early 1960s in Brazil, at Columbia University, and later at Arizona State University, influenced by contributions of S. Postlethwaite and C. B. Ferster. Handouts given to students are quoted to identify the major features of the approach (self-pacing, unit mastery, motivational role of lecturers, student proctors), and the experience of a typical student in a PSI course is recounted in detail. PSI courses are found to increase students' academic interactions, involve more individual testing, and yield an upside-down grade distribution. Although the approach draws from animal research by behavioral psychologists, this paper is nontechnical and optimistic that the approach will lead to a new role for the teacher (hence, the title). "I learned one very important thing: the student is always right. He is not asleep, not unmotivated, not sick, and he can learn a great deal if we provide the right contingencies of reinforcement."

111 Keller, Fred S. "Ten Years of Personalized Instruction." *Teaching of Psychology,* 1974, *1*, 4–9.

The first decade of the Personalized System of Instruction is reviewed by the founder of the approach. He describes how PSI evolved and was disseminated, citing a compilation of courses in science, mathematics, engineering, and social science that indicates the number of offerings more than doubled from 1972 to 1974. "Such evidence as we have today makes me believe that personalized instruction is going to survive—that the teacher's verdict will be for it, and that the days of traditional group education may be numbered."

112 Kemp, Jerrold E. *The Instructional Design Process*. New York: Harper & Row, 1985. 301 pages.

An instructional planning method with ten elements is presented and illustrated. Elements include learner characteristics, learning objectives, teaching-learning activities, support services, and so on. Review and application questions for each chapter help readers use the method to develop their own instructional units, and two sample units are given in the appendix. There is also a glossary. The method is easily applied to higher education, and the book is an excellent introduction for college teachers to systematic instructional planning.

113 Kendall, Jane C.; Duley, John S.; Little, Thomas C.; Permaul, Jane S.; and Rubin, Sharon. *Strengthening Experiential Education Within Your Instruction*. Raleigh, N.C.: National Society for Internships and Experiential Education, 1986. 154 pages.

Many colleges offer opportunities for active learning by means of service opportunities, internships, field studies, and so on. This volume differentiates these various forms of experiential education, provides program models and evaluation systems, and discusses costs and innovation strategies. The book is a source of uniquely practical advice and guidelines about experiential education.

★114 Knowles, Malcolm S. *Using Learning Contracts: Practical Approaches to Individualizing and Structuring Learning*. San Francisco: Jossey-Bass, 1986. 262 pages.

A learning contract is a written agreement between a learner and teacher or supervisor, outlining learning needs and objectives, appropriate learning resources and strategies, and the evidence that indicates satisfactory accomplishments. It also states the procedures by which evidence will be judged. The innovative quality of learning contracts is that, rather than specifying content to be covered (content plan), they specify how content will be acquired (process plan). Sample contracts used in a variety of settings, including independent study, academic classrooms, internships, and professional development, are included, along with instructions for their preparation and use. This general discussion, supplemented by concrete examples, illustrates how contracts can increase the independence of learners while recognizing their diversity.

115 LaFouci, Horatio M., and Richter, Peyton E. *Team Teaching at the College Level.* Elmsford, N.Y.: Pergamon Press, 1970. 157 pages.

In 1949, faculty teams began teaching courses in Boston University's College of Basic Studies; subsequently, the entire two-year collegiate program was taught using that method. This volume describes the program in detail: administration, facilities, curriculum, and student and faculty roles. Limitations and prospects of the approach are also discussed, emphasizing that team teaching "promotes close personal relations, invites continuous student involvement, and, above all, respects the autonomy of each student."

116 Lewis, Linda H. (ed.). *Experiential and Simulation Techniques for Teaching Adults.* New Directions for Continuing Education, no. 30. San Francisco: Jossey-Bass, 1986. 111 pages.

Chapters in this sourcebook describe several techniques by which simulations can be used with adult learners. The authors discuss and illustrate such techniques as video, computer simulations, cases, work simulations, work placements, travel, and theater. A final essay discusses each approach in terms of Kolb's experiential learning model. This one volume discusses a variety of techniques that are usually covered only in disparate sources.

117 Locatis, Craig N., and Atkinson, Francis D. "Designing Instructional Simulations: Heuristics for Training College and University Faculty." *Simulation & Games*, 1981, *12*, 333-344.

The authors describe training they provide for faculty who wish to design simulation exercises for instructional use. Components of the training are described, including a flowchart to guide the design of simulations. They emphasize that simulations should be used only for instructional objectives where "student involvement in an activity that represents reality" is both appropriate and preferable to either direct experience or to vicarious learning through books, lectures, and discussion.

118 McLeish, John; Mateson, Wayne; and Park, James. *The Psychology of the Learning Group*. London: Hutchinson, 1973. 221 pages.

Several studies of group development are reported in this volume. In most cases, the research is set in group dynamics or human relations courses at the college level, and the courses follow such models as Tavistock, case-study, and direct communications. Small group teaching is compared with other instructional approaches for higher education. A number of issues pertinent to small groups are discussed, including power relationships, feelings, role development, and leadership. Although results of the research reported here are equivocal, the book offers much useful information about the rationale and practice of small group teaching and about methods for the systematic study of learning groups. A glossary is included.

119 McNall, Scott G. "Peer Teaching: A Description and Evaluation." *Teaching Sociology*, 1975, *2*, 133-146.

Research suggests that when students teach one another there is usually a grade increase for the tutors and sometimes one for the tutees. For both groups, attitudes are likely to become more positive. This article describes a program for sociology students in which tutors are rewarded according to their tutees' improved exam performance.

120 Mager, Robert F. *Preparing Instructional Objectives.* (2nd ed.) Belmont, Calif.: Fearon, 1975. 136 pages.

This short book, written in a semiprogrammed format, is a classic statement of the characteristics of the "usefully stated" instructional objective. Such an objective indicates the performance expected from the learner, the conditions under which that performance occurs, and the criterion that the performance must reach to be acceptable. The book guides readers in practicing and testing mastery of skills needed for writing such objectives. Most examples are appropriate for higher and adult education.

121 Meyers, Chet. *Teaching Students to Think Critically: A Guide for Faculty in All Disciplines.* San Francisco: Jossey-Bass, 1986. 131 pages.

Taking the position that critical thinking should be taught "in different ways by teachers in different disciplines," Meyers uses cognitive science concepts and the work of Piaget to develop a framework for teaching attitudes and skills of critical thinking to students. Chapters deal with developing students' capacities for abstract thought, fostering interest and motivation, and designing effective written assignments. Sample assignments and exercises for students are provided. One chapter discusses how to prepare professors to teach critical thinking. This exposition includes no evaluation of the effectiveness of the approach, and it is not always clear how the methods were derived from the concepts said to underlie them. Nevertheless, the volume is a stimulating guide for those in postsecondary education interested in trying a critical thinking approach.

122 Mullen, J. G. "An Attempt at a Personalized Course in Thermodynamics." *American Journal of Physics,* 1975, *43,* 354-360.

An elementary course in thermodynamics for thirteen students was restructured to become more personalized, applying the approach of Carl Rogers. By centering on projects, the instructor avoided two common "deceptions": (1) that professors doing derivations promote learning and (2) that courses designed for "broad exposure" lead to significant learning. Each of the projects was graded by students, resulting in a grade that the instructor usually agreed with, and students prepared a final report summarizing what they got out of the course. These student reports are quoted at length as evidence of varied but generally positive reactions, even by students who began with negative expectations. The instructor found that students worked hard and well and enjoyed the spontaneity of the approach. This article is one of the relatively few documented attempts to apply a Rogerian approach, particularly in a science discipline.

123 Neale, Daniel C. "Specifications for Small Group Activities in Instructional Design." *Instructional Science*, 1984, *13*, 15-35.

When planning courses and designing instruction, professors find little guidance about how to implement small group methods. This article takes a systematic approach, using seven descriptive categories from which small group activities can be specified. Each category is defined and illustrated in terms of well-known approaches: tutorial, brainstorming, role playing, and so on. The categories include locating the small group activity within the larger design, defining intended benefits of the activity, describing member roles, describing group tasks, and defining reward structures and evaluation procedures. This "specification" approach should be useful for instructional designers and for developing exercises for faculty workshops.

124 Penner, Jon G. *Why Many College Teachers Cannot Lecture: How to Avoid Communication Breakdown in the Classroom.* Springfield, Ill.: Thomas, 1984. 212 pages.

The author's specialization in the field of speech leads to an analysis of classroom communication in terms of three elements from that field: the verbal (word symbols), the vocal (sound qualities of the voice), and the visible (movements and gestures). The author justifies lecturing, when it is well done, and suggests how lectures may be used most effectively. While some of the advice on presentations is commonplace, there are particularly useful sections on gaining and maintaining student attention, clarifying for students why one's course is worthy of study, and specifying the responsibilities of students in the classroom. The book covers more than the title suggests, with a particularly outstanding chapter on motivation.

★125 Postlethwaite, Samuel N.; Novak, Joseph; and Murray, Hal. *An Integrated Experience Approach to Learning with Emphases on Independent Study.* Minneapolis, Minn.: Burgess, 1964. 114 pages.

In his teaching of botany at Purdue, the first author developed the "audio-tutorial approach." Under this approach, students progress through learning units at their individual pace, studying at work stations equipped with exhibits, audiotapes, films, and other materials. Widespread interest in the approach prompted this book, "designed to answer questions and to serve as both invitation and blueprint for your participation in the continuing growth of a program that represents unusual opportunity for improved teaching." According to the authors, grades have risen under the program, "students' attitudes are considerably improved, vandalism is reduced, and at least one-third more information can be presented in an equivalent length of time."

126 Robin, Arthur L. "Behavioral Instruction in the College Classroom." *Review of Educational Research,* 1976, *46,* 313–354.

In this review, behavioral instruction refers primarily to the Personalized System of Instruction. Across thirty-nine studies comparing PSI with other methods, there is a consistent achievement gain (of 8 percent to 11 percent) favoring PSI. More content is retained with PSI, and student attitudes are more positive. When components of the approach are studied, the following emerge as most important: frequent testing, proctoring, unit-perfection requirement, and study objectives. Areas for future research are specified.

127 Rossini, Frederick A. "EARTHNET: The University of the Future." *Technological Forecasting and Social Change*, 1984, *26*, 189–194.

The present university is "about to be trashed because of intellectual, organizational, and technological obsolescence." In its place, Rossini advocates an alternative institution that might more adequately achieve the following goals: (1) effective and efficient transmission of existing basic knowledge; (2) advanced instruction in frontier knowledge in rapidly changing fields; (3) development of new knowledge through research; (4) effective and efficient transmission of research results to the full spectrum of users; and (5) ongoing, fundamental, constructive criticism of our complex technological society. It would be a network (EARTHNET) rather than a place, and it might be established as an independent entity. If successful, it would "assimilate all the activities of today's universities by the old trick of driving the competition out of the market."

128 Rowntree, Derek. *Teaching Through Self-Instruction*. New York: Nichols, 1986. 386 pages.

Practical advice in an admirably straightforward style is directed at those who wish to produce or better use self-instructional material, that is, materials employed by learners without extensive teacher contact for part or all of the work in a course. The book treats selection of media and activities, text production, learner assessment, and other pertinent topics. Especially helpful are the examples of printed materials that are reproduced from self-instructional units. The book is appropriate for study by individual teachers or by faculty groups with or without an instructor. Its systematic approach could benefit virtually any area of teaching.

129 Ruskin, Robert S. *The Personalized System of Instruction: An Educational Alternative.* AAHE-ERIC Higher Education Research Report no. 5. Washington, D.C.: American Association for Higher Education, 1974. 44 pages. (ED 093 256)

The Personalized System of Instruction is seen as an illustration of the "software revolution" that gives systematic attention to the design and use of instructional materials. This essay outlines the history of PSI and its fundamental features—namely, stress on the written word, unit mastery requirement, student self-pacing, lectures as motivators, and student proctors. Courses using PSI are described, and research is summarized that suggests that performance of students under PSI "is equal to or surpasses most traditional lecture approaches." Balanced and generally optimistic, this presentation is an excellent place to begin to learn about PSI.

130 Scholes, Robert E. *Textual Power: Literary Theory and the Teaching of English.* New Haven, Conn.: Yale University Press, 1985. 176 pages.

This book treats the teaching of literature and composition from the perspective of "the pedagogy of textual power: the ways in which teachers can help students to recognize the power texts have over them and assist the same students in obtaining a measure of control over textual processes, a share of textual power for themselves." With illustrations from Hemingway, the discussion defines movement from "submission to textual authority in reading, through a sharing of textual power in interpretation, toward an assertion of power through opposition in criticism." The author argues for a shift from defining the curriculum in terms of a literary canon to construing it as textual studies. The book is concerned more with theory than with instructional applications and deals explicitly only with literary studies. Nevertheless, the practical implications of this position deserve development, and implications could be worked out for other disciplines, particularly any discipline in which the study of texts is considered fundamental.

131 Spear, Karen I. (ed.). *Rejuvenating Introductory Courses.* New Directions for Teaching and Learning, no. 20. San Francisco: Jossey-Bass, 1984. 116 pages.

In eight chapters plus suggested readings, the authors discuss both what to teach in introductory courses and how teaching should be done. Examples of introductory courses in the following fields are discussed at length: life sciences, psychology, philosophy, and general science. The volume is noteworthy as one of the few resources on this topic.

132 Spinrad, Robert J. "The Electronic University." *EDUCOM Bulletin,* 1983, *18* (15), 4–8.

A vision of life in the not-too-distant electronic university is presented in three vignettes portraying the daily life of members of that institution. Students depend on electronic mail, word processing, data banks of old examinations, and so on. Professors revise and display class notes via computer, search the literature electronically, and correspond with colleagues via computer terminals. Administrators are faced with such decisions as defining and paying for equitable access to electronically based information. Spinrad's article provides a provocative vision for university planning and curriculum committees.

133 Thorson, Esther (ed.). *Simulation in Higher Education.* Hicksville, N.Y.: Exposition, 1979. 343 pages.

This book describes and evaluates a broad range of simulations, including many developed and used at Denison University, where most of the authors teach. Chapters discuss simulations appropriate for the general liberal arts context and for the specific fields of chemistry, logic, urban studies, economics, values clarification, geography, history, international relations, psychology, and faculty development.

134 Timpson, William M., and Tobin, David N. *Teaching as Performing: A Guide for Energizing Your Public Presentation.* Englewood Cliffs, N.J.: Prentice-Hall, 1982. 205 pages.

Relationships between teaching and the performing arts, particularly theater, are elaborated according to views of both teachers and actors. Extended quotations from literature show teachers at work through the eyes of novelists and playwrights. Most valuable are the tips and exercises tailored for teachers. These cover warming up, controlling energy, vocal techniques, improvisation, and so on. The book is appropriate for teachers at all levels of education.

135 Tough, Allen. *The Adult's Learning Projects: A Fresh Approach to Theory and Practice in Adult Learning.* Toronto: Ontario Institute for Studies in Education, 1971. 191 pages.

This pioneering study of adult learning, based on interviews with people who have developed and pursued individual learning projects, has significant implications for the teaching of adults. The author discusses what is learned in such projects and why they are undertaken; the planning process, whether in a group or with one other person; and characteristic problems, such as the dilemmas of autonomy and control.

136 Trivett, David A. *Competency Programs in Higher Education.* AAHE-ERIC Higher Education Research Report no. 7. Washington, D.C.: American Association for Higher Education, 1975. 68 pages. (ED 118 023)

Development of competency programs is guided by "a model of what constitutes an educated person." Programs are characterized by "emphasis on behavioral objectives, mastery learning, and testing of competence rather than narrowly defined ideas of academic achievement based on intelligence-type tests." This research report describes features of programs on eight campuses. Most were too new at the time the report was written for their effectiveness to be known, but the author discusses issues in implementing and evaluating such programs.

137 Tucker, Marc S. (ed.). "Computers on Campus: Working Papers." *Current Issues in Higher Education*, 1983–84, Number 2, pp. 1–38.

Imaginative uses of computers on several campuses are described. Three "hothouse" institutions that have made extraordinary commitments to such research and development are Carnegie-Mellon, Brown, and M.I.T. At four others, applications to specific areas of instruction are described: University of Maryland (physics), Colorado State University (economics), University of Illinois (medicine), and Milwaukee Area Technical College (high-technology equipment).

138 van Ments, Morry. *The Effective Use of Role Play: A Handbook for Teachers and Trainers*. London: Kogan Page, 1983. 186 pages.

Role playing is justified and elaborated as a technique with a distinctive place within the systematic approach to teaching. Chapters take readers through the practical steps of writing, running, and debriefing role plays, covering both the single role play and various ways that a series of role plays can be linked. This is a helpful resource for people, in whatever field, who want to develop role play applications.

139 Weimer, Maryellen G. (ed.). *Teaching Large Classes Well*. New Directions for Teaching and Learning, no. 32. San Francisco: Jossey-Bass, 1987. 108 pages.

Eight essays in this book provide sensible and useful advice for those who teach classes of 100 or more students. Topics include objectives appropriate for large classes, student perceptions of large classes, advice about strategies for teaching and managing large classes, techniques for effective communication and student involvement, and ways of giving and obtaining student feedback. A thirty-two-item bibliography lists related publications from a variety of academic fields. This collection is an excellent resource for workshops about teaching and for any teacher new to large classes.

140 Weston, Cynthia, and Cranton, P. A. "Selecting Instructional Strategies." *Journal of Higher Education,* 1986, *57,* 259–288.

This approach differentiates four categories of instructional methods and three characteristics of instructional materials. The categories of instructional methods are instructor-centered (lecturing, questioning, demonstration), interactive (discussion, peer teaching, group projects), individualized (programmed and modularized instruction, independent projects, computerized instruction), and experiential (field/clinical, laboratory, role-playing, simulations). The characteristics of instructional materials are the delivery system or medium, the content or message, and the form or condition of abstractedness. Choice of method and materials depends on such practical matters as class size, the teacher's learning objectives, characteristics of the audience, and so on. While this system is not prescriptive, it can help teachers make more deliberate choices about instructional methods.

141 Wiseman, Michael. "The BIJOU Teaching Support System." *Perspectives in Computing,* 1986, *6* (1), 4–13.

The Berkeley-IBM Joint Office Utility (BIJOU) project developed this system for supporting professors' management of large courses. It assists with six administrative tasks: recording preenrollment data and section assignments; grade recording and record keeping for teaching assistants; preparing student performance evaluations and giving feedback; preparing outlines, handouts, and transparencies; communicating with teaching and support staff; and maintaining archives for subsequent data retrieval. Although this particular system may not become the standard in higher education, it is an interesting example of an attempt to identify the administrative tasks in large classes where some of the routine functions can be potentially ameliorated through computer assistance.

Evaluating and Improving Instruction

142 Abrahamson, Stephen. "Evaluation of Continuing Education in the Health Professions: The State of the Art." *Evaluation and the Health Professions,* 1984, *7,* 3-23.

Problems of evaluation in continuing education for the health professions are discussed. Selection of variables that indicate effectiveness is a critical issue; those variables include attendance and satisfaction, changed professional performance, and patient outcomes. Effectiveness variables are illustrated with reference to the professional literature since 1960. The variety of reasons for evalution are discussed; they are related to the desired "purity" of the evaluation plan, that is, to the use of stringent controls and sophisticated statistical analysis procedures. In some cases, evaluation is appropriately considered to be part of the educational treatment rather than a relatively pure research activity. Since these issues have their counterparts in any evaluation of teaching improvement activities, the article is useful for advisory committees and evaluators in faculty development, regardless of discipline or educational level.

143 Abrami, Philip C.; Leventhal, Les; and Perry, Raymond P. "Educational Seduction." *Review of Educational Research,* 1982, *52,* 446-464.

Considerable research during the 1970s investigated educational seduction, that is, the extent to which student ratings of instruction reflect the expressive personal style of the instructor rather than the instructor's ability to convey educational content. This review and meta-analysis notes that variations in lecturer expressiveness typically had a large effect on student ratings but a small impact on student achievement. By contrast, variations in lecture content had a large effect on student achievement and a small impact on student ratings. The authors argue that these findings need not be seen as evidence against the validity of student ratings but may be useful in investigating teacher characteristics related to correlations between ratings and teacher-produced achievement.

144 American Association of Colleges for Teacher Education. *Improvement of Instruction in Higher Education.* Washington, D.C.: American Association of Colleges for Teacher Education, 1962. 62 pages.

A six-person subcommittee of the American Association of Colleges for Teacher Education surveyed its 577 member institutions and here reports findings in four areas: (1) how institutions recognize and reward teaching (310 returns from institutions), (2) how faculty are recruited and appointed (361 returns), (3) how new faculty are oriented (261 returns), and (4) how teachers evaluate their own teaching (5,303 returns from professors in member institutions). With regard to orienting new faculty, the most popular technique was "talks by key administrative officials" (91 percent), and the least popular was "team teaching with experienced staff members" (15 percent). With regard to faculty evaluating their own teaching, "in general, the tools judged most successful for self-evaluation are teacher oriented in terms of gathering information rather than student oriented . . . the most used tools frequently are not the ones with the highest success ratios."

145 American Association of University Professors. "Statement on Teaching Evaluation." *AAUP Bulletin,* 1975, *61,* 200–202.

Adopted in 1975, this statement sets forth AAUP guidelines on "proper teaching evaluation methods and their appropriate use in personnel decisions." According to the statement, evaluation should include a description of what one does as a teacher, measures of effectiveness, and consideration of the relationship between those efforts and the expectations and needs of the organization. Pertinent data on teaching effectiveness might include information about student learning, reports of classroom visits, student perceptions, self-evaluation, and outside opinions. This statement is a helpful and highly credible resource for those developing campus policies and procedures on evaluation of teaching.

146 Bennett, John B., and Chater, Shirley S. "Evaluating the Performance of Tenured Faculty Members." *Educational Record*, 1984, *65*, 38–41.

Regular evaluations of posttenure faculty are an increasing practice in higher education. Such activities are better thought of as "evaluation" than as "review," since the latter may imply the risk of losing tenure. Care must be taken that procedures are applied universally and uniformly. Advantages of posttenure evaluations outweigh their disadvantages, according to the authors, but "the primary goal . . . must be to foster and maintain excellent performance." Guidelines are given for criteria and evidence, process, feedback, and models for such evaluations.

147 Benton, Sidney E. *Rating College Teaching: Criterion Studies of Student Evaluation-of-Instruction Instruments.* AAHE-ERIC Higher Education Research Report no. 1. Washington, D.C.: American Association for Higher Education, 1982. 50 pages. (ED 221 147)

How closely does student learning, measured by exam scores, correlate with student ratings of courses and teachers? Although conceptual and methodological problems complicate research on this issue, it appears that the relationship is at least moderately positive. Findings are strongest for such dimensions of instruction as teacher skill and course structure. Some research is reviewed where ratings were validated against criteria other than student achievement in courses. These criteria include students' interest in advanced courses and ratings of teachers' classroom behavior by trained observers.

148 Boud, David, and McDonald, R. *Educational Development Through Consultancy.* Guildford, Surrey, England: Society for Research into Higher Education, 1981. 54 pages.

This book is designed for educational professionals asked to serve as consultants to colleagues on teaching issues. The authors advocate no single model of consultation but raise issues and questions to guide consultants through the decisions they must make. The discussion is organized around five stages of the consultancy process: initial contact, defining the consulting relationship, methods of working, reporting, and further action and completion.

149 Bowen, Howard R., and Douglass, Gordon K. *Efficiency in Liberal Education: A Study of Comparative Instructional Costs for Different Ways of Organizing Teaching-Learning in a Liberal Arts College.* New York: McGraw-Hill, 1971. 149 pages.

In this report issued by the Carnegie Commission on Higher Education, the relationship of cost and quality in instruction is examined through a model that includes labor costs, intensity of labor, capital, scale of operations, and other variables. Five methods of instruction, here called modes, are described: conventional instruction, a rational mix of class sizes (the Ruml Plan), independent study, extensive tutorials (the Bakan Plan), and self-paced instruction using audiovisual equipment (the Kieffer Plan). A hypothetical small liberal arts college was simulated to compare these modes in terms of dollar cost per student. Strengths and limitations of individual modes and of eclectic mixes of modes are reviewed. Although today's modes may differ from the ones examined in this report, this simulation model can generate useful data for planning and budgeting decisions and can serve as a means of sensitizing faculty members to the variety and subtlety of cost factors.

★**150** Braskamp, Larry A.; Brandenburg, Dale C.; and Ory, John C. *Evaluating Teaching Effectiveness: A Practical Guide.* Beverly Hills, Calif.: Sage, 1984. 136 pages.

This guidebook suggests that a variety of perspectives should be used in evaluating teaching and that, prior to undertaking evaluation, its purpose must be clearly specified (for example, teaching improvement or personnel evaluation). Most of the book is devoted to how information about teaching can be gathered from students, colleagues, self, alumni, and records, and how that information might be used. The discussion of each of these sources covers the technical quality of the information, includes specimen instruments for information gathering, and offers suggestions about how that information may be used for improving teaching and for personnel decisions. Suggestions for evaluation practices are explicitly linked to research findings, although details of research are not presented. The volume is a readable and convenient resource for administrators, members of review committees, and faculty preparing to be reviewed.

151 Brick, Michael, and McGrath, Earl J. *Innovation in Liberal Arts Colleges.* New York: Teachers College Press, 1969. 173 pages.

This monograph is one of a number published by the Institute of Higher Education at Teachers College, Columbia University, related to the evolving liberal arts in today's colleges and universities. The study reported here was an attempt to "develop a picture of the novel and creative practices that were introduced in the liberal arts colleges in the United States in recent years." All four-year institutions in the United States offering a program in the liberal arts were surveyed. New approaches to instructional methods and to curriculum are discussed together with evidence for new patterns of student involvement and organizational restructuring in liberal arts colleges. Illustrative case studies are presented. The authors provide a comprehensive overview of changes taking place in liberal arts programs up to the publication date.

152 Carroll, J. Gregory. "Effects of Training Programs for University Teaching Assistants: A Review of Empirical Research." *Journal of Higher Education,* 1980, *51,* 167–183.

The number of workshops, courses, and orientation programs for graduate teaching assistants increased dramatically during the 1960s and 1970s, but the author found only seventeen empirical studies of the effects of such training efforts. This research shows that programs have been effective in altering participants' teaching behaviors, but it is less clear what the effects are on attitudes and knowledge and on the students of participating TAs. Considerably more research is called for, and the article discusses the form that research should take and the questions it should attempt to answer.

153 Centra, John A. *Determining Faculty Effectiveness: Assessing Teaching, Research, and Service for Personnel Decisions and Improvement.* San Francisco: Jossey-Bass, 1979. 204 pages.

This volume is a comprehensive overview of issues and procedures for evaluating the effectiveness of faculty members, primarily in their teaching roles, and is written in a style accessible to faculty from all fields. Advantages and disadvantages of several kinds of information are discussed, for both summative and formative purposes. These kinds of information include student ratings, colleague evaluations, student learning data, and self-analysis. One chapter is devoted to assessment of research, advising, and public service, and one to legal considerations. Steps in assembling multiple sources of information and using them to reach decisions are also reviewed.

154 Clader, Linda. "Self-Evaluation and Prospectus." In John F. Noonan (ed.), *Learning About Teaching.* New Directions for Teaching and Learning, no. 4. San Francisco: Jossey-Bass, 1980, pp. 81–87.

As part of the author's tenure review, her committee requested a letter about her teaching. In her response to that request, she discusses her goals as a teacher of classics and her teaching style. Even though stress sometimes inhibits effective communication in such evaluative settings as tenure review, this letter is a model of open and direct communication.

155 Clift, John C., and Imrie, Bradford W. *Assessing Students, Appraising Teaching.* New York: Wiley, 1981. 176 pages.

Please see entry no. 361 for the annotation of this work.

★**156** Cohen, Peter A. "Student Ratings of Instruction and Student Achievement: A Meta-Analysis of Multisection Validity Studies." *Review of Educational Research,* 1981, *51,* 281-309.

To be considered valid, student ratings of instruction should be correlated with teaching effectiveness, and one indicator of teaching effectiveness is how much students learn in a particular course. This meta-analysis considers forty-one studies reporting sixty-eight separate multisection courses where both student ratings and student examination scores were available. The average correlation between overall instructor rating and student achievement was .47. Correlations were strongest for such rating factors as skill and structure and were lower for such factors as rapport and difficulty. This evidence supports the validity of student ratings.

157 Costin, Frank; Greenough, William T.; and Menges, Robert J. "Student Ratings of College Teaching: Reliability, Validity, and Usefulness." *Review of Educational Research,* 1971, *41,* 511-535.

This review was the first comprehensive assessment of research about the use of student ratings for evaluation of college teachers and teaching, which increased dramatically during the 1960s. Arguments for and against student participation in evaluation are briefly stated, and a survey of student opinions on the topic is reported. Empirical research "indicates that students' ratings can provide reliable and valid information on the quality of courses and instruction," but student ratings should not be taken as the complete assessment of an instructor's teaching contribution.

★**158** Davis, Robert H. "A Behavioral Change Model with Implications for Faculty Development." *Higher Education,* 1979, *8,* 123-140.

A model is proposed to describe individual and organizational variables associated with instructional change. The author points out that all faculty development programs seek to change the behavior of faculty who participate in them. Often this change in behavior involves adopting an instructional innovation. The model includes three broad classes of individual variables: energizers of behavior, personal expectations, and the change-related skills of the faculty member. Organizational variables discussed are motivators used by an organization, role expectations of the department and institution where the faculty member works, and organizational resources available to the faculty member. The author presents these variables in the context of the teaching responsibilities of college and university faculty and discusses the potential of the model for predicting change.

159 Donald, Janet G., and Sullivan, Arthur M. *Using Research to Improve Teaching.* New Directions for Teaching and Learning, no. 23. San Francisco: Jossey-Bass, 1985. 109 pages.

This is an exemplary collection of readable essays. The reports are based on extensive, sustained research programs, rooted in theory, and interpreted in ways that inform the work of college teachers. Topics include classroom behaviors of effective teachers (H. G. Murray); instructor expressiveness, that is, the Doctor Fox effect (R. P. Perry); critical thinking (C. Fureday and J. J. Fureday); and operation of an illustrative campus instructional development program (J. B. Boehnert and G. A. B. Moore).

160 Doyle, Kenneth O., Jr. *Evaluating Teaching.* Lexington, Mass.: Heath, 1983. 173 pages.

Focused on postsecondary education, this volume begins with a brief discussion of historical, philosophical, psychodynamic, and psychometric issues. The author's basic conceptual scheme for evaluating teaching distinguishes among the purposes of the evaluation, the sources of information, the focus of evaluation, the methods of information transmission, and the quality of information. This scheme is used to identify variables that should be emphasized when teaching is evaluated with reference to student learning, course characteristics, instructor characteristics, or student characteristics. This treatment is usually comprehensive, careful and critical, and well informed by research.

★**161** Dunkin, Michael J. "Research on Teaching in Higher Education." In M. C. Wittrock (ed.), *Handbook of Research on Teaching.* (3rd ed.) New York: Macmillan, 1986, pp. 754-777.

Please see entry no. 224 for the annotation of this work.

162 Eble, Kenneth E., and McKeachie, Wilbert J. *Improving Undergraduate Education Through Faculty Development: An Analysis of Effective Programs and Practices.* San Francisco: Jossey-Bass, 1985. 248 pages.

The authors report their evaluation of the Bush Foundation Faculty Development Project in Minnesota, North Dakota, and South Dakota. Based on over thirty faculty development programs, the report discusses the nature and purposes of faculty development, gives a detailed analysis of selected programs, and offers the authors' analysis of effective faculty development. Among the many conclusions emerging from the authors' data, the variable nature of the impact of activities stands out. The culture of the institution is a powerful force in determining what will and what will not work in a faculty development program. The authors combine the criteria of objectivity in evaluation studies with the richness that humanistic inquiry can contribute in this seminal investigation of faculty development practices.

163 Feldman, Kenneth A. "Grades and College Students' Evaluations of Their Courses and Teachers." *Research in Higher Education,* 1976, *4,* 69-111.

Do students' actual or anticipated course grades influence their evaluation of courses and teachers? This careful review of research through the mid 1970s finds a "small but not unimportant" relationship between grades and evaluations. But no conclusion is warranted about whether the more positive evaluations are due to greater learning and motivation or to a bias induced by the grade.

164 Feldman, Kenneth A. "The Superior College Teacher from the Students' View." *Research in Higher Education,* 1976, *5,* 243-288.

Careful review of a large body of research shows that students attribute the following characteristics to "superior" college teachers or teaching: clarity and understandability; knowledge of subject matter; preparation for, and organization of, the course; and enthusiasm for the subject matter and for teaching. Under some circumstances students say they also prefer friendliness, helpfulness, and openness to other opinions. The teachers' regulative activities, such as classroom management and fairness of evaluation, seem to be less strongly related to student views of superior teaching. Reservations are discussed regarding the methodological adequacy of these studies.

165 Feldman, Kenneth A. "Consistency and Variability Among College Students in Rating Their Teachers and Courses: A Review and Analysis." *Research in Higher Education,* 1977, *6,* 223-274.

In rating college teachers and teaching, the reliability of a single rater is only moderate at best. But when ratings by twenty to twenty-five students in a class are averaged together, the composite ratings do have substantial reliability. The author discusses how variables that correlate significantly with ratings should be treated, "whether various correlates of within-class ratings are to be interpreted as biasing factors or as natural influences on social perceptions."

166 Feldman, Kenneth A. "Course Characteristics and College Students' Ratings of Their Teachers: What We Know and What We Don't." *Research in Higher Education,* 1978, *9,* 199-242.

A thorough review of research examines relationships between student ratings of teachers and five course characteristics: class size, course level, "electivity," subject matter, and time of day. Small positive relationships between ratings and the first four characteristics have been found in many studies. Higher ratings tend to go to classes that are smaller, upper division, elective, and in the fields of humanities, fine arts, or language. But these associations are complex, and there are many possible reasons for them. Where these variables lie in a "causal network of variables" is unclear from the research so far.

167 Feldman, Kenneth A. "The Significance of Circumstances for College Students' Ratings of Their Teachers and Courses." *Research in Higher Education*, 1979, *10*, 149-172.

Research is reviewed about the relationships between student ratings of their courses and their teachers and several circumstances: student anonymity, purported use of ratings, presence of instructor, format of the rating form, and timing of data collection. Evidence for relationships is more consistent in studies of the first four circumstances than the fifth, but clear conclusions await further research.

168 Feldman, Kenneth A. "Seniority and Experience of College Teachers as Related to Evaluations They Receive from Students." *Research in Higher Education*, 1983, *18*, 3-124.

Studies are reviewed of relationships between students' evaluations of teachers and particular teacher characteristics, namely, academic rank, age, and extent of instructional experience. Some studies have found significant relationships (modest positive correlations with rank but inverse correlations with age and experience), but many others have not. Alternative explanations are proposed for these findings, whether they are positive or inverse.

169 Feldman, Kenneth A. "Class Size and College Students' Evaluations of Teachers and Courses: A Closer Look." *Research in Higher Education*, 1984, *21*, 45-116.

A careful review of research finds weak inverse relationships between class size and (1) students' overall evaluations of courses and teachers and (2) students' ratings of specific instructional dimensions, namely, presenting material and communicating information. Larger inverse correlations are typically found with dimensions pertaining to interaction and relationships with students. Because of research design limitations, the extent to which these relationships exert a biasing influence on ratings cannot be determined from these studies.

170 Feldman, Kenneth A. "The Perceived Instructional Effectiveness of College Teachers as Related to Their Personality and Attitudinal Characteristics: A Review and Synthesis." *Research in Higher Education*, 1986, *24*, 139–213.

After a meticulous review of research, the author finds that those personality characteristics of teachers that are self-reported, as on personality inventories, are less likely to be related to student evaluations of teaching than are personality characteristics as perceived by students or colleagues. Relationships between teaching effectiveness and teacher personality or attitude characteristics are fairly strong when the latter are measured by student or colleague perceptions; but, because of numerous measurement and conceptual problems, it is unclear how that relationship is best explained. This exhaustive review yields few immediate implications for teaching evaluation, but it is an effective stimulus for further research.

171 Feldman, Kenneth A. "Research Productivity and Scholarly Accomplishment of College Teachers as Related to Their Instructional Effectiveness: A Review and Exploration." *Research in Higher Education*, 1987, *26*, 227–298.

Several dozen studies of the relationship between student ratings of teaching effectiveness and the teacher's research productivity almost always find positive correlations, although more often than not, the association is not statistically significant. Several possible explanations are considered, for example, "that faculty of superior ability tend to be good at both research and teaching" and "that effective teachers who are also productive in research would be even more effective were they to do less research." The most justifiable conclusion, on the basis of evidence so far, is that the two variables are essentially independent.

172 Genova, William J.; Madoff, Marjorie K.; Chin, Robert; and Thomas, George B. *Mutual Benefit Evaluation of Faculty and Administrators in Higher Education.* Cambridge, Mass.: Ballinger, 1976. 222 pages.

Mutual benefit evaluation was developed in projects with colleges and universities in Massachusetts. It emphasizes the benefits that evaluation of faculty and administrators can mutually provide all constituencies of the higher education community. Procedures for evaluation are discussed, and various sample instruments are reproduced. One chapter is devoted to faculty evaluation in competency-based programs. This book is a useful, practical, comprehensive guide to one approach to evaluation.

173 Grant, Gerald, and others. *On Competence: A Critical Analysis of Competence-Based Reforms in Higher Education.* San Francisco: Jossey-Bass, 1979. 592 pages.

The competence movement makes college or professional school credits contingent on demonstrated task performance rather than on time spent or courses completed. These twelve chapters are the result of visiting campuses and examining documents from institutions that have experimented with the approach. They cover educational and social origins of the movement, present five institutional case studies, and discuss implications for several areas, notably for the teacher (P. Elbow), for assessment (G. Grant and W. Kohli), for liberal education (T. Ewens), for professional education (V. Olesen), and for those implementing a competence-based curriculum (Z. Gamson). An extensive annotated bibliography is included.

174 Heiss, Ann. *An Inventory of Academic Innovation and Reform.* Berkeley, Calif.: Carnegie Commission on Higher Education, 1973. 123 pages.

The fifteen years preceding this report were unprecedented in growth for higher education. This volume catalogues many of the academic innovations stimulated by that growth. Chapter topics include new innovative institutions, institutions within institutions (for example, cluster colleges), innovative changes by academic subunits within conventional colleges and universities (for example, field study and programs for minority students), procedural innovations (for example, changes in degree requirements, in evaluation of teaching and learning, and in course credit policies), and institutional self-studies. Particular innovations are described, and there are references for further reading. This fascinating snapshot of innovation at the start of the 1970s could stimulate follow-up studies about which of the innovations have endured and how innovations adapt to changing social and institutional circumstances.

175 Heller, Jack F. *Increasing Faculty and Administrative Effectiveness.* San Francisco: Jossey-Bass, 1982. 126 pages.

One influential approach to organizational studies focuses on contrasts between persons' espoused theories and their theories-in-use. That approach, developed by C. Argyris and D. Schön, is illustrated in this book with examples from postsecondary education. A college's attempt, ultimately unsuccessful, at curriculum change is analyzed using this perspective. A seminar is described in which professors and administrators are trained to recognize their ineffective behaviors, which Argyris calls "Model I" behaviors, and to adopt more effective "Model II" behaviors. Behavioral guidelines ("heuristics") from that seminar are included. This book is a provocative application of action science to the work of higher education faculty and administrators.

176 Hildebrand, Milton. "How to Recommend Promotion for a Mediocre Teacher Without Actually Lying." *Journal of Higher Education,* 1972, *43,* 44–62.

A well-written recommendation for promotion or merit salary increase should refer to characteristics possessed by the candidate, characteristics that discriminate between effective and ineffective teachers. The author presents two fictitious letters. One sounds convincing but actually contains little information of critical importance. By contrast, the second contains information that is congruent with research on effective teaching. Some common objections to student evaluation of teaching are also listed and commented upon.

177 Hildebrand, Milton. "The Character and Skills of the Effective Professor." *Journal of Higher Education*, 1973, *44*, 41–50.

In research conducted with R. C. Wilson, an attempt was made to identify "effective teaching." Several hundred students and 119 faculty were asked to identify best and worst teachers; subsequently, more than 1,000 students in fifty-one classes of the nominated teachers were surveyed. There was high agreement between students and faculty both on identifying best and worst teachers and on characterizations of effective performance. Examples are given of characteristics that discriminate (and some that do not discriminate) between the best and the worst. Factor analysis identified five clusters of items that discriminate: command of the subject (analytic/synthetic approach), organization/clarity, instructor-group interaction, instructor–individual student interaction, and dynamism/enthusiasm. The study is notable for its careful procedures. Its findings have been generally confirmed by subsequent research.

178 Hind, Robert R.; Dornbusch, Sanford M.; and Scott, W. Richard. "A Theory of Evaluation Applied to a University Faculty." *Sociology of Education*, 1974, *47*, 114–128.

A theory of evaluation and authority is applied to postsecondary education using interview data from Stanford University faculty. The authors find that evaluations of faculty research have more influence than evaluations of teaching. Because faculty spend more time teaching, they would like greater congruence between the evaluation system and their actual time expenditure. Evaluations by professional colleagues are more influential than the evaluations by administrators. The university's organizational boundaries are permeable, particularly regarding visibility of research to outsiders. More perceived agreement among evaluators and more satisfaction with evaluations was found in fields that operate from a body of theory.

179 Irby, David M. "Clinical Teacher Effectiveness in Medicine." *Journal of Medical Education,* 1978, *53,* 808-815.

Since forms for evaluating classroom teaching are not appropriate for evaluation in the clinic, the author studied clinical teaching directly. Students in one medical school described characteristics of the best and worst clinical teachers in medicine. Best clinical teachers were differentiated from worst on three (of six) empirical factors: enthusiasm, organization, and interaction. This research approach and the resulting evaluation form are appropriate for instructor evaluation in other fields and in undergraduate education where clinical or studio teaching occurs.

180 Kelley, William F. "Twenty Studies of In-Service Education of College Faculty and the Procedures Most Recommended." *Educational Administration and Supervision,* 1950, *36,* 351-358.

The author identified twenty articles published from 1927 to 1948 (seven of them in 1930 or earlier) that suggest procedures for college teachers' in-service education. Of the thirty-one procedures mentioned by the authors of those articles, the following were mentioned in fifteen or more articles: "to supervise teaching as a professional service," "to provide the faculty with time for research, e.g., sabbaticals," "to make use of outside consultants, lecturers, experts," and "to plan for the student evaluation of instruction." There are few surprises in the list; these items could just as easily emerge from a survey today.

181 Kozma, Robert B. "A Grounded Theory of Instructional Innovation in Higher Education." *Journal of Higher Education,* 1985, *56,* 300-319.

Twenty-six instructional improvement projects supported by either the Exxon Education Foundation or the National Science Foundation were studied. A theory of instructional innovation, grounded in the data from these cases, is presented. The theory contends that instructional innovation is an evolutionary process, largely continuous with previous practices, and is more cooperative than confrontational. Adoption of an instructional innovation often depends on the personal decision of one key individual. Results of the innovation often do not correspond to the needs of students or organizations and may have little further impact. Implications are listed for instructional improvement agencies.

182 Kurland, Jordan E. (ed.). "On Periodic Evaluation of Tenured Faculty: A Discussion at Wingspread." *Academe,* 1983, *69* (6), 1a–14a.

The American Association of University Professors and the American Council on Education each invited about forty people to a conference on evaluation of tenured faculty. Several conference documents are reprinted here, including a statement issued by participants. There was majority agreement "(1) that our current procedures for evaluating academic performance are, where properly implemented, quite satisfactory . . . (2) that an overlay of a formal system of periodic evaluation on existing procedures would bring scant benefit and would incur unacceptable costs, not only in money and time but in a dampening of creativity and collegial relationships."

183 Lacey, Paul (ed.). *Revitalizing Teaching Through Faculty Development.* New Directions for Teaching and Learning, no. 15. San Francisco: Jossey-Bass, 1983. 116 pages.

The editor directed the Lilly Endowment Post-Doctoral Teaching Awards Program from 1980 to 1983, and this book describes the teaching experiences and projects involving participants in that program. The topics involve teaching scientific reasoning to underprepared students, analytical skills in a content course, computer-assisted instruction, philosophies and methods of teaching, fiction and fact in an introductory literature course, and a multidisciplinary course on mental illness. In addition, an on-campus teaching fellows program is examined, and the Lilly Program at Indiana University is discussed. The editor contributes his views on the politics of vitalizing teaching and a selection of additional readings. This collection provides a broad picture of faculty development in action.

★184 Levinson-Rose, Judith, and Menges, Robert J. "Improving College Teaching: A Critical Review of Research." *Review of Educational Research*, 1981, *51*, 403–434.

Studies of five types of interventions to improve college teaching are reviewed: grants for faculty projects, workshops and seminars, feedback from student ratings, practice-based feedback (microteaching and mini-courses), and concept-based training (protocols). Although about three out of four of these seventy-one research reports support the intervention being assessed, some studies deserve less confidence than others because of conceptual and methodological problems. Workshops, for example, are the most frequently used but least carefully evaluated approach. They rarely incorporate follow-up activities or funds or other mechanisms that would produce lasting changes in participants. Implications are offered for those who evaluate and implement teaching improvement programs.

★185 Licata, Christine M. *Post-Tenure Faculty Evaluation: Threat or Opportunity*. ASHE-ERIC Higher Education Report no. 1. Washington, D.C.: Association for the Study of Higher Education, 1986. 105 pages. (ED 270 009)

By the late 1980s, it is estimated that 80 percent of faculty at institutions that have tenure will be tenured. Further, it is predicted that the modal age of tenured faculty will be between fifty-five and sixty-five by the year 2000. In such circumstances, according to the author, posttenure evaluation may have significant benefits and need not conflict with the principle of tenure. Successful evaluation programs are likely to be associated with such features as clearly articulated purposes, faculty involvement in planning, flexibility and individualization, and emphasis on rewards and development.

186 Lindquist, Jack. "Social Learning and Problem-Solving Strategies for Improving Academic Performance." In W. R. Kirschling (ed.), *Evaluating Faculty Performance and Vitality*. New Directions for Institutional Research, no. 20. San Francisco: Jossey-Bass, 1978, pp. 17–30.

For improving faculty performance, the author asserts that bureaucratic and political strategies are less effective than approaches based on social learning and problem solving. The former assume that "people must be either forced or outmaneuvered," while the latter assume that professors are motivated by "such desires as social acceptance and status, self-esteem, and achievement." Four approaches that apply social learning and problem solving are discussed: increasing awareness of productivity, learning about ways to improve, encouraging improvement initiatives, and assisting implementation of improvement. A table lists ten specific improvement strategies that, if they are to be effective, must be developed in collaboration with members of the faculty.

187 Lowry, Howard F., and Taeusch, W. *Research, Creative Activity and Teaching: A Five-Year Experiment to Improve Undergraduate Teaching*. Bulletin no. 33, New York: The Carnegie Foundation for the Advancement of Teaching, 1953. 187 pages.

This five-year program grew from the belief that "the surest way to improve instruction is to stimulate creativity among faculty members." Grants for advanced study and research were made to 900 professors (500 of them received more than one grant) at southern colleges or universities. Much work was generated by the grants; an appendix of seventy-two pages lists resulting publications, manuscripts, and creative works. Courses and curriculum projects resulting from the grants are also mentioned along with "abundant testimony" that participants became better teachers. The authors observe that results cannot be conclusive because "the true test and measurement for teaching has not been invented."

188 McPherron, Sharon M. "Report on Teaching, Number 4: Five Years Later." *Teaching Sociology*, 1982, *10*, 46–131.

A number of teaching innovations across all disciplines were reported by *Change* magazine in 1977 (issue number 4). Forty-one of the innovations were by sociologists, and the author asked those persons to comment, four years later, on the status of their innovations. Replies from twenty-seven respondents are reprinted here. Most continue to use the innovative approach or a variation of it, and there is some evidence that innovations were disseminated to other campuses.

★189 Marsh, Herbert W. "Students' Evaluations of University Teaching: Dimensionality, Reliability, Validity, Potential Biases, and Utility." *Journal of Educational Psychology*, 1984, *76*, 707–754.

After reviewing his own and others' research, Marsh concludes that "class-average student ratings are (a) multidimensional; (b) reliable and stable; (c) primarily a function of the instructor who teaches a course rather than the course that is taught; (d) relatively valid against a variety of indicators of effective teaching; (e) relatively unaffected by a variety of variables hypothesized as potential biases; and (f) seen to be useful by faculty as feedback about their teaching, by students for use in course selection, and by administrators for use in personnel decisions." This large body of research makes student ratings one of the best-supported personnel evaluation systems in any profession. Nevertheless, ratings should be used with care and with cognizance of the criticisms that faculty sometimes make of them, some of which the author analyzes. This article is a comprehensive, clear overview of what is known and what needs to be learned about student ratings of teachers and teaching.

190 Marsh, Herbert W., and Ware, John E., Jr. "Effects of Expressiveness, Content Coverage, and Incentive on Multidimensional Student Rating Scales: New Interpretations of the Dr. Fox Effect." *Journal of Educational Psychology*, 1982, *74*, 126–134.

According to the Dr. Fox effect, sometimes called educational seduction, students' positive ratings are likely to be based more on the expressiveness of the lecturer than on the content covered. In this reanalysis of earlier studies, the Dr. Fox effect was not supported when students had an incentive to learn, which is the experimental condition most like real classrooms. Instructor expressiveness affected ratings of instructor enthusiasm, as expected, whereas the amount of content covered was related to ratings of instructor knowledge and to examination performance but not to instructor enthusiasm. The results support the validity of student ratings of instruction.

191 Menges, Robert J. "Evaluating Teaching Effectiveness: What Is the Proper Role for Students?" *Liberal Education*, 1979, *65*, 356–370.

A number of objections to involving students in teacher evaluation are reviewed and countered with findings from research on the validity of student ratings and student evaluative comments. Examples are given of evaluation questions that are appropriate for students to answer (and some that are not). The distinction between using information for improvement of instruction and for personnel review is seen as particularly important and is explored in some detail.

192 Menges, Robert J., and Brinko, Kathleen T. "Effects of Student Evaluation Feedback: A Meta-Analysis of Higher Education Research." Paper presented at the American Educational Research Association, San Francisco, 1986. (ED 270 408)

On many campuses, student ratings of courses and teachers are routinely conveyed to instructors as feedback about their teaching.

This review applies meta-analytic techniques to thirty studies of the effects of student ratings feedback on subsequent ratings. Results indicate that end-of-course ratings of the average teacher who receives feedback at midterm are at about the 59th percentile (the average teacher receiving no feedback would be at the 50th percentile). When ratings information is accompanied by consultation and/or other types of feedback, the effect is considerably larger, about the 85th percentile. Effects on the achievement and affect of students are less clear from available research but appear to be positive.

193 Mentkowski, Marcia, and Doherty, Austin. "Abilities That Last a Lifetime: Outcomes of the Alverno Experience." *AAHE Bulletin*, 1984, *36* (6), 5-6, 11-14.

Alverno College in Milwaukee has been an early and dedicated adherent of competency-based education for liberal arts students. The curriculum is structured around student learning outcomes in eight core areas: communication, analysis, problem solving, valuing in decision making, social interaction, taking responsibility for the environment, involvement in the contemporary world, and esthetic response. Alverno's implementation of this approach underwent unusually close evaluation over the seven-year period preceding the publication of this article. This article summarizes changes in students that are attributed to curriculum, and references are given to more detailed evaluation reports.

194 Miller, Richard I. *Developing Programs for Faculty Evaluation: A Sourcebook for Higher Education*. San Francisco: Jossey-Bass, 1974. 248 pages.

This book discusses general issues and alternatives rather than advocating one particular approach. Chapters cover ways of developing an evaluation system, choosing among evaluation criteria, evaluations by students, and evaluations of administrators. One institution's experience in developing an evaluation system is recounted in detail, and several specimen evaluation forms are reproduced. About half the book is devoted to an extensive annotated bibliography. Although subsequent research has refined some of the issues the book raises, it remains an important early contribution.

195 Miller, Richard I. *Evaluating Faculty for Promotion and Tenure.* San Francisco: Jossey-Bass, 1987. 257 pages.

The economics of higher education in the 1980s has made the faculty promotion and tenure process much more complex than during the days when institutions were expanding. Evaluating faculty is now an acceptable administrative activity to which resources are allocated and which helps to ensure quality. The author states that "the components of the faculty evaluation system constitute the foundation on which credible and effective promotion and tenure systems are built." This is a practical book about implementing an effective faculty evaluation system. The author presents a logical defense of faculty evaluation as the cornerstone of quality decisions about promotion and tenure. Part One discusses developing effective evaluation procedures, Part Two confronts the improvement of the promotion and tenure process, and Part Three presents some practical resources for academic decision makers. The author has written extensively about faculty evaluation in earlier books. This book offers a useful and cogent view of a central issue in higher education that brings together in a new form many of the author's insights and much of his knowledge.

196 Millman, Jason (ed.). *Handbook of Teacher Evaluation.* Beverly Hills, Calif.: Sage, 1981. 356 pages.

Under sponsorship of the National Council on Measurement in Education, this "guide to the practice of teacher evaluation" presents and discusses teacher evaluation strategies for all levels of education. Most chapters can be applied to colleges and universities, but the following are more pertinent to higher education: Michael Scriven on summative teacher evaluation, Grace French-Lazovik on documentary evidence for peer review, Lawrence Aleamoni on student ratings of instruction, J. Gregory Carroll on self-evaluation, and Stephen C. Brock on teacher development. These articles pose issues and summarize research in ways that should be useful for faculty committees dealing with evaluation policy and practice.

197 Murray, Harry G. "Low-Inference Classroom Teaching Behaviors and Student Ratings of College Teaching Effectiveness." *Journal of Educational Psychology*, 1983, 75, 138–149.

Classroom behaviors of college teachers who received either low, medium, or high student ratings were recorded by trained observers. Teachers were found to differ on twenty-six of the sixty rated behaviors. According to factor analysis, teachers in the three groups differed in their behaviors of clarity, enthusiasm, and rapport. These findings support the validity of student ratings and conclude that the rating system may be useful for providing feedback to instructors who wish to improve their student evaluations. An exceptionally careful and ambitious study, this is one of the few with extensive observation in college classrooms.

198 Naftulin, Donald H.; Ware, John E., Jr.; and Donnelly, Frank A. "The Doctor Fox Lecture: A Paradigm of Educational Seduction." *Journal of Medical Education*, 1973, 48, 630–635.

Cognizant of research that suggests that student ratings of instructors are influenced largely by personality variables rather than by educational content, the authors hired an actor to lecture to persons at a continuing education workshop on a topic about which he knew nothing. The hypothesis was that a lecture involving irrelevant, conflicting, and meaningless content can nevertheless induce satisfaction if it is impressively delivered. The hypothesis was supported by positive ratings given Dr. Fox by a significant number of the experienced educators who heard the lecture. Although little can be concluded from this uncontrolled event, it did serve to stimulate a good deal of subsequent research on the phenomenon of educational seduction.

199 O'Connell, Colman. "College Policies Off-Target in Fostering Faculty Development." *Journal of Higher Education*, 1983, *54*, 662–675.

Using a sample of 228 colleges, the author surveyed faculty development programs to identify the characteristics of programs and to ascertain institutional policies for evaluation and rewards for faculty. The study sought to determine the relationship between the degree of faculty participation in faculty development activities and whether or not colleges in the sample systematically evaluated teaching effectiveness and gave weight to changed teaching in allocating rewards for promotion, tenure, and salary increases. No significant relationships were found between these variables. The author discusses the possible reasons why the evaluation and reward policies of the colleges in the sample were not related to the degree of faculty participation in faculty development activities or to the degree of reported change in teaching behaviors.

200 O'Connell, William R., and Meeth, L. Richard. *Evaluating Teaching Improvement Programs.* New Rochelle, N.Y.: *Change* Magazine National Teaching Program, 1978.

A 1977 conference sponsored by *Change* magazine resulted in this nontechnical essay. Customary evaluation approaches are critiqued, and particular evaluation issues are illustrated by case reports. The authors provide lists of criteria for judging program effects on faculty, students, administrators, and the institution. These criteria will vary depending on whether the audience for the evaluation is the college administration, the faculty, or outside authorities. Although more sophisticated documents on this topic are available, this one contains many useful ideas for people with little background or experience in evaluation.

201 Rae, Leslie. *How to Measure Training Effectiveness.* New York: Nichols, 1986. 151 pages.

Although written for persons working in management training and development, this very practical and readable guide can assist evaluation in higher education. It is especially pertinent to evaluating workshops and short courses. Evaluation techniques described include the repertory grid, process and behavior observation, and a variety of formats for paper and pencil questionnaires. These techniques can be used before, during, and after the event being evaluated. Delayed evaluation ("after the euphoria") is also discussed.

202 Redmond, Mark V., and Clark, D. Joseph. "Student Group Instructional Diagnosis: A Practical Approach to Improving Teaching." *AAHE Bulletin,* 1982, *34* (6), 8-10.

This article describes Student Group Instructional Diagnosis, an approach developed by Clark to increase the efficiency of a consultant who gathers feedback from students for improving instruction. After being invited to a class by an instructor, the consultant divides the class into groups of about five students and asks them to reach consensus on what they like about the course, what they think needs improvement, and what suggestions they have for bringing about the improvement. Group reports, if endorsed by most members of the class, are conveyed to the instructor who subsequently discusses them with the group. The approach has been widely disseminated and used with apparent success in a variety of situations.

203 Reed, Anna Y. *The Effective and the Ineffective College Teacher.* New York: American Book Company, 1935. 344 pages.

Based on information gathered from questionnaires or interviews with administrators at more than 400 institutions, the author describes characteristics of those faculty who are perceived as effective or as ineffective. There are sections on "probable causal factors of rustiness in teaching" and on "suggested methods for the rehabilitation of rusty teachers." About 30 percent of respondents agreed that rusty teachers can be rehabilitated. This is an early and relatively ambitious study, reported in considerable detail, with an annotated bibliography of more than forty items. It deserves comparison with what today's research characterizes as effective and ineffective teaching.

204 Reisman, Bernard. "Performance Evaluation for Tenured Faculty: Issues and Research." *Liberal Education,* 1986, *72,* 73–87.

As Brandeis University was establishing an evaluation program for tenured faculty, the author surveyed twenty-six other universities about similar activities. Performance reviews on most campuses appeared to be relatively unsystematic and decentralized, especially with regard to senior faculty. About 40 percent of responding faculty at institutions without evaluation activities for tenured faculty thought the benefits of such a program would outweigh its costs. At the nine schools that did have programs, 90 percent of respondents agreed that benefits outweighed costs. None of the latter noted threats to tenure from the program. The author recommends experimentation with performance-focused reviews of tenured faculty.

205 Remmers, Hermann H. *The College Professor as the Student Sees Him.* Purdue University Studies in Higher Education XI. Purdue, Ind.: Purdue University, 1929. 63 pages.

This monograph describes an early attempt to consult "consumers" of education about the "teaching personalities" of their teachers, and it introduces the Purdue Rating Scale for Instructors. Results from 115 instructors (293 classes) at Purdue and from two other institutions contribute to the construction of norms and to studies of reliability, validity, and stability of results. Problems with the scale and areas for future research are noted. The results of this pioneering study hold up well in comparison with more recent research.

206 Riegle, Rodney P., and Rhodes, D. M. "Avoiding Mixed Metaphors of Faculty Evaluation." *College Teaching,* 1986, *34,* 123–128.

Distinctions are drawn among five metaphors for evaluation: evaluation as judging, as critiquing, as assessing, as appraising, and as rating. The literature on faculty evaluation is often imprecise regarding which metaphor or metaphors are pertinent. In this article, metaphors are discussed according to their appropriateness for the several combinations of (1) purposes for evaluation (appointment, tenure, promotion, salary, termination, and improvement), (2) functions being evaluated (research, teaching, and service), and (3) sources of evaluative information (other faculty, administrators, students, outside consultants, laypersons, and self). Evaluators sometimes disagree because they operate under different metaphors; therefore, specifying the metaphor appropriate for a particular combination of purpose, function, and source should improve both communication and the ultimate decision.

207 Rodin, Miriam, and Rodin, Burton. "Student Evaluations of Teachers." *Science,* 1972, *177,* 1164–1166.

Students in a multisection calculus course assigned a grade to their teaching assistants' "total teacher performance." Across twelve sections (eleven TAs), the average correlation between ratings of the teaching assistant and student learning (measured by final grade), with initial ability controlled, was -.746. The authors conclude that "students rate most highly instructors from whom they learn least." The article was subsequently carefully critiqued and rather well discredited on conceptual and methodological grounds. It continues to be cited from time to time, sometimes with approval, partly because of its prominent place of publication. It has also stimulated considerable additional research.

208 Seldin, Peter O. *Changing Practices in Faculty Evaluation: A Critical Assessment and Recommendations for Improvement.* San Francisco: Jossey-Bass, 1984. 200 pages.

For this report, the author surveyed deans of more than 600 liberal arts colleges regarding their faculty evaluation practices. When compared with results from his surveys five and ten years earlier, these responses show that evaluations of both teaching and research have become more highly structured and systematic. Student ratings are used even more widely than evaluations by deans, and data from classroom visits, course materials, and self-evaluations have also become more common. Commentaries on the survey by seven educational researchers and a chapter on legal issues in evaluation round out the book. Nine instruments for student, peer, or self-evaluation are reproduced. This is are readable volume with eminently practical advice on building feasible evaluation programs.

209 Shore, Bruce M.; Foster, Stephen F.; Knapper, Christopher K.; Nadeau, Giles G.; Neill, Neill; and Sim, Victor. "Guide to the *Teaching Dossier:* Its Preparation and Use." Ottawa: Canadian Association of University Teachers, 1980. 12 pages.

In these large newsprint pages, a study committee of the Canadian Association of University Teachers offers a tool that they hope will improve faculty evaluation procedures. "A teaching dossier is a summary of a professor's major teaching accomplishments and strengths. It is to a professor's teaching what lists of publications, grants, and honors are to research." This guide discusses teaching evaluation in general and lists six steps for the creation of a useful teaching dossier. Most helpful are the lists of several dozen possible items to be included and the samples of hypothetical dossiers. Administrative and personal uses of the dossier are also covered. A guide like this, perhaps personalized for a particular campus, is indispensable for younger faculty members facing their first performance reviews.

210 Smock, H. Richard, and Crooks, Terrence J. "A Plan for the Comprehensive Evaluation of College Teaching." *Journal of Higher Education,* 1973, *44,* 577–586.

A matrix is presented for collecting and classifying teaching evaluation data. It illustrates the complex decisions that must be made when systems for evaluating teaching are being planned. Three major levels of evaluation are specified: general summary for comparison across departments, specific attributes of courses and instructors, and detailed diagnostic feedback. Several sources of information (students, colleagues, and departmental administrators) and several audiences for evaluation results are differentiated.

The kind of information collected and the uses made of it should vary with the level of the evaluation, and these distinctions are discussed in some detail.

211 Sork, Thomas J. (ed.). *Designing and Implementing Effective Workshops.* New Directions for Continuing Education, no. 22. San Francisco: Jossey-Bass, 1984. 96 pages.

Workshops have several distinctive features that receive little attention in the literature of higher education. These seven chapters examine those features and discuss ways that workshops can be effectively planned, conducted, and evaluated. Defined as "a relatively short-term, intensive, problem-focused learning experience that actively involves participants in the identification and analysis of problems and in the devising of solutions," the workshop is obviously a valuable instrument for higher education's instructional and continuing education mission.

212 Stein, Leonard S. "The Effectiveness of Continuing Medical Education: Eight Research Reports." *Journal of Medical Education,* 1981, *56,* 103–110.

Eight studies published during the 1970s are reviewed to identify principles associated with effectiveness in continuing medical education. The author concludes that programs are more likely to influence physician behavior and patient outcomes when they go beyond didactic instruction and use participative methods designed in light of participants' expressed needs. One problem in these studies is that information on program effectiveness "is likely to be obscured by the form in which . . . literature is presented." Faculty development programs in any college or university can be strengthened by attention to the issues raised here.

213 Sullivan, Arthur M. "The Improvement of University Teaching." *Canadian Psychology,* 1983, *24,* 119–124.

Three types of teaching improvement are defined. Remedial improvement (type R) involves detection and elimination of errors in teaching. Facilitative improvement (type F) involves application of generally recognized principles, such as frequent testing to facilitate student learning. Optimizing improvement (type O) involves use of research to determine which techniques produce greatest student achievement in a particular setting. Movement from one type to another requires increasing attention to student performance. Appropriate techniques for improving teaching differ according to whether the aim is type R, type F, or type O improvement. Illustrations are drawn from the author's own teaching and research.

214 Sweeney, John M., and Grasha, Anthony F. "Improving Teaching Through Faculty Development Triads." *Educational Technology*, 1979, *19* (2), 54–57.

The teaching improvement approach outlined in this article involves teams of three faculty members working for a term or longer in a five-phase process. They identify individual change goals in their teaching, discuss the goals with each other, visit one another's classes, discuss the visit, and plan their next steps. The authors give details on each phase and on the six- to eight-hour training program in which faculty participate. An evaluation based on 120 participating faculty yielded positive results for the program. This carefully detailed approach to peer consultation could easily be adapted to most campuses.

215 Tiberius, Richard G. "Metaphors Underlying the Improvement of Teaching and Learning." *British Journal of Educational Technology*, 1986, *17*, 144–156.

The author asserts that efforts to improve the teaching and learning process have been dominated by a "transmission" metaphor, which implies essentially a transfer of information from teacher to students, and by an educational engineering approach to change. More recently, a competing metaphor has emerged, the metaphor of dialogue or conversation that emphasizes the interactive cooperative and relational aspects of teaching and learning. Using a Kuhnian analysis, the author finds evidence of a shift toward dialogue as the prevailing metaphor and notes "profound implications" for teachers, learners, instructional consultants, and researchers. This is a thoughtful analysis with interesting implications; for example, it can help us understand how the same teacher behavior is sometimes regarded positively by some students and negatively by others.

216 Wahlquist, John T. *Innovations in the Preparation of College Teachers.* Bloomington, Ind.: Phi Delta Kappa, 1970. 61 pages.

This essay synthesizes information about innovative degrees for those preparing to teach at the college level. There are institution-by-institution descriptions of intermediate degrees (Master of Philosophy, Candidate of Philosophy, and Specialist), the Doctor of Arts, Modified Doctor of Education and Doctor of Philosophy degrees, and innovations in the teaching assistantship. The author sees the latter as potentially most significant. This article presents an interesting snapshot of approaches during higher education's boom years.

217 Whitman, Neal, and Weiss, Elaine. *Faculty Evaluation: The Use of Explicit Criteria for Promotion, Retention, and Tenure.* AAHE-ERIC Higher Education Research Report no. 2. Washington, D.C.: American Association for Higher Education, 1982. 50 pages. (ED 221 148)

Since 1970, faculty evaluation programs are more likely to include explicit written criteria. This review reports studies of evaluation programs of the Oregon State System of Higher Education, the State University of New York Faculty Council of Community Colleges, and the Southern Regional Education Board. Results of these self-studies reflect four common issues. First, regarding the purpose of evaluation, these systems appear more successful for informing personnel decisions than for helping faculty improve their teaching. Second, all systems evaluate teaching, research, and service, although the relative weights given to each vary and are often not explicit. Third, although evaluations have become more objective and usually more quantitative, use of student learning measures and of peer review of classroom teaching remain controversial sources of evaluative evidence. Fourth, explicit written criteria may move faculty toward easy-to-measure objectives, slighting areas that are more complex and possibly more valuable.

218 Witte, Stephen R.; Daly, John A.; Faigley, Lester; and Koch, William R. "An Instrument for Reporting Composition Course and Teacher Effectiveness in College Writing Programs." *Research in the Teaching of English,* 1983, *17,* 243-261.

The authors believe that evaluation of courses should be distinguished from evaluation of teachers and that the evaluation instrument should take into account the logic and idiosyncracies of particular disciplines. Development of an instrument for use in composition courses is reported here. It followed four stages: collecting from student interviews a pool of items for a preliminary questionnaire, pilot tests of this pool of items from which a shorter questionnaire was developed, administration and factor analysis of the revised questionnaire, and retest and reanalysis. The resulting instrument includes eighteen general items and sixty-two specific items distributed across nine factors. The items reproduced here are ready for use in composition courses; the process described can be followed to produce an instrument for other fields.

Research on Instruction

219 Clark, Richard E. "Reconsidering Research on Learning from Media." *Review of Educational Research,* 1983, *53,* 445-459.

The author reviews primary sources and meta-analyses of research about media's influence on learning and concludes that "there are no learning benefits to be gained from employing any specific medium to deliver instruction." Apparent benefits are better explained by novelty, learner's beliefs about media, teacher effects, and so on. Clark suggests that future research should emphasize cost benefits (which may be real), task characteristics, learner characteristics, method of instruction (distinct from the medium that delivers instruction), and other nonmedia variables.

220 Conrad, Clifton F. "Undergraduate Instruction." In H. E. Mitzel (ed.), *Encyclopedia of Educational Research.* (5th ed.) New York: Free Press, 1982, pp. 1963–1973.

This article provides a concise review of research in two areas: techniques and methods of instruction and evaluation of instruction. Considerable attention is given to uses of technology for instruction, to the need for more multivariate research designs, and, with regard to evaluation, to the desirability of using evaluative data from sources in addition to student ratings. Approximately 100 references are cited.

221 Cooper, Coleen; Orban, Deborah; Henry, Rebecca; and Townsend, Janet. "Teaching and Storytelling: An Ethnographic Study of the Instructional Process in the College Classroom." *Instructional Science,* 1983, *12,* 171–190.

A successful professor's teaching was studied through classroom observation, video recording, questionnaires, and interviews with the teacher and with students. Much of his success is attributed to planned use of stories. Other key factors of his style were structure and clarity, planned redundancy, practical examples and common language, and ways of inviting student participation. In addition to illuminating the role of storytelling in teaching, this study is a fine example of the ethnographic method in classroom research.

222 Douglass, H. R. "Controlled Experimentation in the Study of Methods of College Teaching." *University of Oregon Education Series,* 1929, *1,* 265–316.

These studies attempt to apply controlled experimental methods to college classroom instruction. They include studies of quiz sections, problem or project methods, and variations of independent or individualized study. As their rationale for limited but carefully controlled studies, the authors assert that "only by hundreds and thousands of tiny but reliable accretions can we hope to build a truly scientific knowledge of how to teach and how to learn." This article provides an example of the research approach most popular early in the century.

223 Dubin, Robert, and Taveggia, Thomas C. *The Teaching-Learning Paradox: A Comprehensive Analysis of College Teaching Methods.* Eugene, Oreg.: Center for the Advanced Study of Educational Administration, 1968. 78 pages. (ED 026 966)

These researchers set out to assess the "folklore" of college teaching that certain instructional methods are more effective than others. Rather than just tallying conclusions from studies under review, they applied statistical tests to the data from those studies. They identified ninety-one studies that compare instructional methods (lecture, discussion, independent study, television, and so on) and used final examination scores as the dependent variable. "We are able to state decisively that no particular method of college instruction is measurably to be preferred over another, when evaluated by student examination performance." Although meta-analysis techniques now available are more sophisticated than the techniques of these authors, this is an important early use of statistical integration for reviews of college teaching research. The report was controversial at the time it was originally published, and the findings remain provocative.

★**224** Dunkin, Michael J. "Research on Teaching in Higher Education." In M. C. Wittrock (ed.), *Handbook of Research on Teaching.* (3rd ed.) New York: Macmillan, 1986, pp. 754–777.

Research on various methods of teaching in higher education and on evaluating and improving teaching is discussed in detail. Several innovative teaching methods, particularly the Personalized System of Instruction, appear to be more effective than conventional instruction. The author believes that studies of teaching behavior using observational techniques in natural settings will increase our knowledge if they occur within a broader paradigm than the prevailing process-product paradigm. Student evaluations have been shown to be credible for evaluating teaching, but their utility for improving teaching is not well understood. There appear to be, in fact, a variety of ways to improve teaching; detailed studies of particular teaching skills in higher education and of teachers' beliefs, values, and attitudes are especially needed. Studies of the impact of such research on improving teaching are also needed. As a comprehensive, current, and thoughtful review, this article is essential for graduate students and researchers interested in postsecondary teaching and learning. Approximately 125 references are cited.

225 Dunkin, Michael J. (ed.). *The International Encyclopedia of Teaching and Teacher Education*. Elmsford, N.Y.: Pergamon Press, 1987. 878 pages.

For this collection, experts from throughout the English-speaking world updated their contributions to the *International Encyclopedia of Education: Research and Studies,* published in 1985. Articles are grouped in six sections: concepts and models (fourteen articles), methods and paradigms for research (twelve), teaching methods and techniques (twenty-one), classroom processes (thirty-two), contextual factors (twenty-six), and teacher education (twenty). Most pertinent to higher education are the following articles: Student Evaluation of Teaching (H. W. Marsh); Lecturing and Explaining (G. A. Brown); Group Teaching (D. Jaques); Science Laboratory Teaching (E. Hegerty-Hazel); Clinical Teaching (P. A. Cranton); Keller Plan, a Personalized System of Instruction (J. A. Kulik); and Teacher Education for Higher Education (A. N. Main). The encyclopedia is a useful reference beyond these particular articles, since issues treated in other articles have their parallels in higher education. Comprehensive author and subject indexes are included.

226 Ellner, Carolyn L.; Barnes, Carol; and Associates. *Studies of College Teaching: Experimental Results, Theoretical Interpretations, and New Perspectives*. Lexington, Mass.: Heath, 1983. 222 pages.

This publication reports interesting findings about classroom teaching in higher education based on studies using either process-product or educational criticism approaches. Several chapters rely on the same data base: transcripts of four sessions of each of forty classes at two public and two private undergraduate institutions, with an average class size of forty-seven students. Transcripts were analyzed with such tools as the Florida Taxonomy of Cognitive Behaviors and the Aschner-Gallagher System. Chapters include C. G. Fischer and G. E. Grant on intellectual levels of discourse in these classrooms, C. P. Barnes on questioning, D. G. Smith on the relation between instructional variables and student outcomes, P. J. Foster on clinical-discussion groups in medical education, and G. E. Grant on community college teaching. Although light on theory and interpretation, the volume provides unusually provocative descriptive information. Some examples: About 80 percent of classroom time was devoted to professor talk rather than to student talk, and most of that talk conveyed factual knowledge. Asking questions accounted for less than 4 percent of class time, more than 80 percent of the questions were at the lowest level of cognitive complexity, and there was no student response for about one-third of the questions.

227 Goldberg, Lewis R. "Student Personality Characteristics and Optimal College Learning Conditions: An Extensive Search for Trait-by-Treatment Interaction Effects." *Instructional Science*, 1972, *1*, 153–210.

This study investigated the common assertion that effectiveness of an instructional method is related to the personality predispositions of the students taught by it. More than 800 students in two large courses were assigned to methods that varied in instructor input (lecture versus self-study) and in student output (quiz versus papers). Results showed no systematic relationships between these methods, the extensive personality measures (which yielded more than 350 scores), and three outcome variables—student knowledge about course content, amount of extracurricular reading, and student satisfaction. Further, scales reflecting relationships among these variables for students in one course failed to withstand cross-validation to the other course. During the 1960s and 1970s, this "intuitively reasonable" trait-method interaction hypothesis received a good deal of research attention, but it has yet to gain strong support.

228 Good, Carter V. "Colleges and Universities: Methods of Teaching." In Walter S. Monroe (ed.), *Encyclopedia of Educational Research*. New York: Macmillan, 1941, pp. 242–248.

The first edition of the *Encyclopedia of Educational Research* devotes about five pages (forty-four references) to college teaching methods research, compared with about four pages (ten references) to college curriculum and much greater attention (seventy-eight pages) to college student personnel work. Most of the studies were completed in psychology or education classes and published in psychological journals. They are discussed under the following headings: instructional procedures, study procedures of students, testing procedures, motivation, and remedial instruction. Suggestions are made for future research. The article gives a glimpse of the state of research during the period from the 1920s to pre–World War II, before higher education's great expansion.

229 Hofstein, Avi, and Lunetta, Vincent N. "The Role of the Laboratory in Science Teaching: Neglected Aspects of Research." *Review of Educational Research*, 1982, *52*, 201–217.

Much less research has been conducted on the effects of laboratory instruction in introductory science courses than on other methods of instruction. In this article, the history and goals of laboratory teaching and learning are reviewed, and research findings are summarized. Evidence suggests that laboratory instruction can facilitate students' logical development, such as inquiry and problem-solving skills, positive attitudes, and skills of cooperation and communication. Nevertheless, many studies fail to demonstrate advantages for laboratory instruction over parallel classroom instruction, perhaps because of methodological problems. Most of this research has been done at the precollege level, but the suggestions for additional improved studies are appropriate for higher education as well.

230 Hudelson, Earl. *Class Size at the College Level.* Minneapolis: University of Minnesota Press, 1928. 299 pages.

Heralded at the University of Minnesota as "a new approach to the study of its own problems, namely, that of experimental investigation," this volume reports an interdisciplinary committee's investigation into class size. Based on faculty testimony, student testimony, student achievement data, and cost information, the researchers found that small classes cannot be justified on the basis of student achievement. "In light of all available evidence, class size seems to be a relatively minor factor in educational efficiency, measured in terms of student achievement. In fact, students in smaller classes tend to lean too heavily on their instructors instead of trying to dig things out for themselves." Taken at face value, as by the writer of the book's introduction, the report is "little short of epoch-making in its implications" for campus construction, organization of instruction, and makeup of the teaching faculty. A more critical appraisal of the study sees some limitations because of the narrow qualitative criteria it employed. Its greatest contribution is to reveal numerous interesting researchable problems, including the need to assess the quality of student and faculty experience.

231 Jones, Harold E. "Experimental Studies of College Teaching: The Effect of Examinations on Permanence of Learning." *Archives of Psychology,* 1923, *10* (68), 5-70.

This monograph reports an early attempt to turn the methods of laboratory investigation of learning toward the classroom. Students in psychology classes were tested on the content of brief lectures and more comprehensive forty-minute lectures for immediate recall, longer-term recall, and effects of examinations on recall. It was found that "the retention of classroom materials obeys the law of slowing decrement after swift initial loss." Recall of the content of forty-minute lectures, initially 62 percent, declined to 45 percent after three to four days and to 24 percent after eight weeks. An immediate examination retarded this decrement, however, keeping the forgetting curve almost level for four days, with retention after eight weeks of almost twice as much material as without the examination, an effect that holds both for "thought questions" and for "fact questions." The author recommends concluding the class hour with a "terminal review," including an examination to be immediately scored and discussed.

232 Kulik, Chen-Lin C.; Kulik, James A.; and Cohen, Peter A. "Instructional Technology and College Teaching." *Teaching of Psychology*, 1980, 7, 199–205.

Conclusions are summarized here from the authors' previously published meta-analyses of 312 research reports covering five uses of instructional technology: Personalized System of Instruction, computer-based instruction, programmed instruction, audio-tutorial instruction, and visual-based instruction. Overall, when courses taught by these methods were compared with conventionally taught courses, the former showed small but consistently positive effects on student achievement and attitudes, but they had negligible effects on course completion rates and on correlations between aptitude and achievement. Effects were strongest for PSI.

233 McCord, Michael T. "Methods and Theories of Instruction." In John C. Smart (ed.), *Higher Education: Handbook of Theory and Research*. Vol. 1. New York: Agathon Press, 1985, pages 97–131.

This chapter reviews research on instruction, for both conventional approaches (lecture, discussion, seminar, and independent study) and innovative approaches (programmed instruction, audio-tutorial instruction, personalized instruction, and computer-based instruction). Although no general theory is offered, several theory-based approaches to instructional planning and organization are described. Problems with quality of this research are also noted. Approximately eighty-five references are cited. This chapter is an accessible discursive review leading readers to primary sources that deal with areas of their own interest.

234 McKeachie, Wilbert J. "Research on Teaching at the College and University Level." In N. L. Gage (ed.), *Handbook of Research on Teaching.* Skokie, Ill.: Rand-McNally, 1963, pp. 1118-1172.

Contending that changes in students, indicated by problem-solving skills and attitudes, are the ultimate criterion of effective college teaching, the author reviews research on the following methods: lecturing, discussion, laboratory teaching, project methods/ independent study, and automated techniques. Pertinent student characteristics, faculty attitudes, and principles from learning theory are also discussed. He emphasizes methodological problems in the research, such as ignoring individual differences among students and using very narrow criterion measures (for example, using examinations based on the textbook). More than 200 references are cited. A readable essay by a prominent contributor to the field, the chapter makes accessible a large volume of post–World War II research.

235 McKeachie, Wilbert J. (ed.). *Learning, Cognition, and College Teaching.* New Directions for Teaching and Learning, no. 2. San Francisco: Jossey-Bass, 1980. 116 pages.

In these varied essays, several areas of research in cognitive psychology are presented in terms of their implications for college teaching and learning. Topics include student aptitude (R. E. Snow, P. L. Peterson), what goes on in the minds of learners (A. Norman), lecturing (W. J. McKeachie), problem solving (J. H. Larkin, J. E. Heller, J. G. Greeno), writing (G. M. Olson, S. A. Duffy, R. L. Mack), and teaching from notes (R. S. Day).

236 McKeachie, Wilbert J., and Kulik, James A. "Effective College Teaching." *Review of Research in Education,* 1975, *3,* 165-209.

In this update to the review in the first *Handbook of Research on Teaching,* the authors discuss research under five headings: individualized instruction, primarily the Personalized System of

Instruction; educational technology; methods emphasizing student interaction and autonomy; student characteristics; structure, content, and information processing strategies. They note that research has contributed to important progress in knowledge in several areas: the importance of student participation and interaction, the aptitude-treatment approach to research, and the "increasing interpenetration of laboratory experimental psychological research and research on human education." Many methodological problems, however, persist with this research. More than 200 references are cited.

★**237** McKeachie, Wilbert J.; Pintrich, Paul R.; Lin, Y.; and Smith, D. *Teaching and Learning in the College Classroom: A Review of the Research Literature.* Ann Arbor: National Center for Research on Improving Postsecondary Teaching and Learning, University of Michigan, 1986. 106 pages.

Focusing on studies in postsecondary settings, this review citing approximately 500 references summarizes research-based knowledge about teaching and learning. Regarding teaching, the review deals with each of the common instructional methods and also considers influences on learning from assignments and evaluation. Regarding learning, a cognitive perspective is used to organize research findings about motivation (an expectancy-value model) and about student knowledge structures, their techniques for learning, and critical thinking. As one of the first products from the National Center for Research on Improving Postsecondary Teaching and Learning, this review is a balanced survey of current knowledge.

238 Mann, Richard D.; Arnold, Stephen M.; Binder, Jeffrey L.; Cytrynbaum, Solomon; Newman, Barbara M.; Ringwald, Barbara E.; and Rosenwein, Robert. *The College Classroom: Conflict, Change and Learning.* New York: Wiley, 1970. 389 pages.

This classic study of interpersonal and emotional events of the college classroom created a conception of the classroom's complexity that had only been hinted at in previous research. The cluster of student characteristics these authors derived has been a major theme in the literature of the college student. They labeled students as compliant, anxious-dependent, discouraged workers, independents, heroes, snipers, and attention seekers. While these labels have tended to be the most frequently used reference to the study, the book has much to offer in the analysis of the natural history of the classroom and classroom organization as a social force. The book is now out of print but is still frequently cited, and the effort to locate it is rewarded by the relevance of its contents.

239 Mathis, B. Claude. "What Happened to Research on College Teaching?" *Journal of Teacher Education,* 1980, *31* (2), 17–21.

The author argues that research on college teaching is hampered by the reluctance of the disciplines to "examine their mysteries and make them public." The complexities of teaching in higher education are not reflected by the univariate approaches to research about a topic that is essentially multivariate in nature. Four guidelines are advanced for researchers in all disciplines who might be interested in the study of college teaching and adult learning. First, recognize that teaching and learning activities in higher education represent both training and educational models. Second, use the literature about teaching and learning at other levels of education to guide thinking about research on teaching and learning in colleges and universities. Third, plan research that tests interactions among variables rather than merely testing the impact of single variables in isolation. Fourth, encourage creative use of models and paradigms in planning studies of teaching and learning in higher education. Illustrations of these guidelines are provided.

240 Pressey, Sidney L., and Associates. *Research Adventures in University Teaching: Eighteen Investigations Regarding College and University Problems.* Bloomington, Ill.: Public School Publishing, 1927. 152 pages.

Practical problems of college administration or instruction are studied, using methods "as might have been carried on by almost any college instructor, no matter how limited the resources at his command." Investigations cover a variety of topics, in some cases more than one topic per chapter: identifying critical studying skills and training poor students in those skills; adjusting curriculum on the basis of examinations given at the beginning of courses; identifying students' personality and character problems and how students use their time; students' precollege preparation in composition, reading, science, and math; students' reading load in courses; characteristics of good courses, and how to use them for course revisions; characteristics of text materials; and preparation for college teaching. These studies, primarily of historical interest, illustrate the traditional psychological empirical approach, but they turn that approach toward practical problems using manageable methods.

241 Schramm, Wilber. "Learning from Instructional Television." *Review of Educational Research,* 1962, *32,* 156-167.

This review of 400 studies comparing televised instruction with conventional instruction concludes, as had previous reviews, "that about as much learning takes place in a TV class as in an ordinary class." The author suggests that "the pertinent question is no longer whether a teacher can teach effectively on television, but rather how, when, for what subjects and with what articulation into classroom activities instructional television can most effectively be used." The importance of this review lies in the fact that, though frequently cited, it failed in its attempt to stimulate greater sophistication in subsequent research.

242 Siegel, Laurence, and Siegel, Lila C. "A Multivariate Paradigm for Educational Research." *Psychological Bulletin,* 1967, *68,* 306-326.

After a critical appraisal of traditional instructional research that typically assesses the relative efficiency of two or more instructional techniques, the authors propose an alternative multivariate paradigm. The four classes of variables making up this "instructional gestalt" are classroom environment, instructor, learner, and course. All these variables and their interactions are measurable, and the results are far more sensitive and informative than simple instructional technique comparisons. Illustrative findings are presented and they show the power of the approach and how it might contribute to meaningful instructional theory. This article influenced the emergence of more sophisticated research designs after the early 1960s.

243 Solomon, Daniel; Rosenberg, Larry; and Bezdek, William E. "Teacher Behavior and Student Learning." *Journal of Educational Psychology*, 1964, 55, 23–30.

On two occasions, classroom observers used a thirty-eight-item questionnaire to rate behaviors of twenty-four evening school instructors in their introductory American government courses. Audiotapes were subsequently scored, using additional categories. Students completed a sixty-item questionnaire, and the teachers themselves completed a brief questionnaire. At the beginning and again at the end of the term, students took a test measuring factual knowledge and comprehension. Factor analysis revealed eight dimensions of teacher behavior. Factual gains were related to the factors of teacher clarity, expressiveness, and lecturing, but the pattern differed for large and small classes. Comprehension gains were associated with moderate permissiveness-control and with teacher energy, aggressiveness, and flamboyance. Student evaluations were significantly related to teacher clarity, expressiveness, and warmth. This study is unusual for its time in the variety of data collected, the care taken in data analysis, and the findings (1) that different kinds of learning are influenced by different teacher behaviors and (2) that effective teacher behaviors differ in large and small classes, perhaps because in small classes students "depend on each other for various social-emotional gratifications."

244 Thielens, Wagner, Jr. "Teacher-Student Interaction, Higher Education: Student Viewpoint." In L. C. Deighton (ed.), *The Encyclopedia of Education*. Vol. 9. New York: Macmillan, 1971, pp. 54–63.

This review of research about the college classroom begins by emphasizing the "ubiquitous and firmly established normative standards" that exist prior to the first meeting of students with a teacher and that influence such things as permitted activities, role of participants, place and time of meeting, and so on. Researchers have emphasized three approaches to the systematic study of the college classroom: classroom method of instruction, primarily comparisons of novel and traditional methods; traits of student, teacher, class, and environment (for example, searching for patterns of traits that differentiate high participants in class discussion from low participants); and classroom styles, that is, the multivariate relationships among natural combinations of traits occurring in the classroom group. Since classroom styles are empirically defined, this third approach is more likely than the others to lead to "the discovery of the unrecognized." Approximately fifty references are cited.

245 Tierney, William G. "Ethnography: An Alternative Evaluation Methodology." *Review of Higher Education*, 1985, *8*, 93–105.

Please see entry no. 466 for the annotation of this work.

246 Trent, James W., and Cohen, Arthur M. "Research on Teaching in Higher Education." In R.M.W. Travers (ed.), *Second Handbook of Research on Teaching*. Skokie, Ill.: Rand McNally, 1973, pp. 997–1071.

The "marked and steady" growth in research since the publication of the first *Handbook* is reviewed in this article. It has five sections: teaching environments; student characteristics and the learning process; teaching techniques and methods; teaching recruitment, training, and resources; and evaluation of teaching. The largest section deals with students, in part reflecting the influence of student dissidents during the late 1960s. The article also reflects influences of technology on teaching and the increasing interest in systematic evaluation of teaching. Problems are addressed regarding the quality of much of this research, its fragmentary nature, and the minimal effect it has had on practice. Nearly 400 references are cited.

3

Learners and
the Learning Process

Relationships between teaching and learning are subtle and complex. Although learning is ordinarily thought of as the consequence of teaching, it also occurs in the absence of deliberate instruction. Learning is sometimes self-directed, takes place in informal as well as formal settings, and does not require the presence of a teacher. Further, much learning is incidental; what is actually learned is not necessarily what was intended by the teacher.

The term *learner*, which we use in this chapter, captures these complexities somewhat better than the term *student*. Unlike student, learner extends beyond the relatively formal roles played in teacher-controlled settings. Learners are diverse individuals who pursue a wide range of activities in a variety of settings. The changes in learners that interest us are not limited to effects of courses and curricula. No less important are changes resulting from nonacademic aspects of higher education. Further, these changes can be seen in many domains, including the intellectual, the emotional, the social, and the moral.

Even though higher education declares that its primary commitment is to learners and it could not exist without them, learners have been studied more as the recipients of services, more for how higher education shapes them, than as active agents who themselves shape higher education. Learners typically have the lowest status and least power of all members of the higher education community. Rudolph (1966, no. 308) documents this neglect of students and their influence. He observes that learners have influenced the extracurriculum far more than the curriculum, and

131

he suggests that contemporary colleges could benefit from historical study of the types and extent of student influence.

This chapter covers literature on several topics related to learners and learning, including developmental theory, the effects and outcomes of college, the processes by which learning takes place, and how these processes are evaluated. Developmental theory is a topic also included in the companion key resources volume about students and student services, and we do not deal here with student personnel services and with the interventions they provide unless implications for teaching, learning, curriculum, or faculty development are explicit.

In the first section of this chapter, we include studies of learners and their development. The second section deals with learning processes. These processes include influences in the instructional and institutional environment as well as processes within the learner. The third section looks at issues related to evaluation of learning and learners, primarily at the levels of individual students and courses. Evaluation at the levels of programs and curricula is taken up in the third section of Chapter Four.

Learners and Their Development

Systematic research with learners who are enrolled as students in colleges and universities goes back many decades. Newcomb, Koenig, Flacks, and Warwick (1967, no. 295), for example, conducted an exemplary longitudinal study of students attending Bennington College from 1935 to 1939. Many studies center on students at a single institution; they include Sanford's (1956, no. 309) work at Vassar; Becker, Geer, and Hughes (1968, no. 252) at Kansas; Heath (1968, no. 280; 1976, no. 281) at Haverford; Perry (1970, no. 303) at Harvard; and Katchadourian and Boli (1985, no. 285) at Stanford. Other studies involve comparisons across institutions, such as Chickering's (1969, no. 260) statement of his theory of student development and Stern's (1970, no. 313) inquiry into effects of the match between individual needs and environmental press.

The boom years of higher education, the late 1960s and

early 1970s, yielded a distinctive literature about and by students. Although student protest is not a major topic for this volume, our index will lead readers to several entries on that subject, including a faculty perspective (Hook, 1970, no. 283), a curriculum perspective (Schwab, 1969, no. 427), and a student perspective (Farber, 1970, no. 271). More than one study of student development during those years was affected by campus disruptions; Suczek (1972, no. 314) presents an example of one such experience at Berkeley. Intense public and scholarly attention to higher education resulted in several collections of popular and scholarly writings about students. The most comprehensive research-based anthologies are those edited by Yamamoto (1968, no. 323) and by Feldman (1972, no. 272). They are excellent introductions to the education and social science literatures about learners through the early 1970s.

Readers interested in special groups of learners may use the index to locate key resources on adult and older students, women, minorities, commuters, and graduate and professional students.

At the most general level, the major question for research about learners is "How do learners change and what is responsible for those changes?" The voluminous literature on this question has been reviewed both in general and with regard to particular areas of change. Most comprehensive of the general reviews is Feldman and Newcomb's (1969, no. 273) two-volume work that, along with Bloom and Webster (1960, no. 255), covers early research critically and thoroughly. Subsequent general reviews of research on the outcomes of college include Withey (1971, no. 322) for the Carnegie Commission, Bowen (1977, no. 257), Astin (1977, no. 249), and Pace (1979, no. 298). Parker and Schmidt (1982, no. 299) are critical of the dominant metaphor underlying much of this research. They suggest that better than the mechanistic "production" metaphor would be "dialogue," which implies a more active role for students.

Studies focusing on specific aspects of the impact of higher education are indexed under "student." They include changes in several areas: student attitudes, cognitive development, peer group influence, personality development, psychological needs, self-concept, student-faculty contact, and values. Students' values and attitudes in particular have been given much research attention; studies on these topics can be traced from Jacob (1957, no. 284) through Levine (1980, no. 292) to Astin, Green, and Korn (1987, no. 250). Critical, integrative reviews specific to other areas include Pascarella (1985, no. 300) on cognitive development, Nucci and Pascarella (1987, no. 297) on moral development, Pascarella, Smart, Ethington, and Nettles (1987, no. 301) on self-concept, and Lenning and Associates (1974, no. 291) on a variety of nonintellective characteristics.

Persons interested in research on the impact of college should also consult chapters in *The American College* (Sanford, 1962, no. 310) that deal with personality development and chapters in *The Modern American College* (Chickering and Associates, 1981, no. 263) that discuss change from a variety of perspectives. A comparison of these two comprehensive and significant compendiums reveals how research about learners has evolved in recent decades. *The American College* adopts an orientation toward personality development, informed both by psychological and social views. By contrast, *The Modern American College* assumes a life cycle or developmental perspective. It encompasses nontraditional as well as traditional learners and sees development over time in all of the areas mentioned above as the proper concern of higher education.

The years between these volumes (the 1960s and 1970s) saw a flowering of student developmental theory. For a readable, comparative introduction to the major theories of student development, see Knefelkamp, Widick, and Parker (1978, no. 289). Among the significant primary sources for these theories are Chickering (1969, no. 260) on identity and education and Perry (1970, no. 303) on intellectual and ethical development. Personality-oriented research like that of *The American College* typically applied preexisting theories of personality to students. More recent scholarship derives developmental theory from responses of students themselves, usually stimulated by fairly general and open questions.

It is often unclear how developmental research about learners should affect the teaching/learning process. Little is known about how a learner's developmental level limits or facilitates specific learning in courses. It is known that the demands of instruction and the expectations of faculty are greater than the developed capacities of many learners (see, for example, Kitchener, 1983, no. 288; Fuller, 1987, no. 95). Nevertheless, that knowledge does not reveal how one can bring about the proper match between learner and instruction or even what the proper match should be.

Methods employed in this research have also changed over time. Quantitative data reported in conventional ways have characterized this literature from its beginning. Recently, the incidence of individual case reports has increased. Some of these case reports are intended to stand alone (Cottle, 1977, no. 267; Harvey, 1982, no. 278), while others are intended to illustrate particular views or positions (Schuman, 1982, no. 312; Daloz, 1986, no. 329). Case portraits of individuals, along with participant observation reports (for example, Becker, Geer, and Hughes, 1968, no. 252), add particularity and concreteness to a style of scholarship that some find excessively general and abstracted. The details of student life conveyed by this recent work constitute an important contribution. We need to know more, for example, about how students spend their time (see Bolton and Kammeyer, 1967, no. 256, for an example of how such studies can be done) and about the intensity of students' cognitive and affective involvement in various activities. Such empirical information complements theories based on epistemological investigations, since the latter usually depend on data from rather general questions about how learners make sense of their experience.

Learning Processes

All learning creates changes within the learner, and perhaps one day we will understand the neurochemical processes associated with learning. For now, however, research focuses on observable learner behaviors, on reports by learners of their thoughts and feelings, and on characteristics of the environment that exert significant influences on learning outcomes.

Many studies of learning processes spring from the developmental point of view. As indicated in the previous section, this viewpoint provides an organizing structure for *The Modern American College* (Chickering and Associates, 1981, no. 263). Theories of student development discussed there and in other resources usually imply at least an informal theory of learning and sometimes explicitly state conditions thought to facilitate learning. Additional theories or viewpoints about learning include the humanistic approach of Rogers (1983, no. 345), which had considerable influence in the 1960s and 1970s; the Socratic approach of Ross (1981, no. 346), which aims at discovery; and the androgogical model of Knowles (1984, no. 336). Still other approaches can be inferred from the key resources on teaching in the previous chapter; see, for example, the compendium by Joyce and Weil (1986, no. 30). The book by Daloz (1986, no. 329) represents an interesting blend: attention to developmental processes internal to the learner on the one hand and, on the other hand, a major external influence, namely, the influence of a mentor.

Adult students and their learning processes are the subject of several publications (Houle, 1984, no. 334; Smith, 1983, no. 349), some of which give special attention to motivation (Cross, 1981, no. 328; Wlodkowski, 1985, no. 357). Summaries of the considerable work on learning styles have been published by Claxton and Ralston (1978, no. 327) and by Kolb (1984, no. 337).

Most American research on learning is based on the study of cognitive processes, involves the production of developmental schemes, or emphasizes teaching. A number of researchers in Europe, by contrast, have studied how learners deal with particular learning tasks. Most of these tasks are realistic classroom activities, so learners might be required to cope with textbook excerpts rather than, as in developmental interviews, asked to reflect about their experience in general. Wilson (1981, no. 355) introduces the array of "approaches to studying" that have been revealed by this research. Particular research programs in this tradition are recounted by Marton, Hounsell, and Entwistle (1984, no. 340) and by Entwistle and Ramsden (1983, no. 331). Ford (1981, no. 333) examines implications of this research for the improvement of learning.

Subject matter to be learned is the special interest of Donald (1986, no. 330), in terms of academic disciplines, and of Richardson, Fisk, and Okun (1983, no. 344) with respect to literacy issues. Thomas and Rohwer (1986, no. 351) analyzed students' studying activities to identify characteristics peculiar to academic settings.

Other items in this section discuss the institutional milieu in which learners are socialized (Bragg, 1976, no. 326). They report the perceptions about institutions held by people in different types of institutions, perceptions likely to be related to learning (Pace, 1971, no. 342). Entwistle and Wilson (1977, no. 332) describe a board game for helping students understand the institutions in which they study and live. Ways of helping students improve their learning, such as learning center facilities, are described and evaluated in publications by Keimig (1983, no. 335), Lauridsen (1980, no. 338), Roueche (1983, no. 348), and Walvekar (1981, no. 468).

Interpersonal influences on learning have also received considerable scholarly attention. Several items in the previous section deal with the influence of peers. Studies of consequences of contact with faculty are reviewed by Wilson and others (1975, no. 356). Other aspects of the teacher-student relationship are examined by Morrill and Steffy (1980, no. 341), Rossman (1972, no. 347), and Thielens (1977, no. 350).

Evaluating Learners and Learning

Formal assessments of the quantity and quality of student learning serve several purposes. Evaluative information can be useful as feedback to learners. Evaluations are sometimes defended as motivational devices that encourage learners to persist with difficult tasks. But the most evident and significant use of evaluation is institutional, that is, grades as a record of achievement. Smallwood (1935, no. 374) traces the venerable history of grading and testing from the early forms of oral examinations to comparatively recent written and practical examinations; she describes how grading became more and more precise, at least in terms of numerical scales employed.

Doubts persist about the accuracy and fairness of grades. For example, the validity of grades is questioned in light of their weak relationship with subsequent adult achievement (Baird, 1985, no. 359). This key resources volume does not cover the extensive technical psychometric literature on validity and reliability of learning assessments, although that literature is referenced in several of the annotated items. Our focus is more on guidelines and techniques for evaluation at the individual student and course levels. The final section of Chapter Four deals with evaluation at the levels of curricula, programs, and institutions.

Because evaluating student learning is reportedly one of the least enjoyed aspects of faculty work, professors comprise a ready audience for practical guides and handbooks. Among the most useful are books by Clift and Imrie (1981, no. 361), Heywood (1977, no. 363), and Milton (1982, no. 367). Of the general books on teaching annotated in the previous chapter, several have sections on evaluation techniques and on grading; see, for example, Eble (1988, no. 14), McKeachie (1986, no. 36), and Fuhrmann and Grasha (1983, no. 18).

A number of items address evaluation in particular teaching-learning settings. These settings include the discussion class (Armstrong and Boud, 1983, no. 358), the clinic (Risley, 1978, no. 372), the laboratory (Clift and Imrie, 1981, no. 361), and the doctoral candidacy examination (Mechanic, 1978, no. 366). Still other items exemplify the literature on evaluation applied to particular instructional approaches—for example, collaborative learning (Wiener, 1986, no. 376), self-directed learning (McGaghie and Menges, 1975, no. 365), and use of student journals (Wagenaar, 1984, no. 375).

Effective guidelines and handbooks reduce faculty anxiety about evaluation tasks. Unfortunately, they may also divert attention from the larger influences of evaluation and grading, most of which are negative. Grading is not simply a set of skills that faculty master through appropriate training programs. It has a powerful influence on the teacher-student relationship and on institutional climate. A classic participant observation study (Becker, Geer, and Hughes, 1968, no. 252) found that most students view academic life through the grade point average perspective. That perspective may have had a softer focus during the permissive seasons of the 1960s and early 1970s, but now it is back, apparently focused more sharply than ever. Some suggestions for reforming evaluation techniques and systems are offered by Milton, Pollio, and Eison (1986, no. 368) in their wide-ranging and enlightened book. Their recommendations invariably provoke lively faculty discussion.

Learners and Their Development

247 American Association of University Professors. "Joint Statement on Rights and Freedoms of Students." *AAUP Bulletin,* 1968, *54,* 258-261.

Adopted by the AAUP in 1967, this statement addresses "minimal standards of academic freedom" that are needed if students are to "develop the capacity for critical judgment and to engage in a sustained and independent search for truth." The following topics are covered: freedom of access to higher education; classroom issues (for example, freedom of expression and standards for academic evaluation); student records; student affairs (for example, freedom of association and student publications); off-campus freedom; and standards for disciplinary proceedings. This AAUP statement is the standard resource for deriving campus policies regarding student affairs.

248 Astin, Alexander W. *Who Goes Where to College?* Chicago: Science Research Associates, 1965. 125 pages.

The research reported here was completed while the author was a member of the staff of the National Merit Scholarship Corporation. The data include a study of freshmen who entered 248 colleges and universities at the beginning of the academic year in 1961. The author cautions that the report "should be regarded primarily as a source of relatively objective information about colleges" rather than as a guide about how to pick a college to attend. The major goal of the study was to learn more about the characteristics of students who enroll at various kinds of institutions. Six "freshman input factors" tended to be associated with specific institutional types: intellectualism, estheticism, status, leadership, pragmatism, and masculinity. The author discusses these factors and how they relate to types of colleges and universities. The monograph presents a comprehensive profile of the 1961 freshman class and serves as a useful comparative index for those interested in how the freshman has changed since that time.

249 Astin, Alexander W. *Four Critical Years: Effects of College on Beliefs, Attitudes, and Knowledge.* San Francisco: Jossey-Bass, 1977. 293 pages.

During the first ten years of the Cooperative Institutional Research Program, longitudinal data were collected from 200,000 students at more than 300 institutions. Results are reported here along with analyses of the literature on college impact and a discussion of related methodological issues. Among many changes in students attributed to the college experience are the following: increased personal and intellectual self-esteem, decreased business interest, and, to a lesser extent, decreased religiousness and increased hedonism. Differences are explored with respect to institutional characteristics and student sex, race, ability, and age. These findings suggest the value of policies that give more emphasis to student progress and less emphasis to economic considerations than do most colleges and universities today. This study is a careful, illuminating contribution to understanding a decade of student data.

★250 Astin, Alexander W.; Green, Kenneth C.; and Korn, William S. *The American Freshman: Twenty Year Trends.* Los Angeles: Cooperative Institutional Research Program, University of California, Los Angeles, 1987. 140 pages. (ED 279 279)

For twenty years, the Cooperative Institutional Research Program with the sponsorship of the American Council on Education has conducted annual surveys of students as they begin their freshman year at some 550 institutions of higher education. In this monograph, survey responses from some six million students are reported regarding academic skills and preparation, demographic characteristics, high school activities, plans for majors and careers, political and social attitudes, and personal goals. Regarding political attitudes and values, the report suggests that "a widely discussed 'conservative' mood on college campuses really reflects a rising tide of materialism coupled with student concern about an uncertain economic future, rather than strong support for conservative political and social policies." This monograph includes an overview chapter of about twenty-five pages, followed by about seventy-five pages of tables that present normative data for men, women, and all freshmen. Appendixes discuss methodological issues, reprint the survey questionnaire, and show in what years each institution participated.

251 Astin, Helen S., and Hirsch, Werner Z. (eds.). *The Higher Education of Women.* New York: Praeger, 1978. 182 pages.

This volume of articles about women and higher education was dedicated to Rosemary Park at the time of her retirement from the University of California, Los Angeles. Part One contains chapters by Rosemary Park on the higher education of women, Esther Raushenbush on studies of three women who are "creators of change," Susan Kaplan on the single-sex college, and Robert Pace on liberal arts education and women's development. Part One continues with chapters on women's studies by Sheila Tobias, the undergraduate woman by Alexander Astin, university policies and women by Margaret Gordon and Clark Kerr, and women's scholarly productivity by Helen Astin. Part Two includes chapters on intellectual quality by Hilde Hirsch and Werner Hirsch, responsibility and public policy by Alan Pifer and Avery Russell, and civil rights and the women's movement by Theodore Hesburgh. An introductory section includes an interview with Rosemary Park. Of interest to anyone studying women and higher education, these chapters are also a fitting tribute to the outstanding scholar and administrator to whom they are dedicated.

252 Becker, Howard S.; Geer, Blanche; and Hughes, Everett C. *Making the Grade: The Academic Side of College Life.* New York: Wiley, 1968. 150 pages.

These researchers produced thousands of pages of field notes doing this participant observation study of life at a large public university (University of Kansas). They find that undergraduates view academic work through what is best termed the grade point average perspective. This perspective is congruent with the major characteristic of the teacher-student environment, that is, "a relationship of subjection in which the higher echelon dictates what will be institutionalized as valuable; . . . members of the lower echelon must, if they are to act effectively and remain members of the organization, accept that judgment and shape their own actions accordingly." This study is significant because of its attention to how social factors exert greater influence on student behavior than does faculty rhetoric or such individual characteristics as student ability and interests. The findings and interpretations hold as true for the 1980s as they did for the early 1960s when the study was conducted.

★**253** Belenky, Mary F.; Clinchy, Blythe McV.; Goldberger, Nancy R.; and Tarule, Jill M. *Women's Ways of Knowing: The Development of Self, Voice, and Mind.* New York: Basic Books, 1986. 256 pages.

Extensive interviews with 135 women yielded over 5,000 pages of text from which the authors discuss "the ways of knowing that women have cultivated and learned to value, ways we have come to believe are powerful but have been neglected and denigrated by the dominant intellectual ethos of our time." Women in the study came from a variety of backgrounds; ninety of them were students in one of six varied postsecondary institutions. The interviews included several questions based on theories of W. Perry, C. Gilligan, and L. Kohlberg. Women's perspectives on knowing are grouped into five major epistemological categories, each elaborated in a chapter in the book: silence, received knowledge, subjective knowledge, procedural knowledge, and constructed knowledge. Other chapters treat family life issues, formal education for women, and "connected teaching." The latter is seen as an approach appropriate for helping women to develop their own authentic voices; it emphasizes "connection over separation, understanding and acceptance over assessment, and collaboration over debate," among other features. The book is eminently readable. It contains ideas for much more research and for instruction that, if implemented, would yield student experiences very different from conventional education.

254 Bess, James L. "Integrating Faculty and Student Life Cycles." *Review of Educational Research,* 1973, *43,* 377–403.

Please see entry no. 479 for the annotation of this work.

255 Bloom, Benjamin S., and Webster, Harold. "The Outcomes of College." *Review of Educational Research,* 1960, *30,* 321–333.

In an issue devoted to research on higher education during the 1950s, this article reviews studies of the outcomes of college. Research on the following topics is summarized: "mortality and survival" of students, changes in students' information and intellect, changes in their personality, and the persistence of changes. Technical problems and measurement issues are also discussed. Fifty references are cited. The article provides convenient access to research during this decade.

256 Bolton, Charles D., and Kammeyer, Kenneth C. W. *The University Student: A Study of Student Behavior and Values.* New Haven, Conn.: College & University Press, 1967. 286 pages.

These authors studied student behavior rather than campus culture or student personality, which were popular research approaches at the time. Near the middle of the 1962 fall semester, 210 randomly selected students at the University of California, Davis, were interviewed regarding their use of time during the previous twenty-four hours; they also completed background and attitude questionnaires. "Even by the most general definition, intellectual activities (other than regular academic work) took up only about three and one half hours a week or half an hour a day of student time. Fifty-five percent of the students had no intellectual time on the day of the interview." Role orientations (privatist, vocational, conventional, and academic) accounted for a good deal of the differences among students in their reported activities. Detailed findings about the extent and content of student bull sessions are also reported. The authors contend that colleges make little conscious effort to influence student interaction toward educational goals.

★**257** Bowen, Howard R. *Investment in Learning: The Individual and Social Value of American Higher Education.* San Francisco: Jossey-Bass, 1977. 525 pages.

Bowen's training as an economist and his experience as an administrator and researcher in higher education give him appropriate credentials for answering critics who contend that the cost of higher education in the United States is not justified by the return on investment. The book is an encyclopedia of facts and reliable judgments about the outcomes of higher education. The point is made that the allocation of resources to higher education must be made on the basis of judgments arrived at in the context of a sound data base. The use of incomplete criteria for making decisions about resources stems from an overdependence on quantifiable and irrelevant outcomes that ignore much of the long-range impact of higher education on society. The author calls for a broader definition of outcomes by presenting facts and judgments based on sound data about the higher education enterprise.

★**258** Boyer, Ernest L. *College: The Undergraduate Experience in America.* New York: Harper & Row, 1987. 328 pages.

Reform movements usually follow periods of expressed dissatisfaction with institutions that affect the lives of the many rather than an elitist few. This book is the most publicized of recent critiques calling attention to problems of the undergraduate experience in higher education in the United States. The study that forms the basis for the book was sponsored by The Carnegie Foundation for the Advancement of Teaching. Twenty-nine institutions representative of the broad range of four-year colleges and universities were visited to obtain information about the status of undergraduate education. The book deals with all aspects of undergraduate life, from admissions to graduation. Both academic programs and campus life are evaluated. The author concludes that colleges suffer from conflicting priorities and competing special interests. Points of tension that appeared most frequently in campus visits include competence in language skills, general education, specialization, teaching, campus life as a community, evaluating students, and student values. The author's recommendations for change further fuel the debate about undergraduate education. This report is essential reading for anyone who wishes to be informed about reform in higher education.

259 Chase, J. L. *Graduate Teaching Assistants in American Universities: A Review of Recent Trends and Recommendations.* Washington, D.C.: U.S. Office of Education, 1970. 70 pages. (ED 043 274)

Please see entry no. 489 for the annotation of this work.

260 Chickering, Arthur W. *Education and Identity.* San Francisco: Jossey-Bass, 1969. 381 pages.

This major theoretical statement about students is based on the Project on Student Development in Small Colleges and on other research. Students are said to develop by completing tasks along seven major dimensions of change: developing competence, managing emotions, developing autonomy, establishing identity, freeing interpersonal relationships, finding purpose, and developing integrity. Institutional conditions associated with change are also discussed, including institutional objectives, size, faculty, curriculum, student culture, and residence hall arrangements. This approach has influenced institutional research and student development projects on many campuses and is a useful framework for discussion of institutional and instructional priorities.

261 Chickering, Arthur W. "Undergraduate Academic Experience." *Journal of Educational Psychology,* 1972, *63,* 134–143.

As part of the Project on Student Development in Small Colleges, academic environments of thirteen institutions were documented from questionnaires completed by students and faculty. Of particular interest is the Experience of College Questionnaire developed for this research. Systematic relationships within institutions were found among such elements of the objective environment as students' mental activities in class, ways of preparing for class, and role of the teacher. Those features vary among colleges and depend on the measuring instrument used. Expectations and student-faculty relations seem much more influential in these matters than are faculty demographics and features of the physical plant.

262 Chickering, Arthur W. *Commuting Versus Resident Students.* San Francisco, Calif.: Jossey-Bass, 1974. 150 pages.

In this pioneering comparison of commuter and resident students, the author finds remarkable consistency among several surveys. "Commuters and residents begin their college careers with an unequal start which strongly favors the residents. The gap between them grows." Students living in college dormitories exceed commuters in learning and in personal development and are much more fully involved in academic, extracurricular, and social activities. A discussion of how student and college characteristics can be more closely matched integrates these findings with other behavioral science research, and a concluding chapter presents policy recommendations for orientation and admission, program planning and evaluation, curriculum, and teaching and learning procedures.

★263 Chickering, Arthur W., and Associates. *The Modern American College: Responding to the New Realities of Diverse Students and a Changing Society.* San Francisco: Jossey-Bass, 1981. 810 pages.

In the foreword to this volume, Nevitt Sanford, who edited *The American College,* links the two works. He commends the contributors to the present volume for organizing it around the concept of life cycle development. *The Modern American College* is divided into three parts. Part One is about today's students and their needs. Included are chapters by Arthur Chickering and Robert Havighurst, Rita Weathersby, William Perry, K. Warner Schaie and Joyce Parr, Carol Gilligan, Robert White, William Torbert, Elizabeth Douvan,

Donald Blocher and Rita Rapoza, David Kolb, Jessie Bernard, Jacqueline Fleming, Allen Tough, and Richard Peterson. Implications for the curriculum is the theme of Part Two, with chapters by Lois Lamdin and Lois Fowler, Larry Friedlander and Martin Esslin, William Bondeson, Paul Ward, George Dawson, Richard Mann, James Gibbs, Elof Axel Carlson, David Halliburton, Paul Grambsch, Dean Griffith, Robert Saunders and Dorcas Saunders, Audrey Cohen, and Rhoda Miller and Carol Wolff. Part Three presents chapters on consequences for teaching, student services, and administration. Authors in this section are Thomas Green, Robert Menges, Thomas Clark, John Duley, Francis Keppel and Arthur Chickering, Morris Keaton, Jerry Gaff and Sally Shake Gaff, Theodore Miller and John Jones, Harold Riker, Jane Shipton and Elizabeth Steltenpohl, Louis Benezet, Harold Hodgkinson, Jack Lindquist, and Timothy Lehmann. The volume concludes with an editor's commentary. The book is a significant resource for persons seeking information about the role of higher education as a setting for lifelong learning. The selection of life-span development as an organizing concept for the discussion of teaching/learning alliances in colleges and universities reveals much about the probable direction for higher education in the years ahead.

264 Clinchy, Blythe, and Zimmerman, Claire. "Epistemology and Agency in the Development of Undergraduate Women." In Pamela J. Perun (ed.), *The Undergraduate Woman: Issues in Educational Equity.* Lexington, Mass.: Heath, 1982, pp. 161–181.

Interviews with ninety women during their undergraduate years at Wellesley College contributed to this developmental study. The students' positions in William Perry's scheme of intellectual and ethical development are documented by quotations, mostly concerning the transition from multiplism to contextualism. This study goes beyond the Perry scheme by introducing the concept of "agency," defined as "the capacity to decide and to act and to trust one's decisions and actions." Agency is especially critical for seniors as they make decisions about life after college, decisions that force them from the passivity of earlier positions.

265 College Board. *Academic Preparation for College: What Students Need to Know and Be Able to Do.* New York: College Board, 1983. 46 pages.

Please see entry no. 396 for the annotation of this work.

266 Cones, James H., III; Noonan, John F.; and Janha, Denise (eds.). *Teaching Minority Students.* New Directions for Teaching and Learning, no. 16. San Francisco: Jossey-Bass, 1983. 97 pages.

Ten essays review relationships between race and teaching. Of special interest are reports from minority students at predominantly white institutions (R. W. Sauffley, K. O. Cowan, and J. H. Blake), reflections of a minority professor (J. Mitchell), an analysis of interviews with white faculty (J. Katz), and a summary of research about minority students (W. E. Sedlacek). Other chapters present ideas or discuss approaches at the organizational level for teaching minority students.

267 Cottle, Thomas J. *College: Reward and Betrayal.* Chicago: University of Chicago Press, 1977. 190 pages.

These nine essays comprise psychosocial portraits not only of students and their families but also of institutions (Earlham College and Columbia College, Chicago) and of faculty, including the author's own tenure struggle at Harvard. Regarding the latter, he writes, "I still rely on marginality and am nourished by the flames of the periphery; but I hunger, too, for the security and the bosom of the center, the traditional and well-established, and of course, the guaranteed destiny." The theme that unifies this volume is an exploration of "how conflicts about education and achievement emerge and are resolved in the working out of a single life or single place of learning."

268 Cross, K. Patricia. *Adults as Learners: Increasing Participation and Facilitating Learning.* San Francisco: Jossey-Bass, 1981. 300 pages.

Please see entry no. 328 for the annotation of this work.

★**269** Daloz, Laurant A. *Effective Teaching and Mentoring: Realizing the Transformational Power of Adult Learning Experiences.* San Francisco: Jossey-Bass, 1986. 256 pages.

Please see entry no. 329 for the annotation of this work.

270 Davis, James R. *Going to College: The Study of Students and the Student Experience.* Boulder, Colo.: Westview, 1977. 248 pages.

This book begins with a brief review of the research on college students. It then presents a fictionalized first-person narrative of experiences during the four undergraduate years, focusing on friends, lovers, teachers, and family. Research on students is linked to people and events in the narrative. This case rings true, at least for students in the 1970s. It serves in a novel way to portray college experiences concretely while also emphasizing their complexity and their difficulty. The narrative further illustrates the influence of chance in the events that a particular person experiences during college.

271 Farber, Jerry. *The Student as Nigger: Essays and Stories.* New York: Pocket Books, 1970. 142 pages.

The title essay first appeared in 1967 in the *Los Angeles Free Press* and was subsequently widely reprinted in the underground press. It explores education as an embodiment of the master-slave relationship. Students have "got that slave mentality: obliging and ingratiating on the surface but hostile and resistant underneath." College students embraced the essay since, as the author says, there is little in it they didn't already know very well; but others denounced it as, among other things, "obscene, pornographic smut." Ten additional selections in the volume include several fiction pieces as well as discussions of the grading system and the drug culture and a satirical piece on educational research and academic politics.

272 Feldman, Kenneth A. (ed.). *College and Student: Selected Readings in the Social Psychology of Higher Education.* Elmsford, N.Y.: Pergamon Press, 1972. 492 pages.

This reader explores social psychological issues in higher education, reprinting or adapting thirty-two selections, continuing many of the themes from the editor's *The Impact of College on Students* (with T. M. Newcomb). The book has seven sections: introduction, from high school to college, change and stability during the college years, assessing influence of college environments, college substructure, student cultures and teachers, innovations and recommendations. Bibliographies from the original articles are reprinted along with bibliographies prepared by the editor for each section. These selections comprise an excellent introduction to the most important areas of empirical work about students through the 1960s.

★**273** Feldman, Kenneth A., and Newcomb, Theodore M. *The Impact of College on Students.* Vol. 1: *An Analysis of Four Decades of Research.* Vol. 2: *Summary Tables.* San Francisco: Jossey-Bass, 1969. Vol. 1, 474 pages. Vol. II, 171 pages.

These two volumes comprise a review, analysis, and compendium of empirical research from the 1920s to the mid 1960s. The authors ask, "Under what conditions have what kinds of students changed in what specific ways?" The painstaking review gives appropriate attention to methodological problems in the research. In the concluding chapter, nine generalizations are offered, which address, for example, the "considerable uniformity" of changes that have been found to occur between the freshman year and the senior year; how college impacts vary with the characteristics of their entering students; how impacts of particular majors vary with the characteristics of those who choose that major; the role of colleges in maintaining existing values or attitudes that might otherwise have been weakened; the negligible role that faculty typically play in campus-wide impact; the notable, desirable impact of small, residential, four-year colleges; and the persistence after college of attitudes held by students when they leave college. The most general proposition is that "processes of attracting and selecting students are interdependent with processes of impact." Seventy-five pages of references are included in the first volume. The second volume provides tables that summarize selected studies. The comprehensiveness and care reflected in these volumes make the work indispensable for any serious discussion of higher education's value for individuals and for society.

274 Freedman, Mervin B. *The College Experience.* San Francisco: Jossey-Bass, 1967. 202 pages.

This book is best approached as a series of observations on personality development during and after college. Some essays deal with specific topics—for example, sex, drugs, and education of women. Data are derived from such personality measures as the California F Scale and interviews with students and alumni, notably from Vassar College. In general, the author stresses "the beneficial social and cultural consequences of the effects of college attendance." There is little material to integrate these fourteen essays, some of which were previously published, but individual contributions illustrate the topic of personality as a focus for research on the college student.

275 Graham, Patricia A. "Women in Academe." *Science,* 1970, *169,* 1284–1290.

Please see entry no. 564 for the annotation of this work.

276 Greenberg, Elinor; O'Donnell, Kathleen; and Bergquist, William (eds.). *Educating Learners of All Ages.* New Directions for Higher Education, no. 29. San Francisco: Jossey-Bass, 1980. 110 pages.

These articles describe viable programs in higher education that were designed for learners of all ages. Chapters cover major trends in achieving a serious commitment to adult learners, the use of life cycle and stage theories in program development, the process of transformation in adult life, and examples of specific programs. The final chapter includes a list of organizing principles that can serve as guidelines for designing quality programs for younger and older learners. The value of this volume is more in the description of programs than in the theories discussed. Persons seeking examples of exemplary departures from traditional practices will find the book useful.

277 Hall, Roberta M., and Sandler, Bernice R. *The Classroom Climate: A Chilly One for Women?* Project on the Status and Education of Women. Washington, D.C.: Association of American Colleges, 1982. 22 pages. (ED 215 628)

This widely circulated paper from the Project on the Status and Education of Women summarizes published research and interviews that suggest that "women's educational experiences may differ considerably from those of men, even when they attend the same institutions, share the same classrooms, and work with the same graduate advisers." It documents how verbal and nonverbal behaviors of faculty and of men and women students create a classroom climate that women experience as chilly. Several pages of recommendations for faculty, administrators, and students list suggestions that climate issues be included in student evaluations of courses and in merit evaluations of faculty, and that faculty be assisted in examining gender-based biases in their own teaching. An annotated list of publications and organizations adds to the paper's value as a stimulus for discussion and policy development.

278 Harvey, Harriet (ed.). *Stories Parents Seldom Hear: College Students Write About Their Lives and Families.* New York: Delacorte, 1982. 423 pages.

During the 1970s, the editor taught a writing seminar at Yale University. These contributions are from eleven of her students whose course requirement was "to find an important event in their lives and write about it in a chapter-length story—thirty to forty pages." The stories are strikingly diverse, because the backgrounds of these students are so highly varied, yet each treats the common transition of passing from childhood to adulthood, that is, of both declaring independence from parents and establishing a new relationship with the family. The editor contributes information on how the writing seminar was structured to help students find their own voice in writing and provides several pages of background introduction to each contribution. These honest and affecting stories portray college students far more vividly and compellingly than most conventional scholarship.

279 Harvey, James. *The Student in Graduate School.* AAHE-ERIC Higher Education Research Report, 1972. 74 pages. (ED 057 258)

In this first of the AAHE-ERIC series of Higher Education Research Reports, the author reviews studies of doctoral students in the arts and sciences. Graduate students are often regarded more as hired help than as junior colleagues. Both faculty and other students should attempt to deal with that issue of status. Special problems of research and teaching assistants, part-time students, and women are noted. Among the controversial topics covered in this book are the relative roles of students and advisers in choosing dissertation topics and the extent of desirable general education requirements. The author concludes that financial aid should be distributed more equally and the excessive length of doctoral programs should be reduced.

280 Heath, Douglas H. *Growing Up in College: Liberal Education and Maturity.* San Francisco: Jossey-Bass, 1968. 326 pages.

Randomly selected Haverford College (Haverford, Pa.) undergraduates were studied through personality tests, interviews, and other instruments. Results documented increasing maturity in symbolic representation ability and in personality alocentrism (contrasted with egocentrism), integration, and stability. Studies of alumni support the persistence of such changes. The author draws implications for how colleges can enhance such changes in their students.

281 Heath, Douglas H. "What the Enduring Effects of Higher Education Tell Us About a Liberal Education." *Journal of Higher Education*, 1976, *47*, 173–190.

Most of the students at Haverford College (Haverford, Pa.) who were studied earlier by the author participated in this ten-to-fifteen-year follow-up investigation. For these men, the principal effects of a liberal arts education were the stabilization, symbolization, and integration of their values. Among suggestions for increasing the power of liberal education further is the following: "Balance its excessive analytical, logical, critical, and deductive bias by nurturing synthetic, intuitive, appreciative, and inductive forms of judgment."

282 Heath, Roy. *The Reasonable Adventurer: A Study of the Development of Thirty-Six Undergraduates at Princeton.* Pittsburgh: University of Pittsburgh Press, 1964. 163 pages.

Thirty-six members of Princeton University's class of 1954 who became the author's advisees were visited at home prior to matriculation, were interviewed and observed extensively during their undergraduate years, and were contacted for a brief follow-up nine years after college. Based on interview transcripts, students were rated on scales measuring development and temperament. The apex of development (the "reasonable adventurer") was attained by seven freshmen and by a total of sixteen students later in the study. Other students were termed noncommitters, hustlers, and plungers. Participation in the project appeared itself to enhance development, compared with control students.

283 Hook, Sidney. *Academic Freedom and Academic Anarchy.* New York: Cowles, 1970. 269 pages.

This book is a reasoned and trenchant commentary on the proper role of students, faculty, and administration in confronting disorder on college campuses. At the time this book was written, the author was a professor of philosophy at New York University. He argues for a commitment to reform on defensible educational, rather than political, grounds. With compelling logic he demolishes the claims of groups committed to radicalizing the university as one step toward the overthrow of society. The book's value today, aside from the details of disruption it contains, lies in the model of an academic community that emerges from its critical discussions of academic freedom, freedom to learn, and the causes of transition in higher education.

284 Jacob, Philip E. *Changing Values in College: An Exploratory Study of the Impact of College Teaching.* New York: Harper & Row, 1957. 174 pages.

This review of several hundred highly varied resources, listed in a thirty-six-page bibliography, covers studies on outcomes of general education courses, particularly in the social sciences. According to these studies, changes in students' values could *not* be traced to specific characteristics of the curriculum, to particular courses, to the instructor, or to teaching methods. When change was documented and the influence for that change could be traced, it seemed to lie primarily with the distinctive climate of a few institutions, with a teacher who had strong value commitments, or with the value-laden personal experiences of individual students. Although by contemporary standards this volume is not a rigorous research review and many of the studies predated World War II, the book stimulated a great deal of reflection and curriculum revision when it first appeared.

285 Katchadourian, Herant A., and Boli, John. *Careerism and Intellectualism Among College Students: Patterns of Academic and Career Choice in the Undergraduate Years.* San Francisco: Jossey-Bass, 1985. 324 pages.

Motivated by a need to learn more about Stanford University students' academic experiences, these investigators used yearly interviews and questionnaires with a random sample of 420 students, both incoming freshmen from the class of 1981 and some transfer students. Questionnaire items yielded a fourfold typology: intellectuals (high intellectualism, low careerism), strivers (high intellectualism, high careerism), careerists (low intellectualism, high careerism), and unconnected (low intellectualism, low careerism). Chapters devoted to each orientation report differences about how students move through their undergraduate experiences and how they evaluate those experiences. The authors acknowledge that the diversity of students extends beyond the categories of the typology. In fact, most of their recommendations deal with handling that student diversity, for example, making sample programs of study available to freshmen and sophomores and increasing students' interactions with faculty and advisers. The approach of the study is of interest even though the findings may not generalize beyond Stanford itself.

286 Katz, Joseph, and Associates. *No Time for Youth: Growth and Constraint in College Students.* San Francisco: Jossey-Bass, 1968. 463 pages.

Students at Stanford University and at the University of California, Berkeley, were studied through personality tests and questionnaires. A subsample of 274 students on the two campuses was also interviewed at least twice each year from their freshman year (1961) to their senior year (1965). Conclusions about how students change are conveyed through reports of aggregated data and through detailed case studies of individuals. Some chapters focus on special topics including the curriculum, career choice, residential living, drinking, authoritarianism, and student activism. The undergraduate campus is found to be "a learning environment in which, for many students, coercion predominates over curiosity and initiative." Recommendations include making "the student, not the course, the primary interest of the professor." Ways are discussed for institutions to better accommodate and foster student individuality, both within and outside of classrooms.

287 Katz, Joseph, and Hartnett, Rodney T. *Scholars in the Making, The Development of Graduate and Professional Students.* Cambridge, Mass.: Ballinger, 1976. 287 pages.

In this collection of articles about students in graduate and professional education, the authors note that "the student has rarely been the focus of systematic attention in the over one hundred years of graduate and professional training in the United States." In Part

One the authors present the history and trends for postbaccalaureate education. In Part Two Leonard Baird covers the reasons students go to graduate school and how they get there. Rodney Hartnett and Mary Jo Clark discuss environments for advanced learning and the meaning of quality in graduate and professional education. Part Three includes chapters by Joseph Katz on the development of the mind, Anne Robinson Taylor on becoming observers and specialists, and Marjorie Lozoff on interpersonal relations and autonomy. Emotional problems of the graduate student are discussed by Seymour Halleck, and Kay Hartshorn presents a day in the life of a graduate student. Part Four contains articles by Nancy Adler on women students and Birt Duncan on minority students and concludes with an essay by Nevitt Sanford on graduate education. The final section of the book contains recommendations by the authors. One provocative conclusion is that "graduate student relations with members of the faculty is regarded by most graduate students as the single most important aspect of the quality of their graduate experience; unfortunately, many also report that it is the single most disappointing aspect."

288 Kitchener, K. S. "Educational Goals and Reflective Thinking." *Educational Forum*, 1983, *48*, 75–95.

The reflective thinking approach to intellectual development draws on notions of John Dewey and William Perry and encompasses a sequence of seven stages that lead to reflective judgment. Each stage has characteristic metaphysical and epistemological assumptions and concepts of justification. In the final stage, "beliefs reflect solutions that can be justified as most reasonable, using general rules or inquiry or evaluation." Research shows that higher stages are associated with greater education. Upper-division college students typically score between positions 3 and 5, a point of "practical skepticism" where beliefs often rest on "a somewhat haphazard review of evidence in combination with emotional commitment." Discrepancies are discussed between the typical orientations of students and the more demanding educational goals characteristic of academic programs.

★**289** Knefelkamp, Lee; Widick, Carole; and Parker, Clyde A. (eds.). *Applying New Developmental Findings.* New Directions for Student Services, no. 4. San Francisco: Jossey-Bass, 1978. 125 pages.

Models for explaining the intellectual, psychosocial, and moral development of individuals are summarized and applied to students in higher education by the editors and their colleagues (P. M. King, A. F. Smith, A. Barna, J. R. Haws). One chapter each is devoted to models originated by E. Erikson, A. Chickering, W. Perry, L. Kohlberg, J. Loevinger, D. Heath, and R. Heath. In addition to describing the model, each chapter provides a critique, discusses related research, and draws implications for teaching and learning. The book provides a concise treatment of perspectives that have significantly influenced work in student services, curriculum development, and instruction.

290 Komarovsky, Mirra. *Women in College: Shaping New Feminine Identities.* New York: Basic Books, 1985. 355 pages.

More than 150 students were followed through four undergraduate years (1979-1983) at an eastern women's college. Using data from questionnaires, diaries, and repeated interviews, Komarovsky describes their experiences in the transition to college; as they face career, marriage, and motherhood decisions; and as they define their roles as women. The report is vividly illustrated with quotations, but it permits no causal inferences. The influence of college is circular, observes the author, since students both shape and are shaped by the college experience. She recommends policy changes designed to increase interactions among students, between students and faculty, and aimed at enhancing equality between the sexes. This is a useful report for teachers and researchers attempting to identify stimuli for change in students.

291 Lenning, Oscar T., and Associates. *The Many Faces of College Success and Their Nonintellective Correlatives: The Published Literature Through the Decade of the Sixties.* Monograph no. 15. Iowa City, Iowa: American College Testing Program, 1974. 551 pages.

Five years were spent in this review of research on the large variety of possible college outcomes, with emphasis on nonintellective factors. For each chapter there is an introduction to criteria for college success in that area, followed by summaries of approximately ten selected studies and then an extensive list of published sources. Chapters cover success viewed as intellectual development; as personal development and adjustment; as motivational and aspirational development; as social development; as esthetic-cultural development; and as moral, philosophical, and religious development.

292 Levine, Arthur. *When Dreams and Heroes Died: A Portrait of Today's College Student.* San Francisco: Jossey-Bass, 1980. 157 pages.

This study of college students portrays them to be relatively inward turning, competitive, materialistic, and cynical about society. In the context of post-Vietnam conditions, these values are seen as similar to other periods of "individual ascendancy" (that is, after World War I and after World War II) and different from periods of "community ascendancy" (that is, the progressive era, the Roosevelt/Depression years, and the Great Society). The author discusses implications of the educational needs of this college generation for liberal education.

293 Manski, Charles F., and Wise, David A. *College Choice in America.* Cambridge, Mass.: Harvard University Press, 1983. 221 pages.

Data from the National Longitudinal Study of the High School Graduating Class of 1972 address the following questions: Who goes to college? Does low family income prevent some from enrolling? Does the available scholarship aid offset financial need?

What roles do SAT scores, class rank in high school, race, and socioeconomic factors play in determining college applications and admissions? Do test scores predict success in college? Major findings are presented in a clear and concise manner with relevant evidence. The transition from high school to college is an increasingly important event for young people. The authors help clarify some of the mystery surrounding who goes where.

294 Murphy, Lois B., and Raushenbush, Esther (eds.). *Achieve-ment in the College Years: A Record of Intellectual and Personal Growth.* New York: Harper & Row, 1960. 240 pages.

All eighty-six members of one class at Sarah Lawrence College were studied during their undergraduate years and for two years thereafter. Data from interviews, tests, faculty reports, and student compositions revealed a variety of ways growth occurs. Writings by these students and accounts by the researchers document growth in intellect, personality, and occupational areas.

295 Newcomb, Theodore M.; Koenig, Kathryn E.; Flacks, Richard; and Warwick, Donald P. *Persistence and Change: Bennington College and Its Students After Twenty-Five Years.* New York: Wiley, 1967. 292 pages.

This study returns the focus of research to Bennington College alumnae who had been studied as undergraduates from 1935 to 1939. During that time, most of them were found to change in a "nonconservative" direction. For the most part, their political points of view were not substantially different in these 1960-1961 data, regardless of the amount of change they had shown during college. A few exceptions to these general findings as well as results for various subgroups and individual case studies are detailed. Appendixes reproduce research instruments.

296 Newcomb, Theodore M., and Wilson, Everett K. *College Peer Groups: Problems and Prospects for Research.* Hawthorne, N.Y.: Aldine, 1966. 303 pages.

Suspecting that "peer group effects are often irrelevant or even opposed to faculty-favored objectives," the editors organized conferences in 1959 and 1960 that produced these papers under the sponsorship of the Social Science Research Council's committee on personality development in youth. Four chapters by the editors, M. Trow and R. Levine, on the characteristics of organizations (colleges) and of individuals (students) set a frame of antecedent conditions that begins the book. Then four chapters present individual studies of student experiences and discussions of research issues: field experiences (B. Willerman), empirical classification of groups (H. Seldin and W. Hagstrom), measurement of peer group influence (P. Rossi), and environmental press (C. R. Pace and L. Baird). Finally, James Colemen and David Riesman each contribute commentaries on the papers. These first-rate scholars apply the best techniques then available for studying students in the higher education setting from a social science, rather than educationist, perspective. They raise problems still worthy of research, such as how to explain differences in patterns of peer group influences found when one campus is compared with another.

297 Nucci, Larry, and Pascarella, Ernest T. "The Influence of College on Moral Development." In John C. Smart (ed.), *Higher Education: Handbook of Theory and Research.* Vol. 3. New York: Agathon Press, 1987, pp. 271–326.

This article reviews evidence related to the traditional claim that American higher education affects students' moral judgments and behavior. Theories of Lawrence Kohlberg underlie much of this research. The authors summarize Kohlberg's theory, discuss the subsequent evolution of that model, and describe techniques used to measure moral growth. Studies show a positive correlation between level of education and growth in moral judgment, although these quasi-experimental research designs do not permit strict causal attributions. Other evidence suggests that there may be distinctive effects from different types of institutions and from different experiences within the same institution, including curricula and courses specifically aimed at influencing moral development. When moral behavior rather than moral judgment is considered, relationships are found to be more complex, and further research is needed before conclusions can be drawn.

298 Pace, C. Robert. *Measuring Outcomes of College: Fifty Years of Findings and Recommendations for the Future.* San Francisco: Jossey-Bass, 1979. 188 pages.

This publication reviews and synthesizes several lines of research to estimate effects of college on students. Studies of students show gains during their undergraduate years in knowledge, understanding, and intellectual skills. Studies of graduates' opinions and career achievements reveal positive effects of the college experience over time. Other studies show how institutional goals affect student outcomes. Overall, findings are favorable to higher education, and the author contends that they would likely be even stronger with more appropriate measurement devices and more powerful research designs.

★**299** Parker, Clyde A., and Schmidt, Janet A. "Effects of College Experience." In H. E. Mitzel (ed.), *Encyclopedia of Educational Research.* (5th ed.) New York: Free Press, 1982, pp. 535–543.

The authors critique prevailing mechanistic metaphors for describing higher education, for example, the "production" metaphor. They favor instead one that acknowledges a more active role for the student, for example, the "dialogue" metaphor. Studies are reviewed that deal with the changes expected to result from higher education. Well-established findings in three areas are summarized: academic gains, psychosocial gains, and economic gains. Illustrative studies of intellectual development of students are discussed in some detail, and problems with research in this area are elaborated, such as difficulties of attributing measured changes to particular causes. Approximately seventy references are cited in this current, succinct, and thoughtful view of research.

300 Pascarella, Ernest T. "College Environmental Influences on Learning and Cognitive Development: A Critical Review and Synthesis." In John C. Smart (ed.), *Higher Education: Handbook of Theory and Research*. Vol. 1. New York: Agathon Press, 1985, pp. 1–61.

This chapter reviews and synthesizes studies, most of them nonexperimental, of postsecondary education's influence on the learning and cognitive development of undergraduates. It seems clear that students' knowledge increases during college years beyond the influence of initial aptitude and that college experiences also affect thinking skills and cognitive development in general. It is not so clear which experiences are unique to college students, which institutional characteristics are responsible for the changes, or how such characteristics differentially influence various types of students. Pascarella presents his own "general causal model" that depicts relationships between college environments and student cognitive development, and he discusses research approaches that may yield stronger conclusions. Although couched in technical language and very cautious in its conclusions, this chapter is a comprehensive survey of research-based knowledge through the early 1980s.

301 Pascarella, Ernest T.; Smart, John C.; Ethington, Corinna A.; and Nettles, Michael T. "The Influence of College on Self-Concept: A Consideration of Race and Gender Differences." *American Educational Research Journal*, 1987, *24*, 49–77.

The authors studied the influence of college on student academic and social self-concept by following a sample of 4,597 students who had enrolled in 379 four-year colleges in 1971 (data from Cooperative Institutional Research Program surveys administered from 1971 to 1980). A causal model was developed by the authors, and separate estimations were made for black and white men and women. The results of the study suggest that the development of a self-concept during the college years is directly influenced by the academic and social experiences of students and that these influences of the college years were quite similar for race and gender.

302 Perkins, D. N. "Postprimary Education Has Little Impact on Informal Reasoning." *Journal of Educational Psychology*, 1985, *77*, 562-571.

To what extent are reasoning skills enhanced by increasing levels of formal education? High school, college, graduate school, and nonstudents (with and without a college degree) participated in ninety-minute interviews. They were asked to construct and present oral arguments on everyday issues, for example, does violence on television significantly increase the likelihood of violence in real life? The influence of education was only very slightly apparent on such indexes as number of sentences in the argument, number of lines of argument, and type of explanation given for the reasons. These discouraging results were attributed to the relatively small amount of attention given in formal education to informal reasoning skills.

303 Perry, William G., Jr. *Forms of Intellectual and Ethical Development in the College Years: A Scheme*. New York: Holt, Rinehart & Winston, 1970. 256 pages.

From extensive interviews with students at Harvard University, Perry proposed a scheme of development revealed in "the forms in which a person perceives his world rather than in the particulars or content of his attitudes and concerns." Movement through the nine positions of the scheme represents movement from a reliance on facts as conveyed by authority, through acceptance of many facts and views, through a struggle to choose among diverse views, to a point of commitment within competing views. This volume recounts research procedures and, using extensive quotations from students themselves, conveys the complex scheme with considerable nuance and subtlety. The research findings, firmly centered on students and their own reports of their experiences, have significantly influenced the fields of faculty development and student personnel services.

304 Peterson, David A. *Facilitating Education for Older Learners.* San Francisco: Jossey-Bass, 1983. 342 pages.

Provision of educational experiences, both formal and informal, for older adults is a rapidly growing phenomenon. As the number of persons in the population over fifty-five years of age increases, the demand for education for this age group becomes more important. Unfortunately, many current educational programs for older adults are extensions of efforts for traditional students. This book brings together relevant research and experience on adult and continuing education, with implications for credit and noncredit programs. Part One deals with the social, economic, and educational consequences of increasing longevity. Part Two covers the implications of changing abilities and attitudes in older persons for teaching these learners. Part Three presents information about developing instructional programs for older learners. Recognition of the older learner as a special type of student entitled to access to higher education brings with it a host of issues and problems relating to the special characteristics and needs of older people. This book provides a useful, informative beginning for those interested in education for older adults.

305 Raushenbush, Esther. *The Student and His Studies.* Middletown, Conn.: Wesleyan University Press, 1964. 185 pages.

For this Hazen Foundation study, the author talked at length with 170 students who entered college in 1958 or 1959, read samples of their papers and other academic work, and kept in touch with them during the undergraduate years. Most of the book centers on four individual cases (students from Harvard, Macalester, Hofstra, and Sarah Lawrence). The notion of "attachment" is presented as an important finding; attachment involves the need to overcome or to counteract student indifference "to the intellectual challenges of college itself and to the social challenges of the historical moment." Ways the curriculum can encourage attachments are discussed.

★**306** Riesman, David. *On Higher Education: The Academic Enterprise in an Era of Rising Student Consumerism.* San Francisco: Jossey-Bass, 1981. 421 pages.

Please see entry no. 423 for the annotation of this work.

307 Rosenberg, Donna A., and Silver, Henry K. "Medical Student Abuse: An Unnecessary and Preventable Cause of Stress." *Journal of the American Medical Association,* 1984, *251,* 739–742.

Data from three groups are reported: medical school deans of student affairs, students at the University of Colorado School of Medicine, Denver, and respondents to an earlier article on this topic. Sixteen of the eighteen deans "denied the existence of the abuse of medical students at their schools." By contrast, all clinical students interviewed reported incidents of "verbal abuse, humiliation, and undermining of self-esteem." Only one preclinical student reported such incidents. The article raises important issues about the definition and incidence of abuse and its relation to stress in students, a topic worthy of study in other fields with undergraduate and graduate students as well as with those in professional schools.

308 Rudolph, Frederick. "Neglect of Students as an Historical Tradition." In Lawrence E. Dennis and Joseph F. Kauffman (eds.), *The College and the Student: An Assessment of Relationships and Responsibilities in Undergraduate Education by Administrators, Faculty Members and Public Officials.* Washington, D.C.: American Council on Education, 1966, pp. 47–58.

Lamenting the neglect of attention to students by both institutions and scholars, the author argues that "unquestionably the most creative and imaginative force in the shaping of the American college and university has been the students." The extracurriculum is the instrument through which students exert their influence for reform, and it deserves more serious study. Such study can help to illuminate differences between nineteenth- and twentieth-century colleges and between the classroom/professor culture and the extracurricular/student culture. A "happy blend of freedom and of guided concern" was apparently achieved by nineteenth-century colleges in their dealings with students; creating its counterpart today is the "greatest challenge" of the contemporary university.

309 Sanford, Nevitt (ed.). "Personality Development During the College Years." *Journal of Social Issues,* 1956, *12* (4), 3-72.

These papers constitute a progress report on studies begun at Vassar College in 1952. Five freshman and four senior classes completed a battery of tests assessing authoritarianism, femininity and masculinity, psychological and physiological well-being, and intellectual functioning and achievement. Results of these tests as well as data from interviews with students are summarized. This extensive research, for which no final report was published, is notable because it combines the perspective of a depth study of personality with focus on a particular institution.

★310 Sanford, Nevitt (ed.). *The American College: A Psychological and Social Interpretation of the Higher Learning.* New York: Wiley, 1962. 1,084 pages.

For many years this book was a basic reference for students of higher education. Although a contemporary flavor is missing from some of the articles, much of the material remains relevant. The editor has organized the articles into eight parts. Part One deals with higher education as a social problem and a field of study, with chapters by the editor, David Riesman, and Christopher Jencks. Part Two discusses the entering student. Authors are Elizabeth Douvan and Carol Kaye, T. R. McConnell and Paul Heist, and Nevitt Sanford again. Academic procedures are the theme of Part Three, which includes chapters by Robert Knapp, W. J. McKeachie, Joseph Katz, Joseph Adelson, Anthony Ostroff, and the editor. Part Four covers student society and student culture and presents work by Theodore Newcomb, John Bushnell, Everett Hughes, Howard Becker, and Blanche Geer. Student performance in relation to educational objectives is the theme for Part Five. Donald Brown, Carl Bereiter and Mervin Freedman, David Beardslee and Donald O'Dowd, and John Summerskill are the chapter authors. Part Six includes chapters by Joshua Fishman, George Stern, Christopher Jencks and David Riesman, and Harold Taylor on the interaction of students and educators. Part Seven on the effects of college education presents chapters by Paul Heist and Mervin Freedman. The final section, Part Eight, introduces the theme of higher education and the social context, with chapters by Campbell Stewart, Frank Pinner, and Christian Bay. An editor's epilogue concludes the volume. As companion volumes, *The American College* and *The Modern American College*, edited by Arthur Chickering, are essential resources for anyone seriously interested in the broad spectrum of issues confronting higher education over recent decades.

311 Sanford, Nevitt (ed.). *College and Character*. New York: Wiley, 1964. 308 pages.

The subtitle for this book is "A Briefer Version of *The American College*," which had been published two years earlier. For this volume, chapters in the complete version were abridged by the authors and a new concluding chapter by the editor was included. The preceding entry for *The American College* gives a more complete description of the chapters.

312 Schuman, David. *Policy Analysis, Education, and Everyday Life: An Empirical Reevaluation of Higher Education in America*. Lexington, Mass.: Heath, 1982. 248 pages.

Intensive interviews with about fifteen people, some of whom completed college and graduated and some of whom did not, provide data for this study of how college experience affects one's everyday life. Extensive quotations illustrate myths regarding higher education and document events in the everyday domains of work and politics. The vivid and complex cases imply many inadequacies in conventional educational approaches. Readers will be provoked both by the author's method, which he terms radical empiricism, and by many of his assertions—for example, "One ironic sign of a 'good' education (in terms of change) appears when people turn their backs on the lessons of our educational system and the powerful myths that surround it."

313 Stern, George G. *People in Context: Measuring Person-Environment Congruence in Education and Industry.* New York: Wiley, 1970. 402 pages.

This extensive program of research is based on a model of the interaction of psychological needs of individuals with the environmental presses they experience. Instruments for measuring needs and presses were developed at Syracuse University and used in a variety of colleges and universities. The results portray interaction of personality dimensions (motivation, orderliness, friendliness) with institutional dimensions (academic climate, group life, impulse control, and so forth) at different types of institutions. This is an important example of cross-institutional research based on quantitative analysis of self-report inventories, a prominent research approach in the 1960s and 1970s.

314 Suczek, Robert F. *The Best Laid Plans: A Study of Student Development in an Experimental College Program.* San Francisco: Jossey-Bass, 1972. 194 pages.

Development of students during the first two years of the University of California, Berkeley, experimental college program (1965–1967) was investigated through interviews, observations, and personality tests. The college was a comprehensive community in which "faculty must tolerate the new and unexpected, for, in any circumstance which permits relationships to develop and grow, the unanticipated paradoxically is inevitable." The college's results were mixed: Faculty expressed a great deal of dissatisfaction, and students' reactions were intensified by the coincidental free speech movement occurring at the same time. Because of that general climate of change, the book may perhaps best be read as an account of how researchers modify their questions and adapt their methods in a dynamic situation.

315 Taylor, Harold. *Students Without Teachers: The Crisis in the University.* New York: McGraw-Hill, 1969. 333 pages.

Please see entry no. 432 for the annotation of this work.

316 Trow, Martin (ed.). *Teachers and Students: Aspects of American Higher Education.* New York: McGraw-Hill, 1975. 419 pages.

Please see entry no. 537 for the annotation of this work.

317 Wallace, Walter L. *Student Culture: Social Structure and Continuity in a Liberal Arts College.* Hawthorne, N.Y.: Aldine, 1966. 236 pages.

During 1959 and 1960, the author studied "Midwest College," a coeducational, nondenominational college with about 1,000 undergraduates. Modified sociometric questionnaires were given to the 327 freshmen on their second day on campus and to all students during their seventh week and during the last week in April. Faculty members were also surveyed. Results showed that freshmen learned organizational values and norms, primarily from nonfreshman students and faculty rather than from their freshman peers. The particular norms of nonfreshmen were often contradictory to those of faculty. Freshman socialization was largely completed during their first seven weeks on campus, although values and norms became more differentiated and complex during the November to April period.

318 Weathersby, Rita P., and Tarule, Jill M. *Adult Development: Implications for Higher Education.* AAHE-ERIC Higher Education Research Report no. 4. Washington, D.C.: American Association for Higher Education, 1980. 58 pages. (ED 191 382)

This unusually concise and comprehensive summary of research on adult development includes life cycle approaches, like those of Roger Gould and Daniel Levinson, and hierarchical approaches, like those of Jane Loevinger and William Perry. Along with each approach, implications for education are presented. A final chapter discusses further applications to program development, curriculum and instruction, faculty development and evaluation, and student support services. An extensive bibliography is also included. This is an excellent overview for those who deal with adults, whether those adults are staff, faculty, or students.

319 Whitman, Neal A.; Spendlove, David C.; and Clark, Claire H. *Student Stress: Effects and Solutions.* ASHE-ERIC Higher Education Research Report no. 2. Washington, D.C.: Association for the Study of Higher Education, 1984. 106 pages. (ED 246 832)

Approaches to defining, measuring, and dealing with stress are explored in this review. Not all persons appraise a particular event as stress-producing and some may even see it as challenging, so definitions of stress must take account of person variables as well as environment variables. Separate sections of the report deal with research about stress on undergraduate students, graduate students, law students, and medical students and residents. Suggestions are summarized for reducing or preventing negative aspects of stress. Particularly helpful are the suggested activities that increase students' "feelings of control over their education, information about what to expect, and feedback regarding what can be done to improve their performance."

320 Whitman, Neal A.; Spendlove, David C.; and Clark, Claire H. *Increasing Students' Learning: A Faculty Guide to Reducing Stress Among Students.* ASHE-ERIC Higher Education Research Report no. 4. Washington, D.C.: Association for the Study of Higher Education, 1986. 87 pages. (ED 274 264)

This report emphasizes stress inoculation, "a preventive approach so that the negative aspects of stress can be avoided. Stress inoculation involves giving people realistic warnings, recommendations, and reassurances." The report provides suggestions to faculty and students for using information feedback and student-faculty interaction to deal with stress.

★**321** Winter, David G.; McClelland, David C.; and Steward, Abigail J. *A New Case for the Liberal Arts: Assessing Institutional Goals and Student Development.* San Francisco: Jossey-Bass, 1981. 247 pages.

Evidence suggests that liberal arts colleges do a better job of preparing students in such areas as critical thinking, leadership capacity, and adaptability than do vocationally oriented colleges and community colleges. From a fourteen-year study of liberal arts graduates, the authors show that "liberal education contributes significantly to success in later life and that it produces benefits for society as well, through the better leadership and management skills and the more vigorous participation in civic organizations of college graduates." The authors' conclusions are derived from a wide range of evidence including tests of thematic analysis, self-ratings of abilities, assessments of thinking skills, and estimates of psychological adaptation to the environment. A model for the liberal arts designed to incorporate the findings of the authors' research is presented. The number of articles and books written in higher education in support of the liberal arts is legion; very few, however, present any empirical data to buttress their arguments. An appendix on the use of educational outcome measures and methodological considerations is a useful resource for those who plan to design similar studies. This book deserves to be read by anyone seeking evidence to support a liberal arts education.

322 Withey, Stephen B. *A Degree and What Else? Correlates and Consequences of a College Education.* New York: McGraw-Hill, 1971. 147 pages.

This book is a report prepared for the Carnegie Commission on Higher Education. Along with chapters contributed by colleagues, the author integrates diverse studies about the consequences and correlates of postsecondary education. Explicit attention is given to economic behaviors of students and alumni, their life-style, their mass media usage, and their political behavior. Despite explosive growth and turmoil in higher education during the 1960s, these studies show that students are generally satisfied with their educational experiences and conclude that students do change significantly in desired ways as a result of college. However, the research does not permit these changes to be traced to particular curricular or institutional characteristics.

323 Yamamoto, Kaoru (ed.). *The College Student and His Culture: An Analysis.* Boston: Houghton Mifflin, 1968. 493 pages.

These thirty-nine selections are drawn from significant theoretical and empirical work, representing higher education research through the mid 1960s from a social science perspective. The book has six sections: the American college; the colleges' clientele; institutional, student, and faculty characteristics; change during college; students who leave; and colleges of tomorrow. Although some of these authors are referenced in this volume as original sources, this edited collection can serve as an excellent introductory overview for a reader new to these topics or to the time period it covers.

Learning Processes

324 Becker, Howard S.; Geer, Blanche; and Hughes, Everett C. *Making the Grade: The Academic Side of College Life.* New York: Wiley, 1968. 150 pages.

Please see entry no. 252 for the annotation of this work.

★325 Belenky, Mary F.; Clinchy, Blythe McV.; Goldberger, Nancy R.; and Tarule, Jill M. *Women's Ways of Knowing: The Development of Self, Voice, and Mind.* New York: Basic Books, 1986. 256 pages.

Please see entry no. 253 for the annotation of this work.

326 Bragg, Ann K. *The Socialization Process in Higher Education.* AAHE-ERIC Higher Education Research Report no. 7. Washington, D.C.: American Association for Higher Education, 1976. 45 pages. (ED 132 909)

It is through socialization that "the individual acquires the habits and modes of thought of the society to which he belongs." This essay describes research from both undergraduate and professional education about the socializing effects that educational settings, faculty members, and peers have on students. Reforms suggested by the author include building small, more autonomous institutions within large ones; capitalizing on the unique qualities of particular institutions and planning change around institutional goals; providing opportunities for increased student-faculty academic interaction; using peer group influence to enhance student life through mutual assistance programs; and providing detailed feedback on student progress in relation to the institutions' goals.

327 Claxton, Charles S., and Ralston, Yvonne. *Learning Styles: Their Impact on Teaching and Administration.* AAHE-ERIC Higher Education Research Report no. 10. Washington, D.C.: American Association for Higher Education, 1978. 68 pages. (ED 167 065)

This essay complements research on teaching methods by reviewing studies of student learning styles, a term which "refers to a student's consistent way of responding and using stimuli in the context of learning." Dimensions of learning style are defined (for example, field dependent–field independent, reflection-impulsivity), and models are described incorporating the instruments commonly used in research at the college level (for example, Myers-Briggs Type Indicator, the Kolb model). Implications for teachers and administrators are stated. This is an excellent introduction to learning style theory and research into the late 1970s.

328 Cross, K. Patricia. *Adults as Learners: Increasing Participation and Facilitating Learning.* San Francisco: Jossey-Bass, 1981. 300 pages.

Addressed to anyone who might work with adults in an educational setting, this book was "motivated by my [the author's] growing conviction that individuals living in today's world must be prepared to make learning a continuing lifelong activity." Chapter One presents information about the growth of the learning society. Issues in recruiting adult learners are covered in Chapter Two. Chapter Three discusses the characteristics of persons who participate in adult learning, and Chapter Four indicates why adults participate in, and avoid, adult education. Chapter Five offers an eclectic model of adult motivation for learning, and Chapter Six presents implications for increasing participation. Chapters Seven, Eight, and Nine discuss patterns of adult learning and development, how and what adults learn, and the facilitation of learning. *Adults as Learners* brings together a wide range of information about adults and their learning needs, including research from the fields of motivation, learning, and life-span development.

★329 Daloz, Laurant A. *Effective Teaching and Mentoring: Realizing the Transformational Power of Adult Learning Experiences.* San Francisco: Jossey-Bass, 1986. 256 pages.

This book is a study of the kind of development that education fosters in adults, focusing on the one-to-one relationship between learner and mentor. Using literary allusions, case studies, and dialogues with individual learners, Daloz argues that teachers and mentors can act as guides when education becomes a "transformational journey." Transformation "means the yielding of old structures of meaning-making to new" and proceeds as a dialectical process. Specific student cases, most of them community college students, are interpreted in light of the developmental theories of Daniel Levinson, Robert Kegan, and William Perry. The author discusses some of the ways that mentors "tilt the mirror they hold up to their students," primarily the ways of giving support, offering challenge, and providing vision in the context of caring teaching. This is a work that all teachers can read with profit. Written in an engaging style, it shows deep understanding of developmental theory and the ability to apply that theory and research to individual instances while remaining consistent with the background of humanistic studies.

330 Donald, Janet G. "Knowledge and the University Curriculum." *Higher Education,* 1986, *15,* 267–282.

Successful assessment of student learning must be guided by a framework "for understanding what and how learning is acquired in different university disciplines." This research examined course content in a variety of disciplines, according to a four-level framework: (1) nature of the concepts used, (2) logical structure of the discipline, (3) truth criteria employed by the discipline, and (4) methods characteristic of the discipline. The approach and methods used here deserve replication in additional courses and at a variety of institutions.

331 Entwistle, Noel J., and Ramsden, Paul. *Understanding Student Learning.* New York: Nichols, 1983. 248 pages.

The projects reported here constituted the largest research efforts ever in Great Britain on the topic of student learning. Influenced by previous work of F. Marton and G. Pask, the authors gathered data using both qualitative analysis of interviews and quantitative analysis of questionnaires. Students' approaches to studying are documented (for example, "meaning" approach versus "reproducing" approach or "deep processing" versus "surface processing"), and students' perceptions of courses are reported. Stable relationships were demonstrated between students' ways of studying and their personal characteristics, and these relationships were found to vary among disciplines. The most successful students were those who could vary their studying approaches appropriately with the task and context. Thus, teaching improvement programs should focus less on teaching techniques and more on the learning and study approaches used by students and on professors' understanding of these approaches.

332 Entwistle, Noel J., and Wilson, John D. *Degrees of Excellence: The Academic Achievement Game.* London: Hodder and Stoughton, 1977. 226 pages.

Studies at Lancaster University and Aberdeen University, reported here, identified variables shown to be important for students' success in higher education and led the authors to a game model of student experience. The object of the academic achievement game is to get a good degree. Each student moves around the game board on one of three tracks: the arts track, the social sciences track, or the sciences track. Starting positions are influenced by several conditions to which students are assigned, including levels of intellectual ability, achievement, and personality characteristics. Moves are influenced by bonus cards ("your practical work is praised by a tutor"), hazard cards ("the course is badly organized"), and chance ("you are injured in a car accident"). Recommendations for higher education drawn from the game include increasing the flexibility of admission to higher education, improving guidance by counselors, and giving more attention to differences among students that affect learning and communication. This model is a provocative portrayal of the complexities of student experience. It also makes clear the desirability of multivariate research designs in studies of student experience.

333 Ford, Nigel. "Recent Approaches to the Study and Teaching of 'Effective Learning' in Higher Education." *Review of Educational Research,* 1981, *51,* 345-377.

When teaching aims at understanding rather than at information and when highly abstract material is being learned, special problems arise. This article reviews models of learning developed by F. Marton and R. Saljo, G. Pask and J. B. Biggs and describes their measuring instruments for studying learning at qualitatively different levels. Two kinds of processes are discussed, both known to be related to effective learning: manipulative approaches, where the subject matter is presented in a way that affects how the learner deals with the task, and metacognitive approaches, where learners deliberately apply techniques they have been taught. Much more research is needed to determine the extent to which these processes can be taught, and the author suggests that in such research the notion of effective learning be expanded to include critical evaluation and personal valuing of information. Although the article is intended for researchers, the concepts it presents are also valuable for college teachers interested in analyzing the goals they have for students and the learning strategies they expect of students.

334 Houle, Cyril O. *Patterns of Learning: New Perspectives on Life-Span Education*. San Francisco: Jossey-Bass, 1984. 243 pages.

This book examines learning as a lifelong activity. Chapter One develops the theme that learning can take place throughout one's life in a variety of contexts and not just in an institutional setting. Chapters Two, Three, and Four focus on individuals who have been able, through their own efforts and management of time, to maintain lifelong programs of self-directed learning and disciplined study. Chapter Five provides an individual example in which collective learning is the central theme for the life of the person used as the example. Chapter Six deals with Florence, Italy, as an example of a center of learning able to maintain its influence up until the present day. Chapter Seven describes the life of a person influential in helping establish systems of education for persons of all ages in the United States. Chapter Eight presents the study of a person who helped to establish the importance of didactic education for physicians in England and the United States. Chapter Nine summarizes some of the principles from these examples, and Chapter Ten suggests implications of the case studies for persons who plan and administer educational activities, especially for adults. The chapters in this book are representative of the work of the author going back to the 1960s, many of them presentations revised for this volume.

335 Keimig, Ruth T. *Raising Academic Standards: A Guide to Learning Improvement.* ASHE-ERIC Higher Education Research Report no. 4. Washington, D.C.: Association for the Study of Higher Education, 1983. 89 pages. (ED 235 696)

Learning improvement programs for students are more likely to be successful when "the developmental concept is perceived as an institutional mission." A four-level hierarchy of learning improvement programs is presented in this report. It posits that isolated courses in remedial skills are least successful and that comprehensive learning systems in academic courses are most successful. Twenty-six critical variables for learning improvement programs have been identified, and they are presented along with possible choices that educators can make regarding them. The variables are grouped into several categories: goals and rationale, instructional methods and content, institutional policies and standards, professional and paraprofessional staff and roles, and evaluation of learning improvement programs.

336 Knowles, Malcolm S. *The Adult Learner: A Neglected Species.* (3rd ed.) Houston, Tex.: Gulf, 1984. 292 pages.

This book presents the author's influential theory of adult learning, which he calls androgogy, and contrasts it with the traditional pedagogical model. Assumptions and design elements of an androgogical model of human resource development are elaborated. Appendixes comprise about half the book, most of them reprints of the author's previous articles on such topics as B. F. Skinner's influence, lifelong learning communities, ways of learning, and learning contracts.

★337 Kolb, David A. *Experiential Learning: Experience as the Source of Learning and Development.* Englewood Cliffs, N.J.: Prentice-Hall, 1984. 256 pages.

The author's significant work on experiential learning receives its most comprehensive and systematic statement in this volume. The model's four-stage cycle (concrete experience, reflective observation, abstract conceptualization, and active experimentation) and two major dimensions (prehension and transformation) are elaborated in detail. Implications are drawn for learner assessment, for various fields of study, and for adult development theories. One chapter is devoted specifically to learning and development in higher education.

338 Lauridsen, Kurt V. (ed.). *Examining the Scope of Learning Centers.* New Directions for College Learning Assistance, no. 1. San Francisco: Jossey-Bass, 1980. 108 pages.

The egalitarian era of American postsecondary education led to programs serving nontraditional students needing assistance with reading and math skills or with more general learning skills. These eight essays describe learning centers in a variety of public and private institutions, how they are organized, and the activities they carry out. The editor believes that in the future separate centers for special students will be integrated into other parts of the academic environment. This is an important compendium of program descriptions through the 1970s.

★339 McKeachie, Wilbert J.; Pintrich, Paul R.; Lin, Y. and Smith, D. *Teaching and Learning in the College Class-room: A Review of the Research Literature.* Ann Arbor: National Center for Research on Improving Postsecondary Teaching and Learning, University of Michigan, 1986. 106 pages.

Please see entry no. 237 for the annotation of this work.

340 Marton, Ference; Hounsell, Dai; and Entwistle, Noel (eds.). *The Experience of Learning.* Edinburgh: Scottish Academic Press, 1984. 242 pages.

Twelve contributors summarize a decade of significant research in Sweden and Great Britain on how students learn in higher education. The basic research approach presents students with a realistic learning task, perhaps an article to read, an essay to write, or a lecture to attend, and subsequently assesses what students learned and how they perceived the experience. Responses are classified into several approaches to studying, such as atomistic/ holistic and surface/deep. There is a good deal of agreement among these independent researchers on the processes that students use, how these processes are related to students' intentions, and how difficult it is to change the views of the world on which approaches to studying are based. This is an important contribution to our understanding of individual differences among students.

341 Morrill, W. T., and Steffy, D. M. "The Ethnography of Collegiate Teaching: Bridging the Student and Academic Culture." *Journal of Thought*, 1980, *15*, 49-75.

The academic, professorial culture is contrasted with the student culture through a number of postulates. For example, the purpose of education according to academic culture is "to enhance the individual's ability to understand the world in which he lives"; according to student culture, the purpose of education is "to increase the student's ability to succeed in the world in which he lives." The authors draw from their experience in teaching anthropology courses to illustrate the implications of these postulates; for example, "if we are correct that student culture postulates the purpose of education as the improvement of manipulability and not increase in understanding, then one way to teach is to show how the subject of study will increase the ability of the student to manipulate his own culture."

342 Pace, C. Robert. "College and University Environments." In L. C. Deighton (ed.), *Encyclopedia of Education*. Vol. 2. New York: Macmillan, 1971, pp. 201-207.

Research on college environments increased greatly during the 1950s and 1960s, establishing the conclusion that college environments "clearly differ greatly from one another in many measurable characteristics." This article, by a major contributor to that research, summarizes the kinds of information and the measuring instruments from which descriptions of environments are developed. Studies yield fairly distinctive environmental characteristics for nine types of institutions: highly selective, private, nonsectarian liberal arts colleges; highly selective public and private universities;

engineering and science institutions; Protestant and Catholic colleges; teacher education institutions; general liberal arts colleges; public and private general universities; state colleges and less comprehensive universities; and junior colleges. There is some discussion about how such information may be useful to students. Twenty references are cited.

343 Pascarella, Ernest T. "Student-Faculty Informal Contact and College Outcomes." *Review of Educational Research,* 1980, *50,* 545-595.

Studies of informal, nonclass contact between students and faculty show that such contact is related to a number of desirable outcomes: satisfaction with college, educational aspirations, intellectual and personal development, academic achievement, and persistence beyond the freshman year. These relationships persist even when the characteristics of entering students are statistically controlled. The greatest impact seems to come from contacts that focus on "intellectual/literary or artistic interests, value issues, or future career concerns," that is, on topics that seem to extend classroom concerns into nonclassroom settings. The author's model that puts student-faculty contact into the broader institutional context can guide further research.

344 Richardson, Richard C., Jr.; Fisk, Elizabeth C.; and Okun, Morris A. *Literacy in the Open-Access College.* San Francisco: Jossey-Bass, 1983. 187 pages.

Three years of study of students' experiences with reading and writing at an open-access community college revealed a highly fragmented process that the authors call bitting. Selected bits of information were transferred by teachers to students without analysis, synthesis, or original expression. This absence of "critical literacy" is traced to features of the curriculum and characteristics of the faculty as well as the students. Although this study is community college-based, the author's recommendations can be helpful to other types of postsecondary institutions as they set policies and requirements related to communication skills.

345 Rogers, Carl R. *Freedom to Learn for the Eighties.* Westerville, Ohio: Merrill, 1983. 312 pages.

Because "teaching is a vastly overrated function," the author chooses to emphasize learning in his writings. He called for a climate of freedom as essential to effective learning, "a way of being with students that was sharply different from conventional education." This volume collects his essays, many concrete case studies, and some research reports, including material from higher education. Chapters deal with responsible freedom in the classroom, the person-centered teacher, attempts at innovation and the resistances they elicit, and issues of freedom and commitment. The volume is a good introduction to Rogers's widely influential writings.

346 Ross, Stephen D. *Learning and Discovery: The University and the Development of the Mind.* New York: Gordon and Breach, 1981. 148 pages.

Learning is discovery, according to Ross, and there are no facts independent of insight and understanding. Analysis of Plato's Meno leads him to emphasize the Socratic model, a collaborative enterprise grounded in the processes of query and discovery. Since those processes are "fundamentally the same for master and student," the university student should see the teacher not as a transmitter of facts but as an exemplar of the cognitive powers that the student is to develop. This is a provocative argument grounded in philosophy of science and epistemology as well as in learning theory.

347 Rossman, Michael. *On Learning and Social Change: Transcending the Totalitarian Classroom.* New York: Vintage, 1972. 384 pages.

A key figure in the free speech movement, the author left Berkeley in 1966 to travel as an education reform activist. In these twelve essays, written from 1968 to 1972, he discusses the major issues of that time of ferment in politics and in higher education. The issues include organizing strategies, free schools, communication networks, technology, and the Tao of education. A basic underlying theme is authority in teacher/student relationships, nicely illustrated in a classroom game entitled "The Totalitarian Classroom."

348 Roueche, John E. (ed.). *A New Look at Successful Programs.* New Directions for College Learning Assistance, no. 11. San Francisco: Jossey-Bass, 1983. 109 pages.

This national study of learning assistance programs revealed that most programs do not collect systematic evaluation data. Nevertheless, Roueche identified approximately a dozen critical features of the subset of successful programs, defined as programs that reported a retention rate of 50 percent or better. These features include strong administrative support, mandatory assessment and placement, structured courses, multiple learning systems, and connections with subsequent courses. Other chapters describe particular approaches and programs for skill training and advising at a variety of institutions. According to the editor, the major issue for college learning assistance lies not with students' aptitude and abilities but with the fact that they have "not been taught very well."

349 Smith, Robert M. (ed.). *Helping Adults Learn How to Learn.* New Directions for Continuing Education, no. 19. San Francisco: Jossey-Bass, 1983. 109 pages.

A great many understandings and skills are required of adults if they are to continue learning in all of the situations and settings they encounter. These essays identify concepts and describe activities intended to lead adults toward more flexibility and autonomy in learning. Subjects covered include collaborative learning, program planning, learning styles and diagnosis, and study skills. The editor concludes that issues of empowerment and consciousness expansion may be particularly fundamental for the success of adult students, but no comprehensive theory of learning yet exists to inform these issues.

350 Thielens, Wagner, Jr. "Undergraduate Definitions of Learning from Teachers." *Sociology of Education,* 1977, *50,* 159-181.

Since much student learning is believed to lie in direct interaction between teachers and students, it is pertinent to examine how students describe those interactions and define their learning. In the interviews reported here, undergraduates seldom mentioned learning when they were discussing their teachers. Students saw themselves as being in college to learn but not to be taught by a teacher. The teacher is sometimes regarded as a peer or a friend but more often as an evaluator. Though properly cautious about overgeneralizing from this small number of interviews, the author probes and speculates in ways that can stimulate faculty discussion and research hypotheses. One provocative conclusion is that "students can readily define interaction with instructors, when it objectively engenders learning, in terms which take no notice of the learning."

351 Thomas, John W., and Rohwer, William D., Jr. "Academic Studying: The Role of Learning Strategies." *Educational Psychologist,* 1986, *21,* 19-41.

This article presents a model of academic studying and discusses the techniques that effective studying requires. Characteristics peculiar to academic studying are presented—for example, studying is an isolated and individual activity, and studying tasks are ill-defined. Major components of the model are student characteristics, course characteristics, study activities, and study outcomes. Four fundamental processes are suggested as affecting learning strategies and their impact on academic study: specificity, generativity, executive monitoring, and personal efficacy. This article is a stimulating presentation, informed by research and rich with implications for researchers and course designers.

352 Tobias, Sheila. "Peer Perspectives on the Teaching of Science." *Change*, 1986, *18* (2), 36-41.

Two master teachers of physics presented lectures that were attended by their nonscientist colleagues. Listeners took notes on content and on what they found difficult about learning the material. They reported feelings of frustration, lack of a framework in which to fit the new learning, discrepancies between word-based learning and the demonstrations, barriers to asking questions, and so on. They also noted their real satisfaction from learning about a new field. This convenient and effective technique for turning teachers into learners should stimulate much reflection about the participants' own teaching.

353 Trent, James W., and Cohen, Arthur M. "Research on Teaching in Higher Education." In R.M.W. Travers (ed.), *Second Handbook of Research on Teaching.* Skokie, Ill.: Rand McNally, 1973, pp. 997-1071.

Please see entry no. 246 for the annotation of this work.

354 Walvekar, Carol C. (ed.). *Assessment of Learning Assistance Services.* New Directions for College Learning Assistance, no 5. San Francisco: Jossey-Bass, 1981. 123 pages.

Please see entry no. 468 for the annotation of this work.

★355 Wilson, John D. *Student Learning in Higher Education.* New York: Wiley, 1981. 194 pages.

This Edinburgh professor regards students as actively developing learners who vary considerably in how they approach academic tasks and how they process content. He describes research on student learning, emphasizing William Perry in the United States; Ferrence Marton in Sweden; Gordon Pask, Noel Entwistle, and others in England. Issues of interest to him include long-term changes in students, content that has personal meaning, individual task strategies, relatively natural learning tasks and research settings, variability across students and settings, and qualitative research methods. The author attempts to tie this research together in his own developmental model, which is presented briefly. The book is most useful as an introduction to predominantly European research through the 1970s on college students' learning.

356 Wilson, Robert C.; Gaff, Jerry G.; Dienst, Evelyn R.; Wood, Lynn; and Bavry, James L. *College Professors and Their Impact on Students.* New York: Wiley, 1975. 220 pages.

Two studies are reported in this volume. The first is a 1968 study of 1,000 faculty from six diverse institutions. The second includes faculty and students at eight institutions between 1966 and 1970. Most faculty said they gained satisfaction from their teaching and believed that their teaching was given less importance in promotion and salary decisions than it deserved. They endorsed formal procedures for evaluating teaching and favored innovation in teaching. Students who changed the most during their college years reported greater interaction with faculty, particularly interaction outside the classroom. Both faculty and students responded to requests to nominate outstanding faculty members; characteristics of the nominees are described as are the environmental conditions associated with student/faculty interaction. Although the late 1960s was an atypical period for American higher education, this study is noteworthy because both faculty and students participated and because of the variety of characteristics that were investigated.

357 Wlodkowski, Raymond J. *Enhancing Adult Motivation to Learn: A Guide to Improving Instruction and Increasing Learner Achievement.* San Francisco: Jossey-Bass, 1985. 314 pages.

Motivation is the central concept around which this practical and well-informed guide for teachers and trainers of adults is organized. "Motivating instructors" are characterized by expertise, empathy, enthusiasm, and clarity; the author states performance criteria for each of those characteristics. Most of the book consists of explanations and illustrations for sixty-eight specific motivational strategies—for example, "When possible, clearly state or demonstrate the advantages that will result from the learning activity. . . . Create opportunities and conditions for the flow experience. . . .

Consider the use of extrinsic reinforcers for routine, well-learned activities, complex skill building, and drill-and-practice activities." These strategies are organized according to a model of motivation that emphasizes the time when learning events occur (the time continuum model of motivation). Applications and guidelines illustrate how the models and strategies can be implemented in a broad range of educational settings at both organizational and course levels.

Evaluating Learners and Learning

358 Armstrong, Merilyn, and Boud, David. "Assessing Participation in Discussion: An Exploration of the Issues." *Studies in Higher Education*, 1983, *8*, 33–44.

When students' grades are based in part on their participation in discussion, the instructor confronts difficult measurement problems. Assessment may be biased by the teacher's personal likes and dislikes, since students cannot be graded anonymously. Assessment may overload the instructor who must simultaneously teach and evaluate. The discussion itself may become artificial because of its role in grading. The authors introduce and critique three types of assessment criteria that can be used to assess participation in discussion: characteristics of a student's contribution, inferred preparation for class, and attendance. Among other topics discussed are when marks should be recorded, what sort of recording format to use, and the pros and cons of external observers. This article is a useful contribution on a difficult topic for which little research-based guidance is available.

359 Baird, Leonard L. "Do Grades and Tests Predict Adult Accomplishment?" *Research in Higher Education*, 1985, *23*, 3–85.

Investigations that relate college grades and ability scores to high-level accomplishments of adults have studied many groups: scientists, technicians, physicians, managers, students, and other highly creative individuals. Some, like the Terman studies, employed longitudinal designs. Relationships are generally positive but low, although they become somewhat stronger as the content of the academic measure and the demands of the field become closer. For example, business school grades, but not admission test scores, were related to managerial success. A better predictor of accomplishment is biographical information showing past accomplishments in areas pertinent to potential future success. Although high academic ability is a prerequisite to entering high-level fields, it is by no means a prerequisite for high-level success in those fields. This detailed research review cites more than 150 references.

360 Becker, Howard S.; Geer, Blanche; and Hughes, Everett C. *Making the Grade: The Academic Side of College Life.* New York: Wiley, 1968. 150 pages.

Please see entry no. 252 for the annotation of this work.

361 Clift, John C., and Imrie, Bradford W. *Assessing Students, Appraising Teaching.* New York: Wiley, 1981. 176 pages.

Acknowledging that assessment "is an activity which arouses anxiety and stress in both teacher and learner," the authors offer this volume as a "practical guide" for teachers in higher and further education. About two-thirds of the book (five of seven chapters) deal with assessing student learning. These five chapters give helpful attention to several rarely discussed topics, such as open-book examinations, oral examinations, and laboratory work. Two chapters suggest ways of gathering information for improving teaching, including how to use students as sources of feedback. Exhibits include sample questions, assessment sheets, and forms for evaluating students' assignments.

362 Ewell, Peter T. (ed.). *Assessing Educational Outcomes.* New Directions for Institutional Research, no. 47. San Francisco: Jossey-Bass, 1985. 128 pages.

Please see entry no. 462 for the annotation of this work.

363 Heywood, J. *Assessment in Higher Education.* New York: Wiley, 1977. 289 pages.

The author has worked for some years at the University of Lancaster and the University of Dublin on the relationships between assessment and teaching/learning. He believes that assessments should be an integral part of teaching/learning and should reflect objectives of the instructor, including complex objectives: problem finding, applying principles to practice, and ability to conduct investigations. For this purpose, he describes his own approach, called the multiple-objectives examination. Other chapters discuss issues of marking, grading, and other examination formats. The book's contribution concerns assessing student attainment of higher cognitive objectives.

364 Jones, Richard M. "Letters of Reflection." In John F. Noonan (ed.), *Learning About Teaching.* New Directions for Teaching and Learning, no. 4. San Francisco: Jossey-Bass, 1980, pp. 1–14.

Jones has developed the practice of commenting on a student's work with off-the-record letters written at midterm. This essay includes several examples of his letters and of student responses to them. Although time-consuming to prepare, letters of reflection can enhance the learning of both students and faculty.

365 McGaghie, William C., and Menges, Robert J. "Assessing Self-Directed Learning." *Teaching of Psychology,* 1975, 2, 56–59.

Instructors whose students complete independent, self-directed projects must derive a measure of success that is comparable for all individuals. Goal Attainment Scaling is a technique developed for that purpose by researchers in the fields of psychotherapy and mental health. To use the technique in the classroom, students in collaboration with the instructor specify their intended learning outcomes and rate their progress. The technique provides an indicator of both how an individual student is progressing and the overall progress of a group of students. It also permits comparisons across groups for researchers who are evaluating, for example, alternative approaches to independent study.

366 Mechanic, David. *Students Under Stress: A Study in the Social Psychology of Adaptation.* Madison: University of Wisconsin Press, 1978. 231 pages.

As a context for studying adaption to stress, this study followed twenty students taking Ph.D. candidacy exams, their spouses, peers, and faculty. How they used both coping and defense devices is illustrated with reference to individual characteristics and group characteristics. This is a largely descriptive study, with some interpretations drawn from social psychological frameworks. Although these data were collected in 1960, the book remains relevant because today's examinations and the justifications given for them are quite similar to the examinations undergone by these graduate students. The author believes such examinations are counterproductive.

367 Milton, Ohmer. *Will That Be on the Final?* Springfield, Ill.: Thomas, 1982. 91 pages.

This volume is a highly critical discussion of teaching and grading practices in higher education. Examples of poor course examination questions are given along with hints for recognizing them and improving them. There are also suggestions about how to use examinations for influencing learning in a positive way.

★368 Milton, Ohmer; Pollio, Howard R.; and Eison, James A. *Making Sense of College Grades: Why the Grading System Does Not Work and What Can Be Done About It.* San Francisco: Jossey-Bass, 1986. 287 pages.

Historical analysis, research reviews, and their own national survey led the authors to view grades as central to student learning. Grades "determine very explicitly how and what students learn." Their own research has identified empirically derived distinctions between grade-oriented students and learning-oriented students. These distinctions include differences in traits and study habits and in what the students think about and do in class. The authors show that a particular grade is context dependent; it holds different meanings for the grade giver, the grade receiver, and the grade user. For grades to promote learning and teaching, rather than merely to place students in rank order, a number of changes can be made. These changes include modifying tests, giving more extensive information to students about their performance, and abolishing the grade point average. Although not a how-to book about testing and grading, the authors present original and provocative thoughts about grades, their functions, and the assumptions underlying them. The book is well documented and written in very straightforward language.

369 Pace, C. Robert. *Measuring the Quality of College Student Experiences.* Los Angeles: Higher Education Research Institute, Graduate School of Education, University of California, 1984. 136 pages. (ED 255 099)

Please see entry no. 465 for the annotation of this work.

370 Perkins, D. N. "Postprimary Education Has Little Impact on Informal Reasoning." *Journal of Educational Psychology,* 1985, 77, 562–571.

Please see entry no. 302 for the annotation of this work.

371 Perry, William G., Jr. "Examsmanship." *Higher Education Bulletin,* 1977, 5, 133–145.

Originally titled "Examsmanship and the Liberal Arts: A Study in Educational Epistemology," this delightful article begins by recounting exploits of a Harvard undergraduate who on a whim wrote final examination essays for a course that he had not taken. What he produced, according to the author, was a pure instance of bull: "relevancies, however relevant, without data." He received an A-. Many of the students properly enrolled in the course wrote essays that are instances of cow: "data, however relevant, without relevancies." They received grades of C. The author discusses relationships between cow and bull and the anomaly of these disparate grades. Implications for our theories of knowledge are also explored.

372 Risley, Betty. "Principles for Developing Instruments to Assess Students' Clinical Skills." *Respiratory Care,* 1978, *23,* 158–166.

This article presents steps for constructing checklists or rating scales to evaluate students' mastery of clinical skills. Special care should be taken with the clarity and the wording of items and with selecting and training raters. Although written for health care workers, these principles are equally appropriate for music, speech, physical education, and other areas of clinical or studio teaching.

373 Saunders, Philip. "The Lasting Effects of Introductory Economic Courses." *Journal of Economic Education,* 1980, *12,* 1–14.

Students who completed a two-semester introductory course in economics were compared at three points with similar students who had not taken the introductory course: at the close of the course, two years later, and five years after graduation (that is, about seven years after the course). Understanding of economics was measured by a special thirty-two-item version of the standardized Test of Understanding in College Economics. "A difference of over three points on the hybrid TUCE some seven years after a sophomore course has been completed, is not only statistically significant, it also seems to be educationally important. This is over 50 percent of the difference associated with taking an introductory course immediately after the course is completed." Various course characteristics, student attitudes, and student evaluations of their course were also investigated. The research questions and methods of this study deserve adaptation for studies of courses in other fields.

374 Smallwood, Mary L. *An Historical Study of Examinations and Grading Systems in Early American Universities: A Critical Study of the Original Records of Harvard, William and Mary, Yale, Mount Holyoke, and Michigan from Their Founding to 1900.* Cambridge, Mass.: Harvard University Press, 1935. 132 pages.

For this dissertation, the author visited the five named institutions and examined faculty minutes, trustee reports, and other documents. Although the study includes no examples of examinations and no systematic information about student and faculty reactions to them, the historical record is sufficient for a chronicle of types of examinations and a chronology of their introduction at particular places. Chapters cover oral, written, and practical examinations; dictated and printed examinations; and public and individual examinations. After examinations became widely used for purposes other than the award of degrees, it was necessary to go beyond descriptive adjectives for conveying results; hence, numerical scales were developed. Some early numerical scales were based on 4 categories, some on 20 categories, and others on 100. Gradually, differential weights assigned to required and optional courses were abandoned. The author remains skeptical of the adequacy of these methods.

375 Wagenaar, Theodore C. "Using Student Journals in Sociology Courses." *Teaching Sociology,* 1984, *11,* 419-437.

The student journal is "an intellectual exercise in reflectively describing and explaining one's own experiences and observations in terms of a sociological perspective." The author describes his use of journals in several courses to increase student involvement and to stimulate higher cognitive learning. He used five criteria for evaluating journals: accuracy, diversity, thoroughness, originality, and range of cognitive levels. This paper is notable as one of the few serious discussions of the student journal as a pedagogic device.

376 Wiener, Harvey S. "Collaborative Learning in the Classroom: A Guide to Evaluation." *College English*, 1986, *48*, 51-61.

Many college English teachers attempt to bring learners together for collaborative learning, but evaluation of such teaching tends to follow a conventional approach rather than an approach that accurately reflects collaborative practice. With reference to evaluating collaborative group work in the classroom, the author emphasizes four aspects of teaching that can guide evaluation: setting the task, implementing the activities, interacting with groups, and synthesizing group reports. Desired teacher behaviors related to each of these aspects are pointed out, and the author argues that such behaviors should be the focus of evaluation.

4

College and
University Curricula:
Traditions, Tensions,
and Directions

The metamorphosis of the higher education curriculum in the United States represents a history of events and philosophies that change as the beliefs, values, and attitudes of society change. One theme remains constant, and that is the responsiveness of the curriculum to the constitutency it serves. This constituency has evolved from the sons, and then the daughters, of the elite in society to include today anyone who wishes to lay claim to a college education. The curriculum has changed from studies that emphasized the classics and religion to the vast cafeteria that now provides a program, and a degree, for almost any need.

Rudolph (1977, no. 424) traces curriculum history, giving a comprehensive tour of the battlefield that JB Lon Hefferlin (1969, no. 464) concludes is at the heart of the institution. To say that the present state of the curriculum for higher education is one of disarray is to recognize the diversity of institutions and of students who attend them. The system of higher education in the United States today consists of colleges and universities that cater to the elitist element in society as well as other institutions whose avowed aim is to deny the elitist image.

Levine (1978, no. 412) deals with this universe by using the 1970 Carnegie Commission on Higher Education typology. That typology divides American colleges and universities into nine categories, although these categories miss much of the diversity in the culture of the institutions. A salient feature of his *Handbook on Undergraduate Curriculum* is the discussion in Appendix A of twelve events noted by Levine as having shaped the curriculum. Both Levine's *Handbook on Undergraduate Curriculum* and Rudolph's *Curriculum* are recommended as essential references for any inquiry about curriculum in American colleges and universities. Other general sources useful for learning about issues and problems in curriculum for higher education are Fincher (1986, no. 403), Bowen (1982, no. 389), Conrad (1985, no. 398), Dressel (1971, no. 401), and Kaysen (1973, no. 410).

This chapter treats curriculum as the totality of educational experiences for learners. It may be both formal and informal, overt and covert, in its influence on the educational process. Any attempt to understand the curriculum certainly should begin with some conception of the nature of higher education. The works by Barzun (1968, no. 381), Bok (1982, no. 387; 1986, no. 388), Kerr (1963, no. 411), Newman (1976, no. 418), Parsons and Platt (1973, no. 420), and Smith (1986, no. 428) present views of the college and university and their missions in society. While these authors analyze different aspects of higher education, they all make a statement about the functions of colleges and universities, in both a descriptive and a critical context. The tensions that emerge from these statements are reflections of tensions that exist in the larger society. The items selected for this chapter represent our attempt to provide some basis for examining the curriculum and its many manifestations as a mirror for larger social, political, and economic issues.

History and Philosophy

The reader may begin with the ideal of liberal education offered by the vision of Cardinal Newman (Newman, 1976, no. 418). His lectures to the Catholics in Dublin set forth an ideal for an academic community of teachers and students dedicated to the pursuit of universal knowledge apart from any practical application it might have. He eschewed research and service as proper callings for higher education, and he stated that in an academic community teachers learn from other teachers just as students learn from other students as well as from the teachers who instruct them. One would relegate Newman's ideas to history were it not possible to identify components of his vision in today's experimental curricula. The great books curriculum, introduced at St. John's College in 1937, is one example of Newman's philosophy in a contemporary mold. In the minds of many, his writings remain a standard for judging the meaning of "a liberal education."

From Newman, the next step in this abbreviated history might be the inaugural address of Charles William Eliot as president of Harvard in 1869 (Eliot, 1969, no. 402). The post-Civil War epoch in higher education in the United States was one of ferment and change. Movement from a common core of courses for all students to a system of free electives is but one part of the philosophy Eliot advocated for his version of curriculum reform for Harvard. The influence of Eliot on higher education in the United States was extensive. By the time he retired, the reforms he pushed for so vigorously had begun to lose their luster, and a more structured curriculum, together with specialization, came to dominate American higher education. The later transformations of undergraduate study at Harvard under Lowell and those who followed him are discussed in Smith (1986, no. 428).

General education as a theme in the curriculum of higher education has a long history. Levine (1978, no. 412) traces the first use of the term to an 1829 article by A. S. Packard of Bowdoin College. General education has many meanings, depending upon the particular frame of reference. General education and liberal education are often used interchangeably to indicate the learning experiences that all students need to have to develop a common understanding of the culture and heritage that links them in a broad social system. Others see general education as nothing more than a core of courses that all students take. The debate over both the definition and the form of general education in the curriculum remains unresolved. Bell's (1968, no. 382) account of general education and its disintegration after World War II indicates the support that scholars who study higher education give to a common learning for all. Boyer and Levine (1981, no. 391) discuss the rationale for common learning and present the historical and social contexts of general education today. The report of a national colloquium on general education sponsored by The Carnegie Foundation for the Advancement of Teaching (1981, no. 394) provides further evidence that serious scholars support the quest for common learning in the college and university curriculum. The Committee on General Education in a Free Society at Harvard University (1945, no. 397) advanced a rationale for general education in its report to James Bryant Conant, the president of Harvard at the time the report was submitted. Gaff (1983, no. 438) describes a specific project that supported models of general education in twelve colleges and universities. General education will continue to have its supporters, and the meaning of general education will vary from one generation to the next as society changes its definition of what is thought essential for the educated person.

Another issue with an honorable historical pedigree is that of liberal education and its translation into a curriculum. Both general education and liberal education are, according to Levine (1978, no. 412), used to indicate the same set of concepts about the curriculum. Liberal education, in its most recent description, refers to courses of study that assist the individual in his or her own liberation from dependence on external authority in the quest for identity. Liberal education is perhaps more a question of style of teaching than it is a collection of specific courses. One can certainly be liberally educated in a professional curriculum, and a curriculum labeled "liberal studies" can function for the most part as preprofessional preparation. Much of the rhetoric of general education and the liberal arts can be found in arguments for the core curriculum as a solution to both needs. Gamson and Associates (1984, no. 439), Martin (1982, no. 413), and Wegener (1978, no. 434) attempt to come to terms with the liberal arts in their own ways. The term remains elusive, however, until course specifications are laid out to implement the philosophy that supports liberal education. Keller (1982, no. 443) reports the recent attempt by Harvard University to define a core curriculum for its undergraduates. What emerged from the melting pot of conflicting and concurring opinions delivered forcefully by the faculty was more a contemporary philosophy for undergraduate study than a set sequence of courses defining the essential education of Harvard undergraduates. Blackburn and others (1976, no. 384), in their study of changing practices in undergraduate education, found that specific course requirements have given way to distribution requirements in which students select courses from several areas of study. This cafeteria approach to general education, the liberal arts, and the core curriculum is not without its critics. Hall and Kevles (1982, no. 441) collected the remarks of twelve scholars who offer alternatives to this conventional approach to common learning.

Graduate education and professional programs have melded with the four-year undergraduate experience in colleges and universities, resulting in programs to meet the needs of a constituency wanting to be trained for the marketplace as well as educated for self-development. These programs introduced curriculum themes into higher education that have more and more been viewed as the tail that wags the dog. From the beginning, colleges had prepared their graduates for work, especially for the calling of the clergy. With passage of the Morrill Land-Grant Act in 1862, the door opened wide for creating multipurpose colleges offering a variety of programs far beyond the dreams of those who, in 1636, established Harvard College.

In 1876, Johns Hopkins University opened its doors as the first American research university with an emphasis on graduate education. By the turn of the century, the United States was well on the way to developing the pattern for higher education that is recognized in the Carnegie Commission classifications of research universities, doctoral-granting universities, comprehensive universities and colleges, liberal arts colleges, and two-year colleges. With additional levels identified within the first four categories, this classification recognized nine different categories of institutions for higher education in the United States. These categories have never been entirely satisfactory for representing diversity in institutions or curricula, and the variation within categories is often as great as the variation between categories, depending upon the criteria used for comparison. Professional education in today's colleges and universities is discussed by Mayhew (1971, no. 415), Mayhew and Ford (1974, no. 416), Nyre and Reilly (1979, no. 419), and Schein (1972, no. 426). Stark, Lowther, and Hagerty (1986, no. 431) point out that undergraduate majors in professional programs outnumber students majoring in the liberal arts. Schön (1987, no. 451) argues for reform in the way professional schools teach their students and organize their curricula.

Professional programs are found at both undergraduate and graduate levels, although the trend in recent years is to upgrade professional curricula to the level of graduate study. The professional master's degree represents a growing area for curriculum development in higher education. Master's of Education, Master's of Business Administration, Master's of Social Work, and Master's of Music are a few of the professional degrees offered by colleges and universities today. This shift toward professional programs at the undergraduate level has left the traditional major in liberal arts far behind. Those who do not wish to be tracked into a career path early during their undergraduate years have fewer curricular opportunities. Trites (1975, no. 433) underscores the increasing demand for career-oriented curricula in today's colleges and universities. He sees the world of work clearly influencing evolution of the undergraduate curriculum.

Graduate programs, particularly at the doctoral level, are associated more with training for research activity. The curriculum of the Ph.D. was traditionally one of days spent doing one's own, or someone else's, research in a laboratory or a field setting. Berelson (1960, no. 383) provides a useful overview of graduate and professional studies in universities. His discussion of the programs represented by graduate curricula show how the Ph.D. has itself evolved into a professional degree, now usually pursued by those whose primary commitment is not to research. Heiss (1970, no. 407) presents a wide range of evidence that the Ph.D. has become an all-purpose graduate degree, a capstone for much that deviates from its original purpose. The number of persons awarded Ph.D. degrees far outnumbers the available academic appointments where competence in research and scholarship in one's field is necessary for advancement. Those Ph.D.'s who do not find a position in academe usually find outlets for their talents in other sectors of the economy. They generally become practitioners of one sort or another and do very little, if any, research after they leave graduate school. This trend will undoubtedly continue as long as a depressed market for academicians persists.

Innovative Curricula

Much recent literature about the college curriculum is directed toward reevaluation and reform. This search for quality is driven by many forces. Perhaps the most influential at the moment is the student who attends a particular institution and creates a need for a specific curriculum to meet his or her needs and aspirations. Riesman (1981, no. 423) may not have had the final word on the influence of students, but his discussion of the rise of student consumerism as a replacement for the tradition of faculty dominance in colleges and universities has already become a classic reference, defining a watershed in higher education. The student as consumer who pays tuition for a product is an influential customer in the general stores that some colleges and universities have become. Creating academic programs for the purpose of becoming more attractive to students is a temptation for any institution that depends on tuition as a major component of a balanced budget.

Many critics of higher education single out the loss of purpose inherent in the curriculum of the modern American college and the willingness of those who make policy to abdicate a sound educational philosophy in favor of an expediency based on economic need. Bloom (1987, no. 386), in his popular critique of American higher education, accuses colleges and universities of caving in to the future economic needs of students with a curriculum that has pushed out all consideration of the kinds of learning that nourish knowledge of self. Hirsch (1987, no. 408) calls for curricula that foster cultural literacy at all levels of schooling. Both content and form of the undergraduate curriculum have been singled out as irrelevant to what a college education should represent. Mattfeld (1975, no. 414) calls for expansion of the curriculum to get beyond the rational to the esthetic and the intuitive. Schwab (1969, no. 427) sees a direct connection between the student protest movement of the 1960s and the contemporary college curriculum. Taylor (1969, no. 432) views the student as the major agent for change in colleges and universities. He places student unrest in the context of a need for academic reform, particularly curricular reform, to alleviate many of the discontinuities that he views as endemic in higher education today. Newman

(1985, no. 448) outlines less radical reforms and develops the theme that obligations for service should be underscored in the college curriculum. He sees a need to encourage public service as a commitment for students. Fincher (1986, no. 403) discusses many of the current statements about reform.

Experiment and reform are, of course, constant themes in the development of higher education in the United States. Perhaps the most radical suggestion comes from Taylor (1971, no. 454), who would allow students to invent their colleges. His challenge to tradition in higher education was quite popular during the time of student unrest on college campuses. One wonders what kind of institution today's students would invent. It would not be the place of intellectual experiences alive with an altruistic commitment to the human experience that Taylor saw. Today's students would probably create a college with a career-oriented curriculum designed to help students attain economic prosperity as quickly as possible after graduation. Reforms for one generation can become forgotten dreams for the next generation.

This chapter contains descriptions of a number of experiments in higher education. Tussman (1969, no. 456) writes about an experimental program at the University of California, Berkeley, that involved developing a problem-centered curriculum. Grant and Riesman (1978, no. 440) evaluate a number of experimental colleges and programs that emerged during the 1960s in response to perceived student needs. These include cluster colleges at Santa Cruz and New College in Florida. Jones (1981, no. 442) reports on the Evergreen experiment and its attempt to bring coordinated studies to a wide range of students. Hutchins (1962, no. 409) presents his educational philosophy that supported the biggest experiment of all at the University of Chicago. Meiklejohn (1928, no. 446) presents a plan to create an experimental college at the University of Wisconsin. Perry (1977, no. 449) describes Great Britain's Open University.

Many of these experiments are placed in an appropriate historical perspective by Levine (1978, no. 412). Reforms and educational experiments will continue to be a part of the tradition of American higher education because the system is closely linked with social need. As society changes, so does our system of higher education. Colleges and universities will continue to lead, and be led by, a constituency reflecting the national conscience, or consciences, that energize social change.

Evaluating Curricula and Programs

Part of higher education's fascination with experiment and reform is its quest for ways to assess and evaluate quality. The monograph edited by Wilson (1982, no. 469) contains a number of articles setting out procedures and considerations for reviewing programs and curricula. Walvekar (1981, no. 468) edited a similar volume on assessing programs that provide developmental and remedial services to students. Ethnography as a method for evaluation is described and assessed by Tierney (1985, no. 466). Gardner (1977, no. 463) describes five approaches for evaluating programs in higher education. Ewell (1985, no. 462) addresses the topic of assessing educational outcomes. Conrad and Wilson (1985, no. 461) discuss academic program reviews and also critique literature and research on assessing program quality in higher education. This fascination with evaluation and assessment is evidence for the increasing maturity of research about higher education.

What clues do these resources about curriculum give for the future of the college curriculum? The clues are not as clear as one might hope, even though the Carnegie Council on Policy Studies in Higher Education (1980, no. 392) attempts to prognosticate. One must look far beyond the bounds of the institution to predict its curriculum even twenty years hence. As Fincher (1986, no. 403) points out, the concern for innovation and reform in the curriculum of higher education has produced changes that have been "gradual, cumulative, and provisional" (1986, p. 304). One might surmise from this statement that the curriculum will remain much the same during the rest of this century. Perhaps, but trends are already hinting at subtle changes. Faculties may finally get beyond thinking of liberal education as a fixed collection of courses and view it as an attitude about learning that can be communicated in almost any educational experience.

The aging of America may mean that colleges and universities will see a wider age range in their students than we see now. The number of people with a college degree increases each year, and the more education a person has, the greater the tendency to seek out further education. Thus, in the years ahead there should be a steady demand for what higher education has to offer, despite a drop in the number of "traditional" students in the population. Diversity in age requires diversity in curricula to accommodate the interests of older persons.

Not only will students represent a wider age range. They will also represent a broader ethnic spectrum. Colleges and universities will be expected to accommodate the needs of blacks and Hispanics, and Asian Americans will be added in increasing numbers. Each group will present its own demands on the curriculum. Age, ethnicity, and amount of previous education are now, and will be in the future, powerful forces to shape the curriculum.

Competency-based curricula and value-added approaches to assessment are likely to continue to be of interest because of their association with evaluation and quality control in educational programs. Economics will continue to have a strong influence on the content of educational programs and on the shape of the curriculum. The temptation to give the public what it wants is an enticement for any institution that depends on tuition for its survival. The world of work will continue to have a forceful presence in any attempt to revise our concepts about general education.

Whatever the future holds for the curriculum in higher education, one thing is certain—a curriculum will be available somewhere for just about anyone who wants to go to college.

References

Fincher, C. "Trends and Issues in Curricular Development." In J. C. Smart (ed.), *Higher Education: Handbook of Theory and Research.* Vol. 2. New York: Agathon Press, 1986.

Taylor, H. *How to Change Colleges: Notes on Radical Reform.* New York: Holt, Rinehart & Winston, 1971.

History and Philosophy

377 American Association for Higher Education. "Liberal Learning and Career Preparation." *Current Issues in Higher Education,* 1982-83, *2,* 1-18. (ED 240 948)

This issue contains briefing papers for presentations made at the annual meeting of AAHE. Mary Ann F. Rehnke served as the guest editor and contributed the introductory statement about liberal learning and career preparation. The topics covered include the economy and the college student by W. Ed Whitelaw; careers, competencies, and liberal education by H. Bradley Sagen; a political approach to creating a career preparation program by John J. Agria; and faculty roles in career advising for liberal arts students by David H. Hiley. The concluding section describes sixty-one career preparation programs for liberal arts students and includes a selected ERIC bibliography on liberal arts and career education. The stress on career preparation at the undergraduate level is viewed by some as conflicting with the aims of liberal education. These papers provide information and points of view aimed at practical resolutions of that conflict.

378 "American Higher Education: Toward an Uncertain Future." *Daedalus: Journal of the American Academy of Arts and Sciences,* 1974, *103* (4), 1-356.

During 1974-75, two *Daedalus* issues contained significant articles brought together by the editors of the *Journal of the American Academy of Arts and Sciences* in an examination of the central importance of higher education for society. The articles range widely across issues that confronted colleges and universities during the 1970s. Among selections most relevant to this volume are Peter Caw's article on instruction and inquiry, Allen Bloom on the failure of the university, Gordon Craig and Derek Bok on undergraduate education, and B. F. Skinner on designing higher education. The curriculum is examined in articles by Steven Muller, Gabriel Almond, and Carl Kaysen. Martin Meyerson writes about the problems of liberal and professional learning, and Talcott Parsons addresses the issue of stability and change in the American university. These examples indicate only a sample of the valuable commentary available in this publication. (The second issue of *Daedalus* is annotated in the first section of Chapter Five of this volume.)

379 Association of American Colleges. *Integrity in the College Curriculum: A Report to the Academic Community.* Washington, D.C.: Association of American Colleges, 1985. 47 pages. (ED 251 059)

The reform movement in higher education has spawned a spate of reports on the health of colleges and universities. This report reflects the interests of the membership of the Association of American Colleges and identifies a number of areas calling for remediation. These include the undergraduate degree, faculty responsibility for the curriculum, minimum curriculum requirements, study in depth, accountability, and the quality of college teaching. A list of readings is included. The report contains no surprises, especially when compared to other reports. Nevertheless, it presents the thinking of a group of scholars who are seriously calling attention to much that is wrong with higher education today.

380 Astin, Alexander W. *Achieving Educational Excellence: A Critical Assessment of Priorities and Practices in Higher Education.* San Francisco: Jossey-Bass, 1985. 254 pages.

American higher education is diverse in many ways, but there is general agreement about its hierarchical nature. That hierarchy is maintained by traditional views of excellence, that is, the reputational view, the resources view, the outcomes view, and the content view. Astin offers his own view of excellence, the talent development view, which he argues is more consistent with higher education's basic purposes and with the goals of educational equity. The key to talent development is Astin's "theory of student involvement," elaborated here at some length. Though much of the presentation lacks rigor by the criteria for good "theory," it does serve to integrate demographic and institutional research data and to suggest innovations worthy of testing. The book also includes a

chapter on teacher education and a summary of the freshman
surveys that Astin has conducted since the mid 1960s.

381 Barzun, Jacques. *The American University: How It Runs,
Where It Is Going.* New York: Harper & Row, 1968. 319
pages.

A noted academician addresses himself to the question of the
survival of the American University and to its future path. In
Chapter One he discusses the new university and the changes that
characterize it as an institution. Chapter Two presents a view of the
professor as a scholar whose activities are limited by the number of
hours in a day. Chapter Three raises the question of whether the
clients of higher education are really students or victims of the
colleges and universities they attend. The author also writes about
administrators above and below; friends, donors, and enemies;
poverty in the midst of plenty; and the higher bankruptcy. The final
chapter is a perceptive essay on the choice ahead for higher
education: "If the university is to save itself by making the changes
that it is already eager and able to make, it must not act singly but
in groups." The book is a practical critique of American higher
education written by a scholar well versed in the rhetoric of
criticism. The reader cannot avoid concluding that the American
university is in a worse state today than when the author first
examined it. One wonders what a second edition might contain.

382 Bell, Daniel. *The Reforming of General Education.* Garden
City, N.Y.: Doubleday, 1968. 330 pages.

This account of the development and apparent disintegration of
general education during the two decades immediately following
World War II has become essential reading for serious students of
the curriculum. It addresses the question of what has happened to
the expectation that *all* who attend college would receive general
education. The author states in his preface that the book "is an
effort to defend the idea of a liberal education against the fragmentation which threatens it both intellectually and sociologically. It
is an effort to affirm liberal education as a significant pursuit of the
confirmation of reality." Columbia University, Harvard University,

and the University of Chicago provide examples for an examination of the contemporary curriculum. The experience of reform initiated at Columbia after World War II is the context for a broad and penetrating analysis of general education and the liberal arts.

383 Berelson, Bernard. *Graduate Education in the United States.* New York: McGraw-Hill, 1960. 346 pages.

Among the publications supported by the Carnegie Corporation and published by McGraw-Hill in their Carnegie Series in American Education, this book is an outstanding contribution to understanding the growth of graduate education and professionalization in the graduate institutions of the United States. The author begins with a review of the history of graduate study and continues with a discussion of the purposes of graduate study, the institutions involved, the students who attend graduate schools, and the programs represented by graduate curricula. The final section of the book presents the author's conclusions, commentary, and recommendations drawn from the data collected as part of the study. This book should be read by anyone interested in the emergence of graduate and professional programs as a dominant force in higher education today. While the data are nearly three decades old, discussions of institutions, students, and problems are still quite contemporary.

384 Blackburn, Robert; Armstrong, Ellen; Conrad, Clifton; Didham, James; and McKune, Thomas. *Changing Practices in Undergraduate Education.* Berkeley, Calif.: Carnegie Council on Policy Studies in Higher Education, 1976. 56 pages.

These authors attempt to define the undergraduate curriculum as it existed at the time this monograph was written. They also ask whether or not the undergraduate curriculum as they found it in the mid seventies represents a change from the past. They identify a number of trends: a shift away from breadth toward depth or specialization, and a move away from specific course requirements in general education to distribution requirements that allow students to select courses from among those that satisfy a requirement. The authors state that "the number of institutions requiring English, a foreigh language, and mathematics as part of everyone's general education declined appreciably from 1967 to 1974." The greatest changes in the undergraduate curriculum were at less selective private four-year colleges. Implications of these changes are discussed. The monograph provides a useful context for assessing changes in the undergraduate curriculum over time.

385 Blackburn, Robert T., and Conrad, Clifton F. "The New Revisionists and the History of U.S. Higher Education." *Higher Education*, 1986, *15*, 221-230.

The authors summarize the traditional history of higher education in the United States as reflected in writings of historians who examined curriculum and instruction, theories of learning, leadership, and exclusiveness in American higher education prior to the Civil War. They then present the revisionists' evidence to refute the traditionalists' view of events. The authors conclude that the revisionists seem more careful in their presentation of data and their qualifications concerning the interpretation of data. Nevertheless, both revisionists and traditionalists may be accused of introducing flaws in their interpretations; neither view is void of error. Much remains to be done by scholars of the history of higher education in the United States. This piece is an interesting and provocative comment on the interpretation of historical data, with a comprehensive list of references.

★386 Bloom, Allan. *The Closing of the American Mind.* New York: Simon & Schuster, 1987. 392 pages.

Occasionally a critic of the American scene produces a book that captures the attention of the general public and becomes a best-seller. *The Closing of the American Mind* is such a book. Professor Bloom, a member of the Committee on Social Thought at the University of Chicago, has written a sweeping analysis of the intellectual themes of this century and has provided a strident indictment of higher education in the United States in the process. The author describes the college student of today as a person who lives in an impoverished present without the benefit of understanding the past or having a vision of the future. Universities, with their emphasis on the future economic comfort of their students, fail to provide a curriculum to nourish the knowledge of self that has always been the basis of humane learning. Informed critics of the book indicate that the author makes a great number of unsubstantiated claims, pointed out by those reviewers who are more knowledgeable than Bloom about the diversity of American higher education. The importance of the book may be less in the validity of its arguments and more in the measure of the contemporary zeitgeist indicated by its popularity.

387 Bok, Derek. *Beyond the Ivory Tower: Social Responsibilities of the Modern University.* Cambridge, Mass.: Harvard University Press, 1982. 318 pages.

The president of Harvard University is expected to use his office as a podium for commenting on higher education issues that affect all campuses, not only his own. This book exercises that expectation. President Bok discusses how a university can respond to social problems without compromising its traditions of objectivity and autonomy. The author's discussion of these issues ranges across academic and nonacademic means for engaging society without being captured by it. The book is a serious exploration of the problems colleges and universities face in a world that holds increasingly complex expectations for higher education.

388 Bok, Derek. *Higher Learning.* Cambridge, Mass.: Harvard University Press, 1986. 206 pages.

In this book the president of Harvard University discusses what is distinctive about the system of higher education in the United States and assesses the performance of colleges against their claims to uniqueness. Five chapters cover the American system of higher education, undergraduate education, professional schools, new developments, and prospects for change. The author avoids the broader issues of educational policy reforms and takes the classroom teacher, students, and learning and testing as his context for change. He believes that colleges and universities should discover again their reason for being—to educate students—by giving greater attention to improving the effectiveness of teaching and learning. The need to keep education uppermost in the minds of those who govern in higher education is a refreshing theme from one who can influence policy in ways that stars from lesser galaxies cannot.

389 Bowen, Howard R. *The State of the Nation and the Agenda for Higher Education.* San Francisco: Jossey-Bass, 1982. 212 pages.

Central to the theme of this book is the shift away from the traditions of liberal education toward vocational training and its consequent effect on higher education. The author argues that narrow educational goals can lead to training students who are not prepared to meet the challenges of a changing society. His agenda for reform is derived from a detailed exploration of tabular data about economic and social progress in the United States from 1950 to 1980, and from information about educational attainments of the American people. The author concludes that, in addition to business as usual, American higher education must: "(1) push on toward the long-range goal of *a nation of educated people,* (2) increase the emphasis on *values* as part of the outcomes of higher education, (3) confront the special and acute problems of youth in our society, and (4) contribute toward the most compelling goal of all, *international reconciliation."* The writing is clear, scholarly, and based on sound data about higher education in the United States today.

★**390** Boyer, Ernest L. *College: The Undergraduate Experience in America.* New York: Harper & Row, 1987. 328 pages.

Please see entry no. 258 for the annotation of this work.

★**391** Boyer, Ernest L., and Levine, Arthur. *A Quest for Common Learning: The Aims of General Education.* Princeton, N.J.: The Carnegie Foundation for the Advancement of Teaching, 1981. 68 pages.

The aims of general education are discussed in the context of reviving interest in common learning for higher education. The authors address the topic by describing weaknesses of the curriculum for general education as it is now conceived and providing a review of its historical and social contexts. A rationale for common learning is presented, and an evaluation of current practices is offered. Finally, the authors propose a form for general education that meets contemporary demands. The essay is thought provoking and provides a useful context for considering general education in the last decades of this century.

392 Carnegie Council on Policy Studies in Higher Education. *Three Thousand Futures: The Next Twenty Years for Higher Education.* San Francisco: Jossey-Bass, 1980. 439 pages.

Carnegie Council publications are designed to offer administrative and faculty leaders information that institutions need to make decisions in an era of rapid change. This report is divided into two parts. The first part presents a general analysis of problems such as enrollment declines, shifting patterns of funding, and changes in the labor market for college graduates. Part Two contains resource documents and supporting data providing a factual basis for the conclusions and recommendations of the council. The discussion of choices to be made focuses on such issues as the quality of education and the integrity of higher education itself.

393 The Carnegie Foundation for the Advancement of Teaching. *Missions of the College Curriculum: A Contemporary Review with Suggestions.* San Francisco: Jossey-Bass, 1977. 322 pages.

These commentaries on selected aspects of the college curriculum focus on the undergraduate experience. The essays seek to inform the college community about curriculum problems and possibilities by providing information on the existing curriculum situation, presenting views of the major contemporary issues, and discussing some effective methods for initiating curriculum change. Chapters cover such topics as diversity, external and internal forces influencing the curriculum, components of the curriculum, and institutional differences. Undergraduate education is emphasized in chapters on mission, general education, the undergraduate major, electives, the place of basic skills, and the relationship of the curriculum to the world of work. Additional chapters cover values and the curriculum and the implementation of curricular policy. Four appendixes contain practical suggestions for those involved in implementing curricular changes. The book is a source of useful information about the many-splendored thing we call the contemporary college curriculum.

394 The Carnegie Foundation for the Advancement of Teaching. *Common Learning: A Carnegie Colloquium on General Education.* Washington, D.C.: The Carnegie Foundation for the Advancement of Teaching, 1981. 146 pages.

These chapters are derived from addresses given at a national colloquium on common learning held at the University of Chicago in April 1981. Approximately 200 participants pursued their interest in general education, which has once again become a priority for higher education. Chapters cover such topics as the quest for common learning, presented by Ernest Boyer; rhetoric and the search for common learning, by Wayne Booth; heritage and traditions, by Frederick Rudolph; contemporary organizations, by Rosabeth Moss Kanter; the natural world, by Lewis Thomas; the high school–college connection, by Fred Hechinger; and prospects for the future as viewed by Arthur Levine. The authors raise more questions than they answer; nevertheless, the collection is valuable as a representation of the critical issues facing colleges and universities as each tries to define general education in a way that represents a best fit for the local culture.

★395 Chickering, Arthur W., and Associates. *The Modern American College: Responding to the New Realities of Diverse Students and a Changing Society.* San Francisco: Jossey-Bass, 1981. 810 pages.

Please see entry no. 263 for the annotation of this work.

396 College Board. *Academic Preparation for College: What Students Need to Know and Be Able to Do.* New York: College Board, 1983. 46 pages.

A ten-year project of the College Board set out to identify what college entrants should know and be able to do. This report summarizes results from deliberations by several advisory committees and from dialogues held with educators throughout the country. Specific learning outcomes (such as the ability to write as a way of discovering and clarifying ideas; the ability to use the Pythagorean theorem and special right triangle relationships) are stated under three categories: six basic competencies (reading, writing, speaking and listening, mathematics, reasoning, studying); computer competency; and six basic academic subjects (English, the arts, mathematics, science, social studies, foreign language). The report's implications are obvious for precollege curriculum as well as for admissions and remedial work in higher education.

397 The Committee on General Education in a Free Society. *General Education in a Free Society.* Cambridge, Mass.: Harvard University Press, 1945. 267 pages.

In his introduction, James Bryant Conant, then president of Harvard University, acknowledges that the twelve scholars responsible for the report explored the status of the American educational system as it existed immediately after World War II as much as they provided a basis for the faculty debate about general education at Harvard at that time. The book begins with a concise overview of education in the United States, followed by a chapter on the rationale for general learning and another chapter on the problems of diversity. The committee points out that "general education must accordingly be conceived less as a specific set of books to be read or courses to be given, than as a concern for certain goals of knowledge and outlook and an insistence that these goals be sought after by many means as intently as are those of specialism." Other chapters place general education in the context of the secondary school, discuss general education in the special context of Harvard University, and then propose an approach that flows from the more generic considerations discussed in the early chapters. The final chapter tackles the issue of general education in the community and the special needs of adults as learners. This report is much more than a prescriptive solution to the problem of general education for colleges and universities in the post–World War II United States. The committee attempted to present a reasoned and persuasive rationale for general education, flexible enough to accommodate the diversity evident in today's institutions. People interested in the recent history of general education in our educational institutions should place this report close to the top of their reading list.

★**398** Conrad, Clifton F. (ed.). *ASHE Reader on Academic Programs in Colleges and Universities.* Lexington, Mass.: Ginn Press, 1985. 387 pages.

The Association for the Study of Higher Education sponsored this volume in order to "illuminate issues related to the purpose, meaning, and content of higher learning and to help faculty, administrators, and their institutions engage in continuous reexamination and renewal." This is accomplished with this collection of twenty-one previously published articles. Part One is devoted to historical and philosophical perspectives and contains excerpts from the works of Frederick Rudolph, Douglas Sloan, Laurence Veysey, John Dewey, and Robert Maynard Hutchins, together with a portion of *The Yale Report* of 1828. Part Two of the volume contains examples of the thinking of Robert E. Roemer, Arthur Levine, Jerry G. Gaff, Betty Schmitz, Anne S. Williams, John Nichols and Zelda F. Gamson, Gerald Grant, and David Riesman. An excerpt of a report from The Carnegie Foundation for the Advancement of Teaching is also included in this section. These selections all relate to contemporary viewpoints about current practices and agendas. Part Three deals with developing and implementing academic programs and includes writings of Clifton F. Conrad, Anne M. Pratt, Philip H. Phenix, Daniel Bell, Arthur W. Chickering and his associates, Jack Lindquist, Don E. Gardner, and Richard F. Wilson. A comprehensive bibliography is included. While these selections by no means represent the full breadth of commentary available on these topics, they provide a useful and insightful introduction to academic programs.

399 Conrad, Clifton F., and Wyer, Jean C. *Liberal Education in Transition*. AAHE-ERIC Higher Education Research Report no. 3. Washington, D.C.: American Association for Higher Education, 1980. 66 pages. (ED 188 539)

Liberal education seems to defy definition in the context of the American college and university. The ambiguity surrounding the concept is exacerbated by the many forms that the liberal arts take in the variety of institutions comprising higher education in the United States. The authors of this interesting monograph state that "our conception of the liberal tradition encompasses the ultimate questions of society and the individual as well as the acquisition of 'skills' and 'knowledge.' " This report presents an overview of the traditions of liberal education and a reexamination of the liberal arts in light of what the authors refer to as "the legacy of the 1970s." They believe that a new meaning must be given to the liberal education curriculum in its entirety rather than piecemeal as seems to be the current fad. Models of liberal education are discussed along with the authors' conception of the "unifying ideals" that provide a foundation for liberal studies. The debate about substance and function of liberal education finds much that is relevant in the provocative perspective of these authors.

400 Culley, Margo, and Portuges, Catherine (eds.). *Gendered Subjects: The Dynamics of Feminist Teaching*. Boston: Routledge & Kegan Paul, 1985. 284 pages.

The authors of these twenty-three chapters want to move beyond mere description to "theory about the dynamics of the feminist classroom." As teachers, they challenge gender-based economic, sociopolitical, cultural, and psychological imperatives and seek to reduce the "schisms between the public and the private, between reason and the emotions." Several essays address definitional issues with regard to gender and feminist teaching. Some deal with particular disciplines (history, law, theater); others concern issues of authority, communicating across differences, and interpersonal relations inside and outside the classroom. While this presentation is not the cogent theory that these authors know is needed, the papers stand as an important progress report on the feminist teaching movement in higher education during the 1970s and 1980s.

401 Dressel, Paul L. *College and University Curriculum.* Berkeley, Calif.: McCutchan, 1971. 325 pages.

The author presents an instructive and articulate view of curriculum in higher education without arguing for the dominance of one best way to organize content. The approach is more that of a textbook than a critique. Chapters cover basic considerations in curriculum development, the structure of knowledge, development and trends in liberal education, the disciplines, professional education, graduate education, instruction, evaluation, curriculum review and control, the student and the curriculum, curriculum models, competencies, and suggestions for improving the undergraduate curriculum. Students of higher education who seek a comprehensive overview of the curriculum in higher education will find it in this book, at least for the period prior to 1971.

402 Eliot, Charles William. *A Turning Point in Higher Education.* Cambridge, Mass.: Harvard University Press, 1969. 30 pages.

This slim volume is the inaugural address of Charles William Eliot as president of Harvard College on October 19, 1869. Nathan Pusey, in an introduction, suggests that "viewed retrospectively . . . his address was a momentous event in the history of American higher education. Majestic in tone and style, striking in metaphor, abounding in new insights, it gave focus to the aspirations and preachments of a small group of restless and impatient college leaders in the post-bellum United States and heralded the beginning of a fresh approach to university studies." The reforms introduced by Eliot at Harvard established a pattern for undergraduate studies that prevails to this day. His ideas played no small part in the creation of universities and colleges devoted primarily to study of the classics. Whether or not one agrees with the philosophy expressed in this address, the influence of Eliot on the direction of higher education in the United States was both seminal and long-lived. He was president of Harvard for forty years, and by the time of his retirement, the university system in the United States had departed from many of the reforms he proposed. Nevertheless, the reader will be hard-pressed to find another university president, with the exceptions of Robert Hutchins and Clark Kerr, whose influence has been as pervasive.

403 Fincher, Cameron. "Trends and Issues in Curricular Development." In John C. Smart (ed.), *Higher Education: Handbook of Theory and Research*. Vol. 2. New York: Agathon Press, 1986, pp. 275–308.

This chapter comprehensively discusses major issues and trends in the study of college curricula. Their relevance to curricular reform is also presented. The author begins with a brief resume of recent reports on undergraduate education in colleges and universities in the United States. The history of curricular development in higher education is summarized, and major issues in curricular reform are discussed. The implications of liberal learning, general education, adult development, and competency-based education are presented in the context of their relevance to curriculum. The author concludes by observing that the concern for innovation and reform in the curriculum of higher education has produced changes that have been gradual, cumulative, and provisional. This article includes a comprehensive bibliography of over eighty items, and citations are used extensively to support the author's assertions.

404 Flexner, Abraham. "The Problem of College Pedagogy." *Atlantic Monthly*, 1909, *103*, 838–844.

The problem of college pedagogy arises in the shift from having students master "an accepted and practically constant subject matter" to a situation where the student is told, in effect, "the iridescent fabric has been unraveled; here are the single threads." The curriculum must somehow take these threads that used to be in organic combination and recombine them with each other and with new knowledge according to proper "intellectual chemistry." This effort exposes "the fundamental antagonism between education and research; for education concerns inevitably organic social components and strives constantly to apprehend relations, significance, function—whereas research abstracts from function, isolates, reduces, analyzes." Flexner does not offer solutions to these problems. By elaborating his concern about whether a teacher can do both education and research, he formulates a dilemma that is still with us.

405 French, Sidney J. (ed.). *Accent on Teaching, Experiments in General Education.* New York: Harper & Row, 1954. 334 pages.

A product of the Committee on General Education of the Association for Higher Education, this book contains chapters that deal with designing curriculum and courses relevant to general education. While the title suggests that teaching is its central focus, chapter authors are more concerned with a structure for education than with a process. Representative chapters include an essay by the editor on the place of general education in the liberal arts, comments by B. S. Bloom about the thought process of students in discussion, and a thoughtful statement by Joseph Axelrod on developing a course in life values. Paul Dressel and Lewis Mayhew address evaluation as an aid to instruction. Chapters are divided into sections on the humanities, the natural sciences, and the social sciences. The reader will find that many of the concerns and views expressed by these authors over thirty years ago are still relevant to today's debate about general education.

406 Handlin, Oscar, and Handlin, Mary F. *The American College and American Culture: Socialization as a Function of Higher Education.* New York: McGraw-Hill, 1970. 104 pages.

This brief essay is one of only a few to address the socialization function of higher education. While college students may organize their time around the demands of a formal educational curriculum, they also participate in a less structured curriculum of socialization. The authors state that "the education administered by the college . . . [is] connected with the desire to adjust the individual to the society within which he [plays] a part." The five chapters cover a statement of the problem, the role of colonial seminaries, the effects of the revolution and the emerging republican culture, the college as a custodian of culture, and the influence of a discipline of scholarship. The authors show how the socialization function varies from one institutional context to another and how it changes as the needs and values of society change. The book clearly articulates what we now take for granted—that American higher education accomplishes much more than the education and training represented by courses in the catalogue.

407 Heiss, Ann M. *Challenges to Graduate Schools*. San Francisco: Jossey-Bass, 1970. 328 pages.

From interviews with graduate deans, academic deans, department chairs, members of graduate faculties, and doctoral students, the author found that reform was needed in graduate study. This book is a presentation of the issues and problems related to that need. Information was gathered from the Ph.D. programs in ten universities. Among the wide range of issues and problems discussed are administration of graduate education, student admission and orientation to graduate study, requirements for the Ph.D. degree, characteristics of faculty and students, student assessment of Ph.D. programs, preparation for research and college teaching, and changes in graduate education. The author's comments and recommendations are as relevant today as when they were written. This book is essential reading for anyone interested in graduate education, especially doctoral study.

408 Hirsch, E. D., Jr. *Cultural Literacy: What Every American Needs to Know*. Boston: Houghton Mifflin, 1987. 251 pages.

In a book that became a best-seller soon after publication and that its publisher calls a "manifesto," the author argues that "only by accumulating shared symbols, and the shared information the symbols represent, can we learn how to communicate effectively with one another in our national community." Research is cited showing that all cognitive skills are knowledge-bound; thus, particularly in reading, content should be emphasized as much as skills. To correct for effects of the romantic formalism that has dominated schools of education for the past fifty years, this volume centers on content and illustrates what the content of cultural literacy might be. About seventy pages are devoted to a "preliminary list of what literate Americans know" (for 90 percent of the items there was agreement by "more than one hundred consultants"). The list foreshadows a planned "dictionary," which will explain each item. Although little of the book deals explicitly with postsecondary education, extrapolation to colleges and universities is inevitable in continuing discussions about core curricula in higher education.

409 Hutchins, Robert Maynard. *The Higher Learning in America*. New Haven, Conn.: Yale University Press, 1962. 119 pages.

The image of the University of Chicago as the maverick among American universities was reinforced by reforms introduced there by Hutchins, the author of these Storrs Lectures delivered at Yale University. His tenure as president of the University of Chicago was marked by conflicts with the faculty over his educational philosophy, and much that he stood for in higher education is no longer identifiable as the "Hutchins model." He provided a "breath of fresh air" as his ideas about university education were debated in this country. His conception of higher education is similar to Cardinal Newman's. He attacks the utilitarian nature of higher learning and states that the mission of the university is "the pursuit of truth for its own sake." The great books as a curriculum for undergraduate education emerged from Hutchins's advocacy of a course of study that would abolish electives and provide a general education for all who matriculated. The ideas brought forth in *The Higher Learning in America* will probably be remembered more for their association with the authentic and forceful personality of the man who advocated them than they will be as the cornerstone of an enduring movement in higher education. The book remains, nevertheless, a significant statement about student learning and curriculum, as well as the role of faculty, in higher education.

410 Kaysen, Carl (ed.). *Content and Context: Essays on College Education.* New York: McGraw-Hill, 1973. 565 pages.

This report from the Carnegie Commission on Higher Education contains chapters by recognized scholars in higher education. The articles by James S. Ackerman, Norman Birnbaum, James S. Coleman, Paul Doty, David Hawkins, Everett C. Hughes, Anthony G. Oettinger, Roger Shattuck, Neil J. Smelser, Laurence Veysey, Nikki Zapol, and Dorothy Zinberg cover issues in undergraduate education, the humanities, the social sciences, the sciences, the arts, and the professions. Attention is also given to information technologies, society's demands and the university, students and professors, and liberal education. While some of the essays are valuable now only for their historical perspectives, others contain information quite relevant to contemporary problems. Browsing through this book can satisfy eclectic interests in higher education.

★411 Kerr, Clark. *The Uses of the University.* Cambridge, Mass.: Harvard University Press, 1963. 140 pages.

The author was president of the University of California at the time he delivered these lectures. These remarks, presented as the Godkin Lectures at Harvard University, point the way to the present-day complexities that confront American universities. Chapter One introduces the idea of the multiversity and points out that "the university [today] is so many things to so many different people that it must, of necessity, be partially at war with itself." The author traces the history of the idea of, and comments on the life in, the multiversity. "The Realities of the Federal Grant University" deals with the federal government's influence on the university, beginning with the Morrill Act of 1862 and the land-grant movement, and points out that the major issue is not one of federal control but one of federal influence. The final chapter discusses the future of universities in the United States. The critique of changes that are taking place in this institution is given in the context of the university as an essential element in American society. *The Uses of the University* charted the future of American universities for the remainder of this century. These lectures are essential reading for anyone interested in the tensions between the educational function of universities and their many other uses.

★**412** Levine, Arthur. *Handbook on Undergraduate Curriculum.* San Francisco: Jossey-Bass, 1978. 662 pages.

Handbooks are generally written to be consulted rather than read through from cover to cover, but this contribution from the Carnegie Council on Policy Studies in Higher Education is a valuable and readable resource for anyone seeking to learn about the structure of higher education in the United States. Part One deals with the undergraduate curriculum at the time of publication. Part Two is a comparative and historical perspective on the undergraduate curriculum. The glossary contains a documented history of twelve salient events in the history of the undergraduate curriculum and a list of the institutions whose catalogues were part of the study reported in the book. This handbook deserves to be consulted by any serious student of higher education curriculum.

413 Martin, Warren Bryan. *A College of Character: Renewing the Purpose and Content of College Education.* San Francisco: Jossey-Bass, 1982. 215 pages.

The author discusses the current status and future prospects of the liberal arts college and of its university counterpart, the college of arts and sciences. A publication of the American Council on Education, the book presents a cogent argument for beginning higher education reform in the four-year liberal arts college. The attempts by liberal arts colleges to pattern themselves after research universities denies the unique function of the liberal arts college in higher education. The author challenges the leadership of these colleges to reject the image of "colleges of convenience" and seek once again their traditional roles of "colleges of character." Martin presents his interpretation of the distinct features of a college of character and discusses the basic purposes and goals he feels such colleges should pursue.

414 Mattfeld, Jacquelyn Anderson. "Toward a New Synthesis in Curricular Patterns of Undergraduate Education." *Liberal Education,* 1975, *61,* 531-549.

The author states, "In this essay, I want to examine contemporary models of undergraduate education and ask whether the many social, political, and intellectual directions of this latter part of the twentieth century demand corresponding curricular responses or whether the greater imperative now is to prepare ourselves for a very different kind of synthesis, a new manner in which the human mind organizes its experience of the world and, as a consequence, one which will require fresh and imaginative approaches." In her attempt to answer this question, the author has written an article that enlightens, educates, and supports restructuring of the curriculum toward feeling and expression, or the esthetic and intuitive, as well as toward the rational. The essay's breadth provides a useful frame of reference for defining liberal education.

415 Mayhew, Lewis B. *Changing Practices in Education for the Professions.* Atlanta: Southern Regional Education Board, 1971. 82 pages.

Preparation for professional fields has become a central issue for those troubled by the intrusion of vocationalism into the groves of academe. After World War II, professional programs expanded far beyond the traditional specializations of medicine, law, and theology. This monograph, according to the author, is "intended to stimulate further thought about the nature of professional education, curriculum reform, and closer cooperation between the various professional schools. It is also intended to be of help to professional faculties considering the range of possibilities for reform." After a discussion of the professions and their educational needs, the author addresses problems of unresolved issues and attempted reforms. The monograph concludes with a presentation of models, guidelines, and criteria to be considered in reforming of professional studies.

416 Mayhew, Lewis B., and Ford, Patrick J. *Reform in Graduate and Professional Education.* San Francisco: Jossey-Bass, 1974. 254 pages.

This book summarizes an investigation into changes in graduate and professional education. Chapters cover such topics as attempted reforms, graduate curriculum and instruction, structure and organization of graduate and professional education, and preparing teachers. The authors found that graduate and professional programs are emphasizing more field experiences at earlier program stages. Greater use of the behavioral sciences is evident. Changes in admissions policies, the availability of more interdisciplinary degrees, improved teacher preparation, and less departmentalism are trends that suggest new models for the future. For those responsible for graduate and professional programs, this book is a useful resource for planning and initiating curricular, teaching, and other reforms.

417 Mayville, William V. *Federal Influence on Higher Education Curricula.* AAHE-ERIC Higher Education Research Report no. 1. Washington, D.C.: American Association for Higher Education, 1980. 55 pages. (ED 187 221)

Greater fear of federal influence on curricula for higher education accompanies the increasing role of the federal government in supporting research, student loans, and facilities. This monograph examines federal influence on curricular development. In the first section, the author discusses direct and indirect curricular influence. Section Two is devoted to the institutional contexts for curricular change. The final section analyzes the impact of federal funding on curricular direction. The author concludes that the direction of federal spending "has supported the vocational/practical end of education . . . by the formation and encouragement of new types of institutions, and by legislation that has supplemented vocational/technical programs at these institutions." This evidence supports the thesis that the federal government has a pervasive influence on defining the nature of higher education in the United States.

418 Newman, John Henry. *The Idea of a University*. London: Oxford University Press, 1976. 684 pages.

Cardinal Newman's vision of an ideal university evolved from his experience as a student, fellow, and tutor at Oxford, and as rector of Dublin's Catholic University. This volume consists of lectures delivered to the Catholics of Dublin and first published as *Discourse on University Education* in 1853, and a second volume of lectures published in 1858 under the title of *Lectures and Essays on University Subjects*. This collection has become a classic theory of university education and a standard for what higher education ought to be. Newman rejects the notion of a university as an institution dominated by research and service efforts. He proposes an educational institution that becomes an academic community of teachers and students dedicated to the "teaching of universal knowledge." This academic cloister follows the historic pattern set by Oxford. Liberal knowledge, not practical knowledge, becomes the justification for learning. These ideas stand as a beacon clouded by the present-day concern for professional studies and vocationalism in colleges and universities. Students of higher education need to read *The Idea of a University*, if only to be reminded of the ideal motivating those who see liberal education, and the liberal arts curriculum, as an expression of Newman's philosophy.

419 Nyre, Glen F., and Reilly, Kathryn C. *Professional Education in the Eighties*. AAHE-ERIC Higher Education Research Report no. 8. Washington, D.C.: American Association for Higher Education, 1979. 51 pages. (ED 179 187)

The authors review the history of professional education in the United States and discuss the changes taking place in the professional school experience. Topics covered include admissions, curriculum development, faculty, accreditation, and the rating game. The authors point out that expansionism in the development of professional schools is a thing of the past, and the future will likely be limited to evolution of already existing practices. Their recommendations cover the integration of theory and practice, cooperation and competition in professional education, and professional development for professional faculty.

420 Parsons, Talcott, and Platt, Gerald M. *The American University.* Cambridge, Mass.: Harvard University Press, 1973. 463 pages.

In their preface the authors point out that *The American University* is both an empirical and a theoretical work. The empirical aspects of the book include factual information about the American university and its place in the larger system of higher education as well as in the broader systems of society. The theoretical aspects of the book relate to the authors' analysis of the university as a social system. After a general introduction, they discuss the "cognitive complex" that provides a basic rationale for higher education. Subsequent sections of the book deal with graduate training and research, general education and student socialization, professional schools, the faculty, the nature of crisis in university systems, and trends in continuity and change. A closing chapter by Neil J. Smelser discusses some social and structural dimensions of higher education. Readers will not find the book an easy one; it is not light reading. The analysis is basically sociological. Contents provide a sound frame of reference for understanding scholarship, teaching, and curricular functions of the American university within the context of a larger social system.

421 Reed, Glenn A. "Fifty Years of Conflict in the Graduate School." *The Educational Record,* 1952, *33,* 5-23.

The value of this article can be found in its brief review of criticisms of graduate education during this century. The author points out that "graduate school problems have a history and a relatedness which deserve careful examination." Among the issues discussed are the proliferation of graduate degrees, specialized versus generalized training, and the improvement of college teaching. The author cites critics who "insist that until teaching is raised to a position equal in importance, in prestige, and in rewards to research, no amount of manipulation of titles or courses or requisites will make much difference." The conflict in graduate education between research and teaching remains as strong today as when this article was written.

422 Rieff, Philip. *Fellow Teachers.* New York: Dell Publishing, 1972. 243 pages.

The role of the scholar/teacher in a university setting provides the theme of this book. The author cites a number of failings that he feels undermine the traditions of the university. In particular, he singles out the permissiveness of the culture that he contends has turned the university into a sanctuary for activities and attitudes responsible for hastening the decline of scholarship and teaching as the major task of higher education. The book has been described by reviewers as an "imposing jeremiad against permissiveness." The author, a sociologist, writes in the style of a social critic with a crusade to defend limits and standards as the essential elements missing from the contemporary university. Within the cultural frame of reference that prevailed in 1972 when the book was first published, the author's prose is convincing and attention getting.

★**423** Riesman, David. *On Higher Education: The Academic Enterprise in an Era of Rising Student Consumerism.* San Francisco: Jossey-Bass, 1981. 421 pages.

In his forward to this volume, Clark Kerr states that *On Higher Education* is "the best single commentary by far on higher education in America at this important transition in its history." This book is anchored in *The Academic Revolution*, authored by Christopher Jencks and David Riesman in 1968. That volume discussed the rise of faculty domination in colleges and universities, which reached its peak during the 1950s and 1960s. *On Higher Education* deals with the decline of faculty influence and charts the rise of a new student consumerism in higher education, which shifts values away from academic merit as a guiding principle for education programs. After discussing the era of faculty dominance and its decline, the author analyzes the rise of consumerism among students, places this movement in the context of several institutional types, and considers different aspects of student consumerism. This book should be read by anyone claiming to be informed about the issues and problems of higher education today. Both scholars and laypersons will find the contents useful and provocative.

★**424** Rudolph, Frederick. *Curriculum: A History of the American Undergraduate Course of Study Since 1636.* San Francisco: Jossey-Bass, 1977. 362 pages.

Prepared for the Carnegie Council on Policy Studies in Higher Education, this book presents a lucid and critical history of the curriculum in American colleges and universities, beginning with the founding of Harvard University. No student of the curriculum of higher education can understand the diversity of issues associated with the elective system, general versus specialized education, subject-based and competency-based programs, elite versus egalitarian education, and mass versus individualized instruction—to name only a few—without knowing their historical contexts. With a scholar's skills and a penchant for clarity, the author captures the essential course of curriculum development in higher education in a way that makes his book essential reading for anyone seriously interested in how higher learning came to be organized the way it is. A comprehensive bibliography is included for each chapter.

★**425** Sanford, Nevitt (ed.). *The American College: A Psychological and Social Interpretation of the Higher Learning.* New York: Wiley, 1962. 1,084 pages.

Please see entry no. 310 for the annotation of this work.

426 Schein, Edgar H. *Professional Education.* New York: McGraw-Hill, 1972. 163 pages.

This report is part of a series of profiles sponsored by the Carnegie Commission on Higher Education. The commission's concern with professional education stems from changes evident in higher education since the end of World War II, particularly professional education laying claim to an increasing proportion of resources devoted to postsecondary education in the United States. Part One of this instructive volume presents the scope of the study and discusses the need for professional programs in higher education. Part Two presents the author's prescription for the perceived ills brought about when professional studies are grafted onto the traditional body of higher education. Among the proposed reforms, flexibility and curriculum revision are emphasized. Anyone interested in professional education should consult this report.

427 Schwab, Joseph J. *College Curriculum and Student Protest.* Chicago: University of Chicago Press, 1969. 303 pages.

The author analyzes the student protest movement of the 1960s as symptomatic of a disease called the contemporary college curriculum. Using a medical model, he presents a diagnosis in the first part of the book and proceeds from there to offer a set of prescriptions addressed to the curriculum. The author argues for a wide-ranging set of learning experiences that would include, as part of the curriculum, many activities we generally think of as extracurricular. The approach goes counter to the "supermarket" theory of universities that seems to be dominant today. The argument is both precise and logical without being outside the realm of possibility. This book should be read as a refreshing departure from the usual debate about liberal arts, general education, and professional studies.

428 Smith, Richard Norton. *The Harvard Century: The Making of a University to a Nation.* New York: Simon & Schuster, 1986. 397 pages.

For many, the history of Harvard University represents the history of higher education in the United States. The publication date of this book marks the 350th anniversary of Harvard College, although the book was not written to commemorate that fact. The author has successfully captured the national presence of Harvard by concentrating on five of the most recent presidents of the university who have guided, and continue to guide, its progress: Eliot, Lowell, Conant, Pusey, and Bok. The curriculum and teaching innovations that first developed under the stewardship of these academic leaders have influenced the directions of educational progress in institutions nationwide. The elective system, academic majors, and general education all have their seeds in activities of the presidents of Harvard and their faculties. The author presents a readable and reliable delineation of Harvard's role in promoting educational reforms that helped to form higher education in the United States.

429 Snyder, Benson R. *The Hidden Curriculum.* New York: Knopf, 1971. 203 pages.

Drawing on his own psychiatric practice and on cases from a research project at Massachusetts Institute of Technology, the author delineates two curricula. One comprises what is formally stated as required; the other is hidden, comprised of the actual expectations of professors and students and institutions. To reduce the dissidence between these curricula, students develop adaptive mechanisms that are more or less successful. One result of the hidden curriculum is an ecological trap in which real success is actually counterproductive; "in the very process of achieving a set of interrelated educational objectives, a number of students appeared to develop both cognitive and adaptive styles which then become so fixed [that] their ability to cope with new tasks or with altered circumstances may be severely limited." Although the book offers little in the way of suggestions for reform, it can stimulate discussions from which reform proposals might emerge.

★**430** Stark, Joan S., and Lowther, Malcolm A. *Designing the Learning Plan: A Review of Research and Theory Related to College Curricula.* Ann Arbor: National Center for Research to Improve Postsecondary Teaching and Learning, University of Michigan, 1987. 88 pages.

The authors review research on higher education and precollege curricula and suggest a model for further research. The monograph emphasizes a perspective for curriculum development broader than that of the individual disciplines. While recent national reports call attention to the need for curricular changes, little research addresses the problem of how these changes might affect teaching and learning or what must be taught to produce educated graduates. The authors present a reasoned argument for including variables that relate to student development in the matrix of concerns that influence research on the college curriculum. This monograph represents a significant attempt to view curriculum research from the multivariate perspective the topic demands. Anyone interested in relationships between teaching, learning, and the curriculum should read what these authors have to say. An up-to-date bibliography contains over 285 items.

431 Stark, Joan S.; Lowther, Malcolm A.; and Hagerty, Bonnie M. K. *Responsive Professional Education: Balancing the Outcomes and Opportunities.* ASHE-ERIC Higher Education Report no. 3. Washington, D.C.: Association for the Study of Higher Education, 1986. 127 pages. (ED 273 229)

Student enrollments in professional programs of higher education have increased to the point that undergraduate professional majors outnumber liberal arts majors. The authors of this monograph discuss intended outcomes in the various fields of professional study. Available literature on professional education provided the data for identifying competencies and attitudes that are the anticipated outcomes of professional study. An overview of professional preparation serves as a prelude to the discussion of competence and attitudes. A concluding chapter presents common themes in professional study together with implications for faculty, administrators, and researchers. A comprehensive and contemporary list of references is included.

432 Taylor, Harold. *Students Without Teachers: The Crisis in the University.* New York: McGraw-Hill, 1969. 333 pages.

This book addresses the student revolution of the 1960s and the legitimacy of the student movement in pressing for changes in how colleges and universities relate to students. Because students are major agents of social change, they should be taken seriously as indicators of needed reforms in colleges and universities. The intellectual origins of this book reflect a strong commitment to progressivism as an educational philosophy. Part One includes chapters about the university and its students and provides a rationale for student unrest. Part Two discusses mass culture and the academic mind. Part Three is a reconsideration of general education in relation to academic and curricular reform. The final section, Part Four, contains specific programs of reform advanced by the author and presented with persuasive logic. This book would be effective beginning reading for those wondering about the importance of student unrest in higher education.

433 Trites, Donald (ed.). *Planning the Future of the Undergraduate College.* New Directions for Higher Education, no. 9. San Francisco: Jossey-Bass, 1975. 105 pages.

During the decade in which this book appeared, projections about declining enrollments and increasing vocationalism among students resulted in concerns about faculty retirement and in demands for more career-oriented educational programs. Changes in the college-age population and in the world of work clearly influence the future of undergraduate programs. Chapters dealing with these topics and with feminine socialization, social change, the scholarly enterprise, regionalism, and the future are, for the most part, still relevant to the problems facing undergraduate colleges.

434 Wegener, Charles. *Liberal Education and the Modern University.* Chicago: University of Chicago Press, 1978. 163 pages.

In his preface, the author states that this book is "an attempt to rediscover and redefine a persistent problem in the interest of encouraging attempts at its solution." The problem is that of reconciling liberal education with the multipurposed institution called the modern American university. The author does more to articulate the problem than he does to present solutions, in the process exposing the reader to a wide range of challenging ideas about higher education. The book is not easy to read, largely because the style is discursive, and the absence of an articulated polemic makes the narrative hard to follow at times. It is worth the effort, however, because the book puts liberal education into an appropriate philosophical perspective. The first two chapters survey the history of institutional and intellectual contexts for solving the problems of liberal education, frequently citing the University of Chicago for illustration. Chapter Three, "Liberal

Education: A Search for a Problem," expands on the ideas presented earlier focusing on the institutional revolution in higher education that grew out of a more basic intellectual reconstruction and orientation. Chapter Four discusses the liberal curriculum and the problem of institutionalizing those intellectual circumstances that define liberal learning. Chapter Five, "Institutionalizing," confronts the major issues of institutional discontinuity and liberal education. Anyone seriously interested in inquiry about a philosophy of liberal education is advised to consult this book.

435 Wolff, Robert Paul. *The Ideal of the University.* Boston: Beacon Press, 1969. 161 pages.

This book provides a rigorous analysis of the uses and misuses of the university that prevailed at the end of the 1960s. In Part One the author discusses four models of the university: emphasizing scholarship, training for the professions, social service, and the reinforcement of Establishment Man. Part Two provides the author's thoughts about such educational controversies as grading, admissions, the quest for neutrality in values, relevance, and efficiency. Part Three addresses governance issues within the university, and the book's conclusion discusses practical proposals for utopian reform. Much of the content remains relevant to contemporary problems even though the context stimulating the author's polemic has changed. The quality of the writing and the excellence of the argument make for interesting reading.

Innovative Curricula

436 Association of American Medical Colleges. "Physicians for the Twenty-First Century." *Journal of Medical Education,* 1984, *59* (11, part 2), 1-208.

This ambitious project attempted to specify the general professional education appropriate for all physicians. Its conclusions ranged across five areas and included recommendations for each. These areas, with illustrative recommendations, are as follows: (1) purposes of a general professional education (reduce emphasis on memorization of information, describe more clearly what is required to enter graduate medical education, increase emphasis on promotion of health); (2) baccalaureate education (include natural and social sciences and the humanities, simplify admission requirements but include skills of writing and of inquiry); (3) learning skills (emphasize independent learning skills, reduce lecture hours and other scheduled time); (4) clinical education (specify outcomes of clinical education and integrate them with work in basic sciences, supervise and evaluate students more carefully); and (5) enhancing faculty involvement (involve faculty in cooperative planning, use faculty as mentors with students, assist faculty to develop new skills). Reports of work groups and lists of those who participated in the project are appended.

437 Bergquist, William H., and Armstrong, Jack R. *Planning Effectively for Educational Quality: An Outcomes-Based Approach for Colleges Committed to Excellence.* San Francisco: Jossey-Bass, 1986. 218 pages.

This book was sponsored by the Council of Independent Colleges (CIC) and grew from the Project on Quality Undergraduate Education (Project QUE). Funded by the W. K. Kellogg Foundation, Project QUE supported the design and implementation at each of sixty CIC colleges of a single academic program, such as a new degree, a core curriculum, an orientation program, and so on. The authors report on "planning and leadership strategies that can be used to help all institutions—public or independent, large or small—build strong, distinctive campus programs." Part One presents standards and strategies for ensuring program quality. Part Two describes a systematic model for academic planning, and Part Three discusses reviewing the success of the planning model. The appendix includes expanded case studies from Project QUE. The authors provide a practical and insightful approach to quality assurance by emphasizing planning and the selective enhancement of individual programs rather than more global strategies that are often difficult to manage.

438 Gaff, Jerry G. *General Education Today: A Critical Analysis of Controversies, Practices, and Reforms.* San Francisco: Jossey-Bass, 1983. 248 pages.

The Project for General Education Models, sponsored by the Society for Values in Higher Education from 1978 to 1981, was a three-year collaboration of twelve different colleges and universities attempting to strengthen their general educational programs. The author directed this project, and this book resulted from his experiences. While the book reports on the outcomes of the project, the author presents an informed overview of the issues and problems in defining general education and implementing general education programs for undergraduates. The history of general education is traced, and a description is advanced that includes elements the author feels would be favored by those who have differing points of view about the nature of general education. The debate about general education is once again becoming a major agenda item for the reform movement in higher education. Gaff's book is essential reading for anyone wishing to participate in this debate as an informed and constructive critic of the undergraduate curriculum in colleges and universities.

439 Gamson, Zelda F., and Associates. *Liberating Education.* San Francisco: Jossey-Bass, 1984. 253 pages.

Based on interviews with students, faculty, and administrators, the author and her collaborators discuss innovative programs at fourteen colleges and universities. The book is much more than a description of these programs. The innovations are discussed in light of rationales for curricula for helping students develop inquiry and analysis skills, become more critically aware of the world around them, and increase feelings of self-assurance and independence. Part One of the book attempts, quite successfully, to discover a new meaning for liberal education in contemporary society. Part Two discusses ways of achieving these goals of liberal study. Part Three presents strategies for making these changes happen. The book is well written, and the authors present challenging ideas as they envision educational programs for

liberating students from obedience to authority and teaching them
to become independent and self-directed persons.

440 Grant, Gerald, and Riesman, David. *The Perpetual Dream:
Reform and Experiment in the American College.* Chicago:
University of Chicago Press, 1978. 474 pages.

The authors evaluate a decade of campus experiments that had their
beginnings in the volatile period of the 1960s. Reform efforts that
are discussed include St. John's and the great books, cluster colleges
at Santa Cruz, New College in Florida, and two experimental public
colleges in New Jersey, among others. A comparison of these efforts
with earlier reform movements places the recent experiments in
historical perspective. Two general types of reforms are identified:
"telic" reforms, which redefine the goals of a college education, and
"popular" reforms, which emerged in response to specific social
and political pressures. The concluding chapter presents the
authors' assessment of the future of undergraduate reform in higher
education. They suggest that undergraduate education needs to
maintain a more focused experimental posture if the perpetual
dream of effective and humane education is to continue as an ideal.

441 Hall, James W., and Kevles, Barbara L. (eds.). *In Opposition to Core Curriculum: Alternative Models for Undergraduate Education.* Westport, Conn.: Greenwood Press,
1982. 235 pages.

The twelve contributors to this volume argue against core curriculum when it means a specific and highly limited set of courses.
Recognizing that social changes have brought greater diversity to
college populations, they explore alternatives to the conventional
core approach, including a human development "core," interdisciplinary approaches, communities of learners, special efforts with
disadvantaged students, and links with vocational education. The
book as a whole is rather loose thematically, but individual chapters
contain insights and provocative ideas that are likely to be helpful
for curriculum committees and course developers.

442 Jones, Richard M. *Experiment at Evergreen.* Cambridge, Mass.: Schenkman, 1981. 163 pages.

Jones reports on ten years of Evergreen's experiment to bring "coordinated studies" to a broad range of students at a public institution. The Meiklejohn-Tussman pedagogical model was employed: "A team of teachers teach the same group of students, who are all studying the same things at the same time, over a prolonged period." Ten teams of three to five faculty members along with 100 students worked together full-time for a year examining multidisciplinary, liberal arts themes. About one-third of the book is devoted to a chapter on evaluation and provides extended examples of the "portfolio," Evergreen's evaluation instrument. The portfolio contains narrative reports, self-evaluations, evaluations of faculty by students, and evaluations of students by faculty. Jones considers this approach to evaluation and the careful execution of collaborative interdisciplinary teaching to be the significant improvements made by Evergreen over previous models. This account is notable for its extended examples and its exhibits and for the author's sensitivity to dilemmas that Evergreen faculty have experienced in their teaching roles.

443 Keller, Phyllis. *Getting at the Core: Curricular Reform at Harvard.* Cambridge, Mass.: Harvard University Press, 1982. 201 pages.

The most recent round of undergraduate curricular reforms at Harvard attempted to define a common core of knowledge thought by the faculty to represent learning necessary for undergraduates to function effectively in today's world. This book places the Harvard Core Curriculum in its historical context as "part of a complex and lengthy institutional history of curricular change." The author tells "how and why it happened." She points out that "a curriculum is ultimately more than a cluster of courses arranged in an institutionally acceptable pattern. It is a statement of a faculty, a college, a generation, as to what they believe to be the character and goals of a college education. So it was with Harvard's Core Curriculum— as with the century and more of curricular change that preceded it." The curriculum received a tremendous amount of attention from the press and the public at the time of its creation, implying that these curricular changes were revolutionary in nature and contemporary in their response to new forms of undergraduate education. The book is fascinating reading for anyone interested in the process of curricular change at a university that frequently sets the pattern for others to follow.

444 Knott, Bob. "What Is a Competence-Based Curriculum in the Liberal Arts?" *Journal of Higher Education,* 1975, *46,* 25-40.

"A competence-based curriculum then is one where the competencies expected of all graduates are agreed upon and defined, and courses or experiences are designed to assist the student in becoming competent." In a liberal education, competencies must be synthesized or integrated and utilized by the learner; thus assessment should be holistic rather than fragmented. Four components of a competence-based liberal education are presented and illustrated: an analytic epistemology of the patterns of human meaning, a special area of advanced expertise, a developmental scheme, and a list of institutional values.

445 Martin, Warren Bryan. "The Limits to Diversity." *Change,* Dec.-Jan. 1978-1979, *10* (11), 41-45.

The author argues that a new two-track system of higher education is emerging in the United States. He indicates that the two systems are characterized "on the one hand, by institutions that are narrowly academic, and on the other by institutions that may be described as broadly educational. As the two tracks diverge, the diversity and pluralism in education that has long been part of our educational rhetoric will be realized as never before." The author discusses reasons for this assertion and provides a listing of common terms associated with the division. Educators often simplify the issues associated with this two-track system by using such labels as traditional and nontraditional, but such diversity breeds further diversity. The limits to diversity may have been reached, and the resulting changes may have led to the creation of a new set of priorities. This article places in perspective changes in curriculum and student values in higher education.

446 Meiklejohn, Alexander. "The Experimental College." *Bulletin of the University of Wisconsin,* 1928, *1284.* 22 pages.

The plan to establish at the University of Wisconsin an experimental college for a cross section of students in their first two years of liberal studies is set forth by its first director. The plan called for 120 freshmen, all males, to live together in newly constructed men's dormitories and to study with members of the regular faculty who devote two-thirds of their time to the college. The program of study will "demand that students take the lead in the making of their own education." Instead of required courses and electives, students will study together two or possibly three great civilizations. As planned, the college affirms democracy against aristocracy, general training against specialization, free choice of studies, professional training, and the small college within the large university. As an inspiration for many subsequent experiments, this description of the college remains important for today's scholars.

447 Meisler, Richard. *Trying Freedom: A Case for Liberating Education.* San Diego, Calif.: Harcourt Brace Jovanovich, 1984. 301 pages.

The author describes the Individualized Degree Program (IDP) at Buffalo State College as a way of presenting his views about the positive and negative interactions between freedom and authority that govern undergraduate education. The first-person narrative traces a commitment to experimental education from his association with Antioch College to his experience as Director of IDP at Buffalo. IDP is a degree program built around independent projects under cooperative alliances between faculty and students. There are no courses or grades. The book provides both philosophical and practical information for those who are interested in nontraditional curricula in higher education.

448 Newman, Frank. *Higher Education and the American Resurgence*. Princeton, N.J.: The Carnegie Foundation for the Advancement of Teaching, 1985. 268 pages.

At the time he wrote this book, the author was president of the Education Commission of the States. He develops the theme that American higher education has a central role to play in national renewal, and he emphasizes the need for college and university graduates to participate in shaping the world around them. Obligations for service are underscored, and he proposes that financial assistance be given to college students who engage in public service. The book contains many provocative recommendations for reforms in higher education, fueling the debate about the future national role for higher education in the United States. Anyone interested in reform movements for higher education will find the book useful.

449 Perry, Walter. *The Open University: History and Evaluation of a Dynamic Innovation in Higher Education*. San Francisco: Jossey-Bass, 1977. 298 pages.

A major success story in developing nontraditional approaches to higher education is the Open University in Great Britain. The author's personal involvement in an innovation first proposed in 1963 is the focus for delineating the background, courses, students, administrative plan, and future of an experiment in higher education that has attracted worldwide attention. The Open University was originally conceived as a degree-granting institution with academic standards equal to other, more traditional, institutions in Great Britain. Students, however, would be taught at home through the use of such media as television and radio. The pressures to compromise on standards and to "popularize" higher education through a less demanding curriculum were great. The story of how the author, the first vice-chancellor of the Open University, resisted those pressures while creating a curriculum and a method that had no parallel in history is an interesting and informative story about a visionary approach to higher education.

450 Riesman, David; Gusfield, Joseph; and Gamson, Zelda. *Academic Values and Mass Education*. New York: McGraw-Hill, 1970. 331 pages.

This book reports a study initiated in 1958 at two experimental public commuter colleges: Oakland University and Monteith College, both in Michigan. Interviews with faculty and administrators were begun in 1960 when both colleges had been in existence for only one year. After an excellent summary of the move toward universal higher education in Chapter One, subsequent chapters discuss the origins of both Oakland and Monteith, recruitment of faculty, academic life-styles in the two colleges and the encounter of faculty with nonelite students, colleagueship and teaching styles, some of the conflicts that emerged over academic standards, and various administrative issues. This book is both a record and an interpretation of the beginning years of an exciting experiment in devising alternative strategies for meeting the needs of the nontraditional student.

451 Schön, Donald A. *Educating the Reflective Practitioner: Toward a New Design for Teaching and Learning in the Professions*. San Francisco: Jossey-Bass, 1987. 355 pages.

Most professional schools, according to the author, teach only "standard scientific theories and how to apply them to straightforward cases and problems." Yet most problems for the professional are complex and not entirely responsive to the scientific and technical knowledge taught in professional programs. The author presents a new approach to educating professionals in all areas. He argues that skilled professional practice depends on the ability to reflect before taking action, at least in those instances where decision making is not dictated by the application of formula thinking. Educating the professional should emphasize enhancing the practitioner's ability for "reflection-in-action." Part One of the book is devoted to understanding the need for artistry in professional education and Part Two to an educational model for reflection-in-action with the architectural studio as an example. Part Three provides examples and experiments showing how a reflective practicum might work. Part Four discusses implications for improving professional education. The book offers a provocative frame of reference for redesigning professional education in all the professions. A comprehensive list of references is provided.

452 Schuster, Marilyn R., and Van Dyne, Susan R. *Women's Place in the Academy: Transforming the Liberal Arts Curriculum.* Totowa, N.J.: Rowman & Allanheld, 1985. 328 pages.

Eighteen essays discuss "the difference it makes" when material about women's experience enters courses across the curriculum. Approaches to curriculum transformation at the institutional level include discussions of coeducation and of relationships between black studies and women's studies. Approaches to faculty development include interdepartmental programs, institutes and regional projects, and dissemination activities. Approaches at the classroom level include examples from courses in humanities, philosophy, literature, interpersonal communication, social science, and biology. Sets of guidelines for redesigning (transforming) traditional courses are appended, drawn from literature and the arts, government and history, and natural science and psychology. They pose questions that help to identify the conventional assumptions underlying courses. There is also a thirty-seven-page bibliography covering women's experience in the liberal arts curriculum.

453 Suczek, Robert F. *The Best Laid Plans: A Study of Student Development in an Experimental College Program.* San Francisco: Jossey-Bass, 1972. 194 pages.

Please see entry no. 314 for the annotation of this work.

454 Taylor, Harold. *How to Change Colleges: Notes on Radical Reform*. New York: Holt, Rinehart & Winston, 1971. 180 pages.

The author's commitment to challenging the traditions of higher education is spelled out in this plan for radical change in colleges and universities. The book responds to the student unrest of the late 1960s and early 1970s. Its theme is the reconstruction of higher education in response to the perceived alienation expressed by students during those troubled years. The author believes that students should be given the chance to invent their colleges and universities so that these institutions can be places of lively intellectual experiences that reinforce a commitment to the cause of mankind. The book is a refreshing challenge to ideas about students and learning that are usually taken for granted.

455 Truxal, John G. "Learning to Think Like an Engineer: Why, What, and How?" *Change*, 1986, *18* (2), 10–19.

Courses in technology for liberal arts students, like these efforts supported by the Sloan Foundation, are typically structured around problem situations—for example, how to get abandoned cars off city streets or deciding on the capacity needed by international satellite communications. Such problems require interdisciplinary analysis and an understanding both of systems analysis, the quantitative approach to decision making, and of artifacts, the structures and machines of technology. How such concepts can be developed and connected with students' everyday experiences is discussed in this article, consideration of which should be useful for persons dealing with curriculum and course development related to technological fields.

456 Tussman, Joseph. *Experiment at Berkeley*. New York: Oxford University Press, 1969. 139 pages.

The experimental program of the University of California at Berkeley, which Tussman directed, redesigned the first two years of college for 150 students, five senior faculty, and a director. The curriculum was problem-oriented, a "variation of the Athens-

America curriculum, focusing on Greece, 17th Century England, and America." It proved impossible to loosen faculty from departments, and after two years the experiment was staffed by faculty visiting from other campuses. Two years later, the experiment closed. Several reports about the college are appended to the volume.

457 White, Alvin M. (ed.). *Interdisciplinary Teaching.* New Directions in Teaching and Learning, no. 8. San Francisco: Jossey-Bass, 1981. 113 pages.

"Significant knowledge is naturally interdisciplinary. If we seek understanding, then we cannot restrict the scope of inquiry." This theme is developed in thirteen provocative essays. Their richness and subtlety defy brief summary, particularly G. Vickers on two modes of knowing, R. Ross on the "transdisciplinary," K. E. Boulding on general systems, and D. Layzer on order in the physical and esthetic worlds. Other chapters deal with particular subject areas or particular teaching activities. This volume should be an effective basis for discussions by curriculum committees and faculty involved in interdisciplinary teaching.

Evaluating Curricula and Programs

458 Bennett, William J. *To Reclaim a Legacy: A Report on the Humanities in Higher Education.* Washington, D.C.: National Endowment for the Humanities, 1984. 32 pages. (ED 247 880)

This report presents the author's assessment of the state of learning in the humanities and is based in part on the work of the Study Group on the State of Learning in the Humanities in Higher Education, although the author clearly indicates his own responsibility for the content. The thoughts put forth in this report constitute a reasoned polemic against the dominance of professional training and vocationalism apparent in higher education today. The author concludes that "the curriculum has become a self-service cafeteria through which students pass without being nourished. Too many colleges and universities have no clear sense of their educational mission and no conception of what a graduate of their institution ought to know or be." Although the report was written before Bennett became President Reagan's Secretary of Education, it reflects much of the conservative opinion that has become the author's hallmark. The report deserves serious attention as a major statement in the reform literature for higher education. The author's ideas about the place of the humanities, and their form, in the curriculum of colleges and universities will be debated for years to come.

★**459** Chickering, Arthur W.; Halliburton, David; Bergquist, William H.; and Lindquist, Jack. *Developing the College Curriculum: A Handbook for Faculty and Administrators.* Washington, D.C.: Council of Independent Colleges, 1977. 313 pages.

When the Council of Independent Colleges was still the Council for the Advancement of Small Colleges, it published a series of handbooks for member institutions to help them engage in development activities necessary for encountering change and maintaining vitality. This handbook on curriculum, part of that series, is divided into four parts. Part One provides a rationale for curriculum development and discusses the major social changes, immediate conditions, and direct pressures that lead to curricular development. Part Two presents information about designing a college curriculum. Practices in curricular development are covered in Part Three, including a description of eight curricular models for higher education. Part Four deals with the practicalities of implementing a curriculum and discusses obstacles to curriculum development, determining curriculum objectives, the formulation of a curriculum, and the implementation and evaluation of the curriculum. This handbook practically and comprehensively covers the issues and problems generally encountered by faculty and administrators when confronted with the need for curriculum development and change.

460 Conrad, Clifton F., and Blackburn, Robert T. "Program Quality in Higher Education: A Review and Critique of Literature and Research." In John C. Smart (ed.), *Higher Education: Handbook of Theory and Research.* Vol. 1. New York: Agathon Press, 1985, pp. 283–308.

The quality of programs in higher education is an enduring topic of interest for students and critics of colleges and universities. The authors point out that indicators of quality have been sought through a "reputational" approach emphasizing rankings, through a search for "objective" indicators of quality, and through identification of quantifiable program characteristics that can be linked with already established quality programs. The chapter reviews statements about the meaning of quality. Critiques of these approaches are balanced and based on evidence from the studies reviewed. A list of over eighty references is included. Program quality and the comparison of departments, professional schools, colleges, and universities will remain a topic of central importance for higher education as accountability efforts increase. While the chapter does not deal directly with the professoriate, faculty are directly involved in determining quality and setting the standards by which quality is judged.

461 Conrad, Clifton F., and Wilson, Richard F. *Academic Program Reviews: Institutional Approaches, Expectations, and Controversies.* ASHE-ERIC Higher Education Report no. 5. Washington, D.C.: Association for the Study of Higher Education, 1985. 96 pages. (ED 264 806)

Program reviews have become common on individual campuses, in multicampus systems, and at state-level agencies. Formal reviews assist in controlling program quality and in making decisions regarding resource allocation and reallocation. In operation, the authors find that program reviews reflect characteristics of one or more of the following models: goal-based model, responsive model, decision-making model, and connoisseurship model. Defining program quality is a complex and controversial issue and definitions usually include a combination of elements from four views about higher education quality: reputational view, resources view, outcomes view, and value-added view. There is presently too little evidence to decide among these models and views or even to reach clear conclusions about the efficacy of program reviews in general.

462 Ewell, Peter T. (ed.). *Assessing Educational Outcomes.* New Directions for Institutional Research, no. 47. San Francisco: Jossey-Bass, 1985. 128 pages.

Student outcomes from higher education are customarily assessed through standardized tests, self-report questionnaires, and expert observers, with a focus on such outcomes as attitudes, achievement, and occupational and career development. Contributors to this sourcebook describe programs in three varied institutions whose programs are explicitly aimed at enhancing these outcomes. One program uses performance-based funding as a major incentive, one applies a value-added approach, and one emphasizes learning gains in a liberal arts setting. Other chapters discuss more technical issues, including use of questionnaires, designing cohort studies, and tracing students for follow-up studies after they leave the institution. For those concerned with mandated assessment of student outcomes at the program or institutional level, the volume highlights the importance of the natural evolution of such research programs and the importance of measuring outcomes in a variety of ways.

463 Gardner, Don E. "Five Evaluation Frameworks: Implications for Decision Making in Higher Education." *Journal of Higher Education,* 1977, *48,* 571–593.

Five of the prominent evaluation systems used in higher education are presented, illustrated, and contrasted with regard to their assumptions, procedures, and expected outcomes. The approaches are evaluation as measurement, evaluation as professional judgment, evaluation as the assessment of congruence between performance and objectives (or standards of performance), decision-oriented evaluation, and goal-free/responsive evaluation. The author applies these approaches to institutional evaluation, program evaluation, and instructional evaluation, and he specifies criteria by which users can select the evaluation approach most appropriate for their purposes.

464 Hefferlin, JB Lon. *Dynamics of Academic Reform*. San Francisco: Jossey-Bass, 1969. 240 pages.

This book reports on the Study of Institutional Vitality completed by the Institute of Higher Education at Columbia University with the support of the Kettering Foundation. Data from 110 representative colleges and universities are used by the author to address the following questions: "Why is change in higher education more difficult than in almost any other social institution? How do academic institutions adapt to new conditions? What are the most common techniques of reform? How influential are faculty members, administrators, trustees, and students in the process? How important are funding agencies in shaping the character of institutions? What are the causes of change in the curriculum—in the redesign of courses and departments and programs of study?" The author addresses these issues in chapters that discuss the problems and processes of reform, changes in the curriculum, the agents of change, the correlates of dynamism, and the sources of reform. Useful appendixes present a summary of the literature on change, a discussion of the sampling procedures and analysis of the data base, and a protocol for the telephone interviews. Although nearly twenty years old, this study has much to offer in its interpretation of data, and it is still quite relevant to the struggle for reform that continues in higher education today.

465 Pace, C. Robert. *Measuring the Quality of College Student Experiences*. Los Angeles: Higher Education Research Institute, Graduate School of Education, University of California, 1984. 136 pages. (ED 255 099)

The author emphasizes the effort that students put into their educational activities and offers a questionnaire to assess the quality of that effort, that is, "how students use the major resources and opportunities for learning and personality growth that are provided by the college." The Quality of Effort Scales deal with use of facilities such as libraries, classrooms, and living units, and with other opportunities, including student acquaintances, faculty, organizations, and so on. The monograph discusses measurement issues and how these scales can be used by institutions for diagnosis and planning.

466 Tierney, William G. "Ethnography: An Alternative Evaluation Methodology." *Review of Higher Education*, 1985, *8*, 93–105.

This article discusses using ethnographic techniques in evaluation of higher education institutions. Ethnography is defined, and its usefulness is explained in terms of the distinct cultures of institutions of higher education. The author states that "ethnographic research attempts to record and describe culturally significant behavior of a particular people. . . . We approach the institution to be studied as if it were an interconnected web that cannot be understood unless one looks not only at the structure and natural laws of that web, but also the actors' interpretation of the web itself." The author points out that ethnography is used infrequently in evaluation studies for higher education and counsels administrators to adopt the alternative research methodology outlined in the article. Persons engaged in evaluation studies in higher education will find both the article and the bibliography useful.

467 Tyler, Ralph W. "Innovation and Productivity: Possibilities, Conflicts, and Resistance." In David T. Tuma (ed.), *Innovation and Productivity in Higher Education*. San Francisco: San Francisco Press, 1977, pp. 10–22.

With regard to the educational functions of colleges and universities, Tyler defines productivity as "the total amount of the desired student learning that actually occurs, summed for all the students involved." Productivity depends on three interrelated systems: the student learning system, the curriculum and instructional planning system, and the system for managing student learning activities. Components of each system are elaborated in a laudably jargon-free discussion that raises issues most college teachers resist confronting—for example, "in many cases, inadequate practice opportunities are provided for the learner to use the new behavior in the varied

settings where it is appropriate" (student learning system), and
"lack of connection between the tests and examinations and the
learning goals" (curricular and instructional planning system).
Sources of faculty resistance to productive innovations are mentioned along with guidelines for developing more constructive
innovations. Any reader of this article gains a new understanding
of the gap between higher education's typical rhetoric and its
practice. The article helps to identify some ways that gap can be
reduced through individual and collaborative faculty action and
should serve as a superb springboard for faculty discussion.

468 Walvekar, Carol C. (ed.). *Assessment of Learning Assistance
Services.* New Directions for College Learning Assistance,
no. 5. San Francisco: Jossey-Bass, 1981. 123 pages.

Concepts of evaluation are applied to programs that provide
developmental remedial services to special students. Experimental
and quasi-experimental designs using both qualitative and
quantitative methods are illustrated. Also deserving careful
evaluative designs are student learning outcomes and staff performance. This is a nontechnical introduction for practitioners in
learning assistance centers who must also deal with evaluation in
order to develop new programs or to justify continuation of their
present programs.

469 Wilson, Richard F. (ed.). *Designing Academic Program
Reviews.* New Directions for Higher Education, no. 37. San
Francisco: Jossey-Bass, 1982. 110 pages.

The recent expansion of cyclical program reviews in colleges and
universities prompted two national conferences sponsored by the
University of Illinois; most of the papers in this sourcebook
originated at those conferences. Contributors assert that institutional evaluations and program evaluations should be interactive
(with each other); should admit their value orientations; should
lead to judgments about both worth and effectiveness, rather than
merely gather information; and should build networks of people
through which educational values and expectations can be disseminated. Special problems of state-level evaluations and of adminis-

trator evaluations are also discussed. This is an accessible, nontechnical volume for those beginning or revising program reviews.

470 Wood, Lynn, and Davis, Barbara G. *Designing and Evaluating Higher Education Curricula.* ASHE-ERIC Higher Education Report no. 8. Washington, D.C.: Association for the Study of Higher Education, 1987. 65 pages. (ED 165 669)

This research report addresses the neglected fields of curriculum evaluation and design in higher education. In their overview, the authors discuss the reasons for this neglect and present six findings that they feel are generalized conclusions about the college and university curriculum. Additional chapters present a view of higher education curriculum at the time the monograph was written and a summary of the state of the art with respect to design and evaluation of educational programs in colleges and universities. Curriculum is defined, and linkages between design and evaluation are discussed. Topics such as needs assessment, curriculum design, curriculum implementation, and curriculum evaluation are presented with reference to pertinent research. A bibliography of some sixty-nine items is included. The monograph is an informative and useful source for those interested in assessing the impact of curriculum models in higher education.

5

Faculty and
Staff Development:
Goals, Trends,
and Approaches

Key resources on faculty and staff development comprise a literature with the study of academic careers as its nucleus. Faculty and staff development represents a relatively new approach to the enhancement of academic careers. Mathis (1982, no. 522) states that "faculty development typically refers to the recent movement in postsecondary education toward more attention to the total development of faculty members in relationship to competence in professional activities. Faculty development interests range from research and scholarship in a discipline and teaching in formal classrooms to the informed management of one's own professional career over time" (1982, p. 646). One report (no. 493) defines faculty and staff development as "the total development of the faculty member—as a person, as a professional, and as a member of the academic community. This definition . . . moves beyond development as a teacher to include development as an individual as well as a group member, and to focus on the person's development and growth in all of his or her professional roles" (Crow, Milton, Moomaw, and O'Connell, Jr., 1976, p. 3).

This chapter is divided into five sections, which cover general resources, career development, development as teachers, individual development, and organizational development. Readers will immediately recognize the futility of treating these classifications as mutually exclusive categories. We have attempted to cross-reference the most obviously overlapping material, but each reference contains more than the theme that justifies its placement in one category. This is particularly applicable to items classified in the general resources section.

Several references are recommended for the reader who is beginning an acquaintance with the literature on academic careers and faculty development. Finkelstein (1984, no. 496) has written a lucid and comprehensive treatment of the American academic profession. Faculty development is an amorphous process, and Bergquist and Phillips (1975, no. 476) capture several facets of that topic in their model of organizational, instructional, and personal factors in the development of the professoriate. Finkelstein's (1985, no. 497) collection of articles on faculty issues, done under the sponsorship of the Association for the Study of Higher Education, provides a sample of issues thought to be important by contemporary scholars. The article in the *Encyclopedia of Educational Research* by Mathis (1982, no. 522) presents a general summary of the literature on faculty development. Baldwin and Blackburn (1981, no. 546) discuss a stage theory for thinking about academic careers, and Bowen and Schuster (1986, no. 550) describe the state of today's professoriate and call for institutions to anticipate difficulty in recruiting the best and brightest scholars in the years ahead. Keller (1983, no. 631) describes the arrival of management techniques in the administration of higher education and, by implication, advocates a different view of an academic career than the one traditionally espoused in academe.

General Resources

Faculty development emerged as a significant movement in higher education during the 1960s. As higher education entered into a time of crisis during the 1970s, concerns by faculty members about the changing natures of their academic roles stimulated both internal and external financial support for programs to help faculty become more productive, especially in their teaching function. The terms *vitality* and *renewal* were frequently used to describe the purposes of faculty development efforts. The book by Gaff (1975,

no. 505) describes many of these basic issues and uses *renewal* in the
title to indicate the conceptual frame of reference he employs. A
more recent effort by Clark and Lewis (1985, no. 491) places faculty
vitality in the context of institutional productivity. Rice (1985,
no. 529) uses the terms *vitality* and *change* as the key words in the
title of his report on faculty development programs. Nelsen's (1981,
no. 525) study for the Association of American Colleges is entitled
Renewal of the Teacher-Scholar.

This focus on renewal and vitality has its origins in the
agenda for educational reform articulated by students during the
time of student protest in the late 1960s and early 1970s. Daniels,
Kahn-Hut, and Associates (1970, no. 494) describe these times in
their discussion of the student-faculty strike at San Francisco State
College. Many students felt that the educational system was remote
and unresponsive to their interests and needs. Faculty were seen as
more interested in their own research careers and the funding they
could obtain than in what students saw as their major concern, the
quality of undergraduate education. The call for more effective
teaching and a more tangible commitment by faculty to educational
issues is a theme that is identified in the literature of this period;
see, for example, Jencks and Riesman (1968, no. 513) and Shils
(1983, no. 533).

The perception of decline from the period of expansion of
higher education following World War II was another factor in
stimulating the growth of faculty development programs. The end
of the growth years in higher education did not arrive as precipi-
tously as some predicted; nevertheless, the specter of retrenchment,
reassessment, and realignment and the shrinking of economic
support have become realities for many institutions in the United
States. The unstable nature of academic careers during this time
created a need for programs that would help faculty examine their
careers and accommodate to the changing nature of the workplace.
Baldwin and Blackburn (1983, no. 475), in their edited volume for
New Directions for Institutional Research, have collected articles
that address the status of faculty in a period of constraint. Much of
what constitutes the content of faculty development programs can
be gleaned from the three volumes that make up the *Handbook for
Faculty Development,* edited by Bergquist and Phillips (1975,

no. 477). Many of the exercises for faculty in these volumes promote expanded self-awareness and reassessment of roles.

The emergence of faculty development as an instituional concern is evident in a literature rich in scholarship about the academician and academic careers. Anderson and Murray (1971, no. 473) edited a collection of essays about the work and life-style of academicians. Bernard (1964, no. 478) has written a classic account of women faculty. Caplow and McGee (1958, no. 486) studied personnel practices and mobility in American universities at a time when higher education was undergoing rapid expansion in this country. Finkelstein (1984, no. 496) examines the history and present status of the academic profession. Ladd and Lipset (1975, no. 515) derive a statistical portrait of the professoriate from the questionnaires they sent to 60,000 professors in 1969 and 1972. An earlier study by Lazarfeld and Thielens (1958, no. 516) describes the backgrounds, political beliefs, and intellectual values of professors in social science fields. More references are in our other chapters. Much of this research confirmed the observation that academicians represent a broad spectrum of society, and their beliefs and attitudes do not identify them as unique among professional groups. Faculty development is one strategy for meeting the need for nurturance in their careers, which is as strong as that of any person in a work setting.

Career Development

Linking faculty development with career development is a direct result of the increasing interest in adult development. The many publications and studies that call our attention to life-span issues in the workplace, together with the increasing age of the population and the change in retirement age for faculty, have sensitized faculty to expect that the institutional environment will give them a range of alternatives in managing their careers. The American Association for Higher Education recognized this in its publication about career development for faculty (1979, no. 544). Career development projects were reviewed by the same association in 1981 (no. 545). Baldwin and Blackburn (1981, no. 546) studied the developmental process represented by a faculty career. Stage theories for faculty careers are discussed by Brookes and German (1983, no. 551). Menges (1985, no. 568) argues for a softening of the boundaries that identify life-span issues in faculty careers, and Patton (1979, no. 640) focuses on retirement and midcareer change as a resolution for the low satisfaction a career sometimes brings in its later stages.

The literature on career development recognizes the need for professionals to become more active in managing their own careers, and for institutions to respond accordingly with support and resources that allow faculty members flexible options in expressing their professional skills. The literature also emphasizes the teaching function in higher education as a route to productivity. One central theme in the citations in this section is the need for institutions to reward teaching in appropriate ways and to recognize the contribution that effective teaching makes to institutional productivity. Eble (1971, no. 557) underscores this forcefully in his study of the career development of the effective college teacher, and Furniss (1984, no. 562) calls for academicians to become more self-reliant in identifying the things they need to do to maintain success in their careers.

Development as Teachers

Teaching responsibilities are an essential element in any academic career; yet, the professoriate has had an ambivalent attraction to teaching exacerbated by dominance of the research ethic in higher education. Nearly all academicians teach, but the reward structure gives greater recognition to scholarship, research, and publication than to teaching. Faculty themselves create this reward structure through a system of peer approval that emphasizes scholarship and research as the most important factor in obtaining the approbation of colleagues. Faculty development literature frequently contains an exhortation to improve teaching and a plea to give effective teaching the recognition it deserves. The Group for Human Development in Higher Education, in their publication *Faculty Development in a Time of Retrenchment* (1974, no. 584), presents a strong argument for including teaching as a central component in any faculty development program. Dressel and

Thompson (1977, no. 579) discuss the Doctor of Arts degree as the ultimate degree for those who wish to make teaching the focus of their careers. Arrowsmith's (1967, no. 574) defense of teaching underscores the opinion that research and teaching are reconcilable only at the expense of teaching. By teaching, he means the molding of men rather than mere production of knowledge. Many of the problems associated with college teaching are much the same as they were over fifty years ago (Munro, 1933, no. 587).

More attention is being given in the literature to effective teaching and to preparation for college teaching. Andrews (1978, no. 572) traces the development of a teacher and contrasts this growth with the growth that takes place in psychotherapy. Bess (1982, no. 576) has edited a volume of articles about motivating professors to teach effectively. Fink (1984, no. 580) discusses the first year of college teaching. The teaching assistant is the subject of the monograph edited by Andrews (1985, no. 573). Gaff's (1978, no. 582) collection of articles focuses on the use of teaching as a renewal strategy for colleges and universities.

Citations in this section are only a small sample of the many works in this book that have teaching as their main theme. The reader is advised to consult the index and Chapter Two on teaching for a more comprehensive selection of books and articles that address college teaching and the college teacher.

Development as Individuals

The most neglected themes in writing about faculty development concern the personal development of individual faculty members. Recent attention to the individual has emphasized the stressful aspects of the workplace. Blackburn, Horowitz, Edington, and Klos (1986, no. 591) write about faculty and administrator responses to job strains in their study of administrators and faculty at the University of Michigan. Melendez and de Guzman (1983, no. 603) treat burnout as a new academic disease. Seldin (1987, no. 609) has collected articles that tell us how to cope with faculty stress.

Not all attention to individual needs is directed at the stressful. Bess (1973, no. 590), in his study of academic departments, looks at organizational achievement and personal satisfaction. Cares and Blackburn (1978, no. 596) examine faculty self-actualization in the context of career success. Martin (1975, no. 602) sees faculty development as an extension of human development, while Hodgkinson (1974, no. 599) casts an academic career in the stages of adult development and discusses parallels that emerge. Near and Sorcinelli (1986, no. 605) relate life at work with life away from work, and Schrecker (1986, no. 608) tells us about the McCarthy era and its influence on the lives of academicians. A collection of individual reflections about the processes that make up intellectual work is edited by Menges (1982, no. 604).

The influence of the field of adult development is apparent in the citations that examine faculty development as a life-course process. Much more is yet to be done in relating the course of a faculty career to the total environment that surrounds us on a daily basis.

Organizational Development

The system of higher education in the United States, and the organizations that make up that system, have stimulated a rich literature that includes much of implicit value for thinking about faculty development. Austin and Gamson (1983, no. 610) present evidence about changes in the academic workplace. Many of these are organizational changes forced on institutions by outside pressures. Scholars question whether academic careers can maintain their attractiveness as the nature of academic work changes. Blau (1973, no. 617) studied bureaucratic growth in colleges and universities and its relationship to scholarship. Clark (1966, no. 622) develops the thesis that the organizational structure of higher education is molded by the needs of professional staff. In another volume, Clark (1983, no. 623) examines academic organizations from an international perspective. Keller's (1983, no. 631) book on management in higher education serves both as a blueprint for organizational change and as a catalogue of what not to do in colleges and universities, depending upon the values of the reader. Bess (1982, no. 616) discusses the organization of faculty work, and Nisbet (1971, no. 637) views the academic entrepreneur as the enemy of all that's right with higher education. Veblen's (1918, no. 645) critique of the University of Chicago shows that tensions between management and scholarship were apparent over fifty years ago.

The role of the president has been given much thought by Cowley (1980, no. 624) and by Kerr and Gade (1986, no. 632). Bennis (1973, no. 613) provides the perspective of a university administrator on the upheavals in higher education that took place during the late 1960s and early 1970s. Bowen (1980, no. 619) applies his expertise to the question of costs in higher education. Tenure and its alternatives are the subject of the work by Chait and Ford (1982, no. 620), and Chronister and Kepple (1987, no. 621) examine early retirement programs for faculty. Patton (1979, no. 640) looks at early retirement, while Yuker (1984, no. 647) discusses faculty workload.

Literature on faculty development will undoubtedly continue to expand, much of it replicating what has already appeared. The interest in faculty development nationally has stimulated an increase in research about faculty and their roles. Future publications about faculty development may be expected to reflect this maturing interest.

References

Arrowsmith, W. "The Future of Teaching." In C.B.T. Lee (ed.), *Improving College Teaching*. Washington, D.C.: American Council on Education, 1967.

Crow, M. L.; Milton, O.; Moomaw, W. E.; and O'Connell, W. R., Jr. (eds.). *Faculty Development Centers in Southern Universities*. Atlanta: Southern Regional Education Board, 1976.

Mathis, B. C. "Faculty Development." In H. E. Mitzel (ed.), *Encyclopedia of Educational Research*. (5th ed.) New York: Free Press, 1982.

General Resources

471 Altbach, Philip C., and Slaughter, Sheila (eds.). "The
Academic Profession." *Annals of the American Academy of
Political and Social Science.* Vol. 448. Philadelphia:
American Academy of Political and Social Science, 1980.
203 pages.

This monograph contains articles on a wide range of issues and
problems concerning faculty in colleges and universities. Of special
interest for higher education in the United States are chapters on the
crisis of the professoriate by Philip G. Altbach, dialectical change
in academe by Logan Wilson, and the status of women faculty by
Lilli S. Hornig. Robert T. Blackburn discusses faculty careers and
Michael A. Faia deals with teaching, research, and role theory for
academics. Sheila Slaughter presents an analysis of academic
freedom and civil liberties, Joseph W. Garbarino's topic is faculty
unionism, and Lionel S. Lewis deals with academic tenure. Robert
C. Johnson, Jr.'s topic is affirmative active and the academic
profession. The articles are not reviews of the literature on specific
topics. They are critical essays reviewing contemporary issues of
concern for today's faculty.

472 "American Higher Education: Toward an Uncertain
Future." *Daedalus: Journal of the American Academy of
Arts and Sciences,* 1975, *104* (1), 1-355.

The second *Daedalus* issue of articles about the problems facing
higher education in the United States, prepared by the editors of the
Journal of the American Academy of Arts and Sciences, continues
the theme initiated by the issue annotated in the first section of
Chapter Four of this volume. The first article, "What We Might
Learn from the Climacteric," is by Clark Kerr. The academic
profession is the subject of an article by Walter Metzger, and both
Kenneth Boulding and Martin Meyerson write about maintaining
quality while, at the same time, meeting a commitment to mass
education. Articles in both issues of this interesting and wide-
ranging inquiry into the future of higher education are of variable
quality. Nevertheless, they offer a splendid opportunity for

browsing through the minds of acknowledged leaders in higher education, whose grasp of the problems is reinforced by their own experiences in bringing higher education to the uncertain paradigm shift of the 1970s.

473 Anderson, Charles H., and Murray, John D. (eds.). *The Professors: Work and Life Style Among Academicians.* Cambridge, Mass.: Schenkman, 1971. 350 pages.

This book consists of essays on topics relating to the work done by academics in pursuit of their profession. It is organized by six general categories of "effort": work as income while on the job, work as income while getting and holding the job, work as leisure, work as alienation, work as community, and work as political responsibility. The topics dealt with by the writers are wide-ranging and, for the most part, still relevant to the expression of academic careers. The editors' introduction is a scholarly and readable advance organizer for the articles that follow. The book is an excellent example of applying sociological thought to issues in higher education.

★**474** Astin, Alexander W.; Green, Kenneth C.; and Korn, William S. *The American Freshman: Twenty Year Trends.* Los Angeles: Cooperative Institutional Research Program, University of California, Los Angeles, 1987. 140 pages. (ED 279 279)

Please see entry no. 250 for the annotation of this work.

475 Baldwin, Roger G., and Blackburn, Robert T. (eds.). *College Faculty: Versatile Human Resources in a Period of Constraint.* New Directions for Institutional Research, no. 40. San Francisco: Jossey-Bass, 1983. 105 pages.

This book consists of chapters by the editors and by Barbara A. Lee, Carl V. Patton, Wilbert J. McKeachie, William C. Nelsen, and William Toombs. They discuss various aspects of the professoriate, in a time of change and limited resources in higher education. The argument is advanced that faculty development programs have failed in their aim of becoming a permanent fixture in the organizational structure of colleges and universities. The issue of maintaining institutional vitality through the development of human resources calls for institutions to change their faculty personnel policies. The book brings together views that have been expressed before, but the value of these chapters is the way the editors mold these collected opinions into a focused thesis for reform.

★**476** Bergquist, William H., and Phillips, Steven R. "Components of an Effective Faculty Development Program." *Journal of Higher Education*, 1975, *46*, 177–211.

This model for effective faculty development provides a comprehensive frame of reference for viewing faculty development as a three-dimensional process: organizational development, instructional development, and personal development. Organizational components provide a structure for faculty activities; instructional components provide a process for these activities; and personal components infuse beliefs, values, and attitudes into the professional lives of faculty. The authors discuss this model and its relationship to changes academicians will undergo during the span of their careers, and they present examples of faculty development initiatives for each dimension. Comprehensive faculty development is an institutional effort to provide support for change through programs that relate to all three dimensions. This article has been cited frequently as a thoughtful and well-reasoned definition of faculty development that outlines how institutions might begin to initiate faculty development strategies.

★**477** Bergquist, William H., and Phillips, Steven R. *A Handbook for Faculty Development*. Vols. 1, 2, and 3. Washington, D.C.: Council of Independent Colleges, 1975, 1977, 1981. Vol. 1, 306 pages; Vol. 2, 313 pages; Vol. 3, 357 pages.

These handbooks are part of a series of publications made available by the Council of Independent Colleges, an organization that began as the Council for the Advancement of Small Colleges. The series is designed to provide practical assistance for colleges engaged in faculty, administrative, and curricular development. Planned under the general editorship of Gary Quehl, the series has been widely used in higher education. Volume One contains five sections devoted to different aspects of faculty development: (1) a comprehensive approach to faculty development that includes organizational, instructional, and personal elements; (2) instructional development, containing exercises and assessment instruments relating to observation and diagnosis, evaluation, microteaching, and faculty and student teaching and learning styles; (3) organizational development, including a number of useful exercises to highlight decision making and conflict management in organizational structures; (4) personal development; and (5) information useful for implementing faculty development programs.

Volume Two continues the themes introduced in Volume One. The first section provides models for faculty development, exercises for assessing faculty motivation, and procedures for developing a portfolio evaluation. The second section, on instructional development, explains procedures used by the Clinic to Improve College Teaching and includes strategies for consultations about course designs. Organizational and personal development are the topics for the third section, and the fourth section covers program development and evaluation. Instructional development, personal and organizational development, and a look at the future for faculty development are the themes of Volume Three. The exercises, simulations, and assessment instruments contained in this volume do not replicate those in the other volumes.

These three volumes of *A Handbook for Faculty Development* are essential resources for practitioners faced with implementing faculty development strategies. While the contents were assembled for use by undergraduate colleges with an emphasis on teaching, faculty in any institution of higher education can profit from the exercises, instruments, games, and practical wisdom contained in these three volumes.

★**478** Bernard, Jessie. *Academic Women.* New York: New American Library, 1964. 330 pages.

Women associated with academe are carefully studied in this sociological analysis of a problem long left unstudied in higher education. The author discusses many of the issues that emerged with the resurgence of feminism during the 1960s. The tone of the book is scholarly and dispassionate, yet it presents a wealth of data and insights about the status of academic women at a time when women were entering the academic marketplace in increasing numbers. Differences between academic men and academic women are presented, the role performance of women is discussed, and productivity issues are dealt with in an interesting and informative manner. This book has become a benchmark for a host of further studies about women in colleges and universities and should be on the required reading list of anyone who teaches about faculty in higher education.

479 Bess, James L. "Integrating Faculty and Student Life Cycles." *Review of Educational Research,* 1973, *43,* 377–403.

This article discusses the developmental life cycles of faculty and students as they interact in the context of their educational roles, with emphasis on the manner and timing of this interaction. A comprehensive review of the literature is presented, revealing the changing nature of developmental needs at different stages of development. The author notes that faculty roles involving teaching, research, and public service are supported by different reward systems and can be made more fulfilling for both students and faculty by the use of different strategies. The author urges better selection of graduate students for academic careers. He contends that more should be done in graduate school to expose students to the psychological hazards of teaching. He also discusses the need for expanding professional opportunities for faculty, especially at midcareer.

480 Blackburn, Robert T., and Lawrence, Janet H. "Aging and the Quality of Faculty Job Performance." *Review of Educational Research*, 1986, *23*, 265–290.

This review of research on faculty performance and the influence of age assesses supportable and nonsupportable assertions about the job performance of older faculty. The prospect of an aging faculty raises questions about performance and about the quality of faculty efforts in higher education. Four theories of aging are considered— biological, psychological, sociological, and social psychological— and inferences about faculty behavior are drawn from each. The major faculty role assessed is that of scholar and researcher. After presenting critical evaluations of the research, the authors conclude that the relationship between age and productivity is not as strong as is generally assumed. The article contains many interesting and challenging statements about the helpfulness of theoretical constructs in conceptualizing research on age and faculty performance.

481 Blackburn, Robert T.; Lawrence, Janet H.; Ross, Steven; Okoloko, Virginia Polk; Bieber, Jeffery P.; Meiland, Rosalie; and Street, Terry. *Faculty as a Key Resource: A Review of the Research Literature.* Ann Arbor: National Center for Research to Improve Postsecondary Teaching and Learning, University of Michigan, 1986. 46 pages.

This monograph is one of a series sponsored by the National Center for Research to Improve Postsecondary Teaching and Learning (NCRIPTAL) at the University of Michigan, a center supported by a grant from the Office of Educational Research and Improvement of the Department of Education. The monograph is divided into six sections. The first presents a historical perspective on research about faculty, beginning with the data reported by Lazarfeld and Thielens in *The Academic Mind: Social Scientists in a Time of Crisis.* Part Two discusses research on faculty at work. The third section presents data about faculty in a teaching role and includes research on the evaluation of teaching. Part Four is a summary of the research literature about faculty. Part Five is a discussion of professionals at work in organizations, and the final section presents the authors' concluding remarks. The authors thoroughly and effectively present a synthesis of the research literature on "the work life of faculty in American Colleges and Universities." The monograph contains a reference list of 215 items, with the most recent citations representing 1986 publications. Anyone interested in faculty careers and the work life of academicians will find the publication indispensable.

482 Boice, Robert. "Faculty Development Via Field Programs for Middle-Aged, Disillusioned Faculty." *Research in Higher Education*, 1986, *25*, 115–135.

The author points out that middle-aged, disillusioned faculty have been neglected by traditional faculty development programs. These faculty are inactive and unenthusiastic as teachers and researchers, are usually depressed and angry about their jobs, and are passive in their campus participation. The article describes a field-based program for forty-five faculty who worked with their department chairs in development activities. Five steps are discussed for working with disillusioned faculty: (1) reestablishing communication, (2) arranging reinvolvement in campus activities, (3) renegotiating for broader reinvolvement, (4) coping with resistance, and (5) getting beyond resistance to implementation of meaningful change. The program was successful for more than two-thirds of the participants.

483 Boyer, Carol M., and Lewis, Darrell R. *And on the Seventh Day: Faculty Consulting and Supplemental Income.* ASHE-ERIC Higher Education Report no. 3. Washington, D.C.: Association for the Study of Higher Education, 1985. 76 pages. (ED 262 743)

Increases in consulting activity have prompted questions about the appropriateness of some forms of consulting as well as about the amount of consulting being done by faculty, particularly in research universities. There is concern with faculty earning supplemental income on university time and fear that consulting detracts from time available to provide appropriate services for the employing institution. This monograph reviews empirical research relating to issues about faculty consulting and discusses numerous issues involved in the topic. In their call for more explicit institutional policies, the authors conclude by pointing out that "steps should be taken to ensure that such policy does not discriminate against the most highly active and valued faculty." This publication is a thorough and rigorous presentation of one of the more complex topics in determining professional responsibilities for faculty.

484 Braskamp, Larry A.; Fowler, Deborah L.; and Ory, John C. "Faculty Development and Achievement: A Faculty's View." *Review of Higher Education,* 1984, *7,* 205-222.

Interviews with forty-eight academicians at the assistant, associate, and full professor levels in a large research university were conducted to ascertain styles of work and achievement, sources of intrinsic and extrinsic motivation, and career goals and aspirations. The researchers found that the interviewed faculty felt that their professional activities were not independent of activities involving family, friends, and leisure pursuits. They regarded professional and personal relationships as the central components of their lives. The authors report common themes associated with faculty rank and categories of adult development. The findings are presented in a table form that permits useful comparison of faculty rank with the major issues and problems summarized from the adult development literature.

485 Buhl, Lance C., and Greenfield, Adele. "Contracting for Professional Development in Academe." *Educational Record,* 1975, *56,* 111-121.

The authors believe that the environment of a faculty member's institution largely determines whether that faculty member finds it worthwhile to commit time for improving learning effectiveness. Performance contracting is suggested as one solution to melding instructional development strategies with the demands of the total environment of the institution. If contracting is to be an effective method of motivating change, it should be characterized by full sharing of information, true negotiability, realistic definitions of roles and performance defined in detail in writing, and a mutual commitment to establish performance contracts. The authors recommend that specific rewards be built into the system and that the contract reflect faculty and administrative equity.

486 Caplow, Theodore, and McGee, Reece J. *The Academic Marketplace.* New York: Basic Books, 1958. 262 pages.

Personnel practices and mobility in American universities are the themes of this sociological study of higher education. The authors illuminate the secrecy, ignorance, and self-deception that governed the working conditions and performance of faculty at the time the study was published. The authors point out that this self-deception is "neither deliberate nor perverse, (but) is yet remarkable in a social group wedded to the norms of truth." How vacancies occur and how performance is evaluated are central questions for the study. While many of the practices reported in the book (largely the "old boy network") have received some degree of amelioration today, the study itself remains a classic in its exposure of the academic profession as one that behaves in much the same manner as other professions. College professors seek status and economic rewards with the same motives as others. The combination of scholarship and wit gives the book a style that is both readable and informative.

487 Centra, John A. "Faculty Development in Higher Education." *Teachers College Record,* 1978, *80,* 188–201.

The upsurge in faculty development programs during the 1970s is examined, and practices and programs are presented and discussed. The author surveyed 1,044 colleges and universities identified as having "an organized program or set of practices for faculty development and improving instruction." Approximately 72 percent, or 756, of the coordinators responded to the survey. The author classifies the practices under these categories: institution-wide policies, analysis or assessment practices, workshops and seminars, media, technology, and course development practices, and a group of miscellaneous activities. Factor analysis identified four factors: (1) practices such as workshops and seminars, faculty consultation, and informal assessment of courses by colleagues that represent high faculty involvement; (2) instructional-assistance practices in which specialists help faculty develop teaching skills or utilize technology; (3) traditional practices such as sabbatical leaves and travel grants; and (4) assessment practices in which the emphasis is on evaluation. The author concludes by pointing out that the effectiveness of these practices is not as yet entirely known.

488 Centra, John A. "Types of Faculty Development Programs." *Journal of Higher Education,* 1978, *49,* 151-162.

The author describes patterns of faculty development practices, and the types of colleges and universities where these practices exist. He also investigates the perceived effectiveness of different faculty development practices and provides some information about how they are organized. The types of faculty development practices identified by Centra include (1) those with higher faculty involvement, found mostly in smaller colleges; (2) those that offer instructional assistance as a major theme, found, for the most part, in larger two-year institutions; (3) traditional activities such as leaves and the use of consultants, found mainly at larger colleges and universities; and (4) an assessment emphasis in two-year institutions. The author discusses funding for these programs, both internal and external.

489 Chase, J. L. *Graduate Teaching Assistants in American Universities: A Review of Recent Trends and Recommendations.* Washington, D.C.: U.S. Office of Education, 1970. 70 pages. (ED 043 274)

The author was commissioned to review and integrate studies of graduate teaching assistants. He describes studies made during the 1960s at Michigan State; University of California, Berkeley; Cornell; Rochester; University of Michigan; and at the Association of Graduate Schools. Support for graduate students as teaching assistants began because of their financial need but has come to serve institutional and even national needs, he observes. His own recommendations include establishing a unified "graduate assistantship" that would carry both teaching and research responsibilities at appropriate times prior to receiving the degree. This book is a useful resource for anyone wishing to learn the history of graduate students as teaching assistants.

490 Chickering, Arthur W., and Associates. *The Modern American College: Responding to the New Realities of Diverse Students and a Changing Society.* San Francisco: Jossey-Bass, 1981. 810 pages.

Please see entry no. 263 for the annotation of this work.

★491 Clark, Shirley M., and Lewis, Darrell R. (eds.). *Faculty Vitality and Institutional Productivity: Critical Perspectives for Higher Education.* New York: Teachers College Press, 1985. 293 pages.

This collection of essays about maintaining and improving faculty vitality in a time of changing demands for faculty covers faculty and institutional career development, aging and productivity in relation to careers and older faculty, and an institutional case study. Also included are chapters on faculty development, midcareer change, professional consulting, collective bargaining, and early retirement options. The editors discuss the implications of the chapter contents for the response of institutions. In addition to the editors, chapter authors include Carol M. Boyer, Mary Corcoran, W. Lee Hansen, Robert T. Blackburn, Barbara F. Reskin, Robert J. Havighurst, John A. Centra, Carl V. Patton, David D. Palmer, William E. Becker, Jr., and Karen C. Holden.

492 Cresswell, John W. *Faculty Research Performance: Lessons from the Sciences and Social Sciences.* ASHE-ERIC Higher Education Report no. 4. Washington, D.C.: Association for the Study of Higher Education, 1985. 73 pages. (ED 267 677)

The question of research productivity for faculty remains poorly understood despite some ninety studies since 1940. The fact that some faculty produce research year after year while others do not is well documented. Why this occurs is not. This monograph reviews the literature on faculty research performance and discusses correlates of research performance. The following conclusions are offered by the author: (1) The power of a correlate to predict is largely a function of the criterion used to measure performance; (2) studies suggest that individual and psychological correlates explain less than do sociological and work-environment correlates; (3) a complete explanation of differences in faculty research productivity is not offered by the literature available; and (4) interaction effects, together with issues of causality, make it difficult to determine precise relationships between some correlates and productivity. A comprehensive reference list is included.

493 Crow, Mary Lynn; Milton, Ohmer; Moomaw, W. Edmund; and O'Connell, William R., Jr. (eds.). *Faculty Development Centers in Southern Universities.* Atlanta: Southern Regional Education Board, 1976. 58 pages.

This monograph presents the status of eleven campus faculty development centers in southern universities as they were organized in 1976. The discussion of these centers is prefaced by an introductory chapter that presents concepts of faculty development applicable to the centers. The final chapter is an overview of faculty development in southern universities. Since 1976, some of these centers have gone out of existence while others have become more comprehensive. The value of the monograph as a historical document is assured by the detailed presentations of each of the centers at the eleven universities.

494 Daniels, Arlene Kaplan; Kahn-Hut, Rachel; and Associates. *Academics on the Line.* San Francisco: Jossey-Bass, 1970. 269 pages.

The student-faculty strike at San Francisco State College during the academic year 1968–69 received national attention as a prominent example of student-faculty protests in colleges and universities during the troublesome years of the Vietnam War. The college has since become a university, and much of the excitement surrounding the event has faded from the campus, but this book recaptures the strike as it was experienced by a group of sociologists who participated in various ways. The book draws attention to the perceived inequities in the California State College System, which at that time led to student and faculty dissatisfactions that motivated the strike. Changes that have taken place in higher education in California, and nationally, make the book essentially a historical account; nevertheless, persons interested in those turbulent years will find this book interesting and informative.

495 Fink, L. Dee. *The First Year of College Teaching.* New Directions for Teaching and Learning, no. 17. San Francisco: Jossey-Bass, 1984. 119 pages.

Please see entry no. 580 for the annotation of this work.

★**496** Finkelstein, Martin J. *The American Academic Profession: A Synthesis of Social Science Inquiry Since World War II.* Columbus: Ohio State University Press, 1984. 289 pages.

This volume brings the extensive and scattered literature on the academic profession up-to-date. It contains a composite profile of the college professor in his or her many roles as both professional and private citizen. After a discussion of the modern academic role, the author presents a demographic portrait of the academic profession; a discussion about academic careers; a portrait of faculty as workers, as people, and as citizens; and a survey of what we know about women and minority faculty. The comprehensive, contemporary bibliography makes this book essential reading for anyone interested in faculty in colleges and universities. The author's adroit handling of available resources and his summary remarks have created a basic resource for students of higher education.

★**497** Finkelstein, Martin J. (ed.). *ASHE Reader on Faculty Issues in Colleges and Universities.* Lexington, Mass.: Ginn Press, 1985. 391 pages.

Sponsored by the Association for the Study of Higher Education, this volume represents an attempt to bring together relevant writings about faculty. The book includes articles on the current status of the professoriate, academic careers, faculty culture, the work role of faculty, and faculty development and evaluation. The authors are all recognized scholars in their fields, and the contents are reprinted from journals, books, and reports. An extensive bibliography is included for each section of the book. This eclectic collection of material about faculty careers and other issues fits well with contemporary concerns about faculty development in colleges and universities.

498 Fox, Mary Frank. "Publication, Performance, and Reward in Science and Scholarship." In John C. Smart (ed.), *Higher Education: Handbook of Theory and Research.* Vol. 1. New York: Agathon Press, 1985, pp. 255-282.

This chapter reviews research relating to scholarship and publication in higher education and the reward structure that accompanies these aspects of faculty performance. The author discusses functions of rewards for publication, rates of publication by academics, factors that account for differential publication, and an agenda for future research on the topic. The chapter concludes with implications for equity and performance. The author's summary of research and commentary about motivational functions of the recognition afforded by publishing provides a useful context for understanding realities of the "publish or perish" philosophy. For those interested in pursuing further this important aspect of professional development for faculty, the chapter is accompanied by a comprehensive list of over 130 references.

499 Francis, John Bruce. "How Do We Get There From Here? Program Design for Faculty Development." *Journal of Higher Education,* 1975, *46,* 719-732.

The author analyzes the stages that define attitudes about faculty development as they evolve over time. Three developmental stages are described: (1) consciousness raising, (2) focal awareness, and (3) subsidiary awareness. Examples of practices for program elements (speeches, conferences, workshops, materials; evaluation of instruction; policy, program, and system changes) are presented for each of the three developmental stages. Coordinating programs with the prevailing institutional climate is recommended for ensuring the maximum impact of faculty development efforts.

500 Freedman, Mervin (ed.). *Facilitating Faculty Development.*
New Directions for Higher Education, no. 1. San Francisco:
Jossey-Bass, 1973. 122 pages.

The editor views faculty development as a process leading to
heightened self-awareness and a broadened world view. The articles
include a review of changes in faculty life since 1965, a consideration of the professor as an artist at teaching, faculty response to
student diversity, the relationship between personal history and
faculty career, a presentation of stages of faculty development, the
career challenges of innovative colleges, some examples of faculty
development programs, interinstitutional cooperation, and ways to
facilitate faculty development. The final chapter discusses additional resources about faculty development. The book is slanted
toward the social psychology of faculty development and its
accompanying theme of personal development as a parallel to
professional and career development views. The articles are
representative samples of this thematic approach to faculty
development.

501 Freedman, Mervin, and others. *Academic Culture and
Faculty Development.* Berkeley, Calif.: Montaigne, 1979.
173 pages.

Using an ethnographic method, the author and his associates derive
their conclusions about stages of faculty development, the relationship between personal history and career development, and patterns
of faculty response to student diversity. The ethnographies are
studies of faculty cultures at Stanford University, Mills College, and
the University of California, Berkeley. Additional information
about innovative colleges is introduced, and the challenges of
innovation for faculty development are discussed. The chapter on
stages of faculty development is especially useful for persons who
work directly with faculty in a one-on-one relationship.

502 Fulton, Oliver, and Trow, Martin. "Research Activity in American Higher Education." *Sociology of Education*, 1974, *47*, 29-73.

This study addresses the division of academic labor between institutions, and within institutions, by investigating the distribution of research activities in higher education in the United States. The authors sought to find out what kinds of institutions and what kinds of teachers contributed most to the activity of research. Data were obtained from the National Surveys of Higher Education sponsored by the Carnegie Commission on Higher Education. The detailed conclusions of the study support the assumption that research productivity at "elite" universities is rewarded by higher salaries. The author also found that "high-quality" four-year colleges are responsible for a relatively high level of research activity. These conclusions and many more make the article an interesting and essential resource for those concerned with the division of academic labor.

503 Furniss, W. Todd. "New Opportunities for Faculty Members." *Educational Record*, 1981, *62*, 8-15.

Please see entry no. 560 for the annotation of this work.

504 Furniss, W. Todd. *Reshaping Faculty Careers*. Washington, D.C.: American Council on Education, 1981. 171 pages. (ED 208 769)

Please see entry no. 561 for the annotation of this work.

505 Gaff, Jerry G. *Toward Faculty Renewal: Advances in Faculty, Instructional, and Organizational Development*. San Francisco: Jossey-Bass, 1975. 244 pages.

This book addresses basic issues in faculty development with an emphasis on the improvement of teaching. The author identifies current college and university programs to improve the quality of teaching and learning, describes the range and variety of these programs, and places the programs in the context of current trends in higher education. He points out that faculty renewal involves enhancement of talent, expansion of interest, improvement of competence, and facilitation of professional and personal growth for faculty. He discusses three basic dimensions in this process: (1) faculty development that takes the professional beyond the boundaries of his or her discipline to include knowledge of higher education and student development, (2) exposure to new pedagogical approaches and instructional innovations for classroom use, and (3) faculty involvement in issues that relate to the development and goals of the institution as an organization. The book reviews many programs and lists faculty development agencies in operation at the time the author's research was completed. While much has changed nationally for faculty development programs in higher education since 1975, Gaff's book remains an anchor for anyone seeking a definition of faculty development.

506 Gaff, Jerry G. "Current Issues in Faculty Development." *Liberal Education,* 1977, *63,* 511–519.

The author reviews many accomplishments of the faculty development movement in higher education. These include establishment of faculty development programs, identification of valuable models, and development of an extensive professional literature. He then identifies various activities remaining to be done. The author discusses faculty development issues for colleges and universities that have just discovered faculty development, for institutions that have gotten started but need to move ahead, and for schools with faculty development programs that have reached maturity but need to continue changing in order to remain vital. Gaff offers the following generalizations: (1) Existing effort should be institutionalized, (2) organizational structures are important but not sufficient for effective faculty development, (3) evaluations of programs should be conducted, (4) administrators must become aware of the need for faculty development, (5) faculty development programs should serve both individual and institutional needs, (6) more attention needs to be given to the personal aspect of faculty development, and (7) students should be included in faculty development efforts.

507 Gamson, Zelda F. "Utilitarian and Normative Orientations Toward Education." *Sociology of Education*, 1966, *39*, 46–73.
"Performance and Personalism in Student-Faculty Relations." *Sociology of Education*, 1967, *40*, 279–301.

Based on the author's doctoral dissertation at Harvard University, the first article reports a study of a "small non-residential college, one of several colleges in a sprawling state university located in the midst of a large industrial city." The article examines the "collective beliefs and norms which emerged among faculty members during the first four years of the college." The belief systems of the two dominant departments, the natural sciences and the social sciences, are described, and their differences discussed. According to the author: "The natural science orientation was predominantly 'utilitarian': it emphasized cognitive effects on students, was unconcerned about developing high student commitment to the College and encouraged faculty to maintain some distance from students. The social science orientation was 'normative': faculty were to 'reach' students personally as well as intellectually, encourage high student commitment, and promote close egalitarian relationships with students."

The second article extends these results to an analysis of faculty behaviors, such as grading, interaction with students outside of class, and selectivity of contact with students. Conflicts between personalism and performance are discussed. "The social scientists' emphasis on personalism in their relations with students led to problems centered around the legitimate exercise of faculty authority. The natural scientists' emphasis on performance . . . produced pressures for changes in natural science curricular and grading standards." Anyone who believes that faculty are all cut from the same bolt of cloth should read these articles.

508 Gouldner, Alvin W. "Cosmopolitans and Locals: Toward an Analysis of Latent Social Roles." Parts 1 and 2. *Administrative Science Quarterly*, 1957, *2*, 281–306; 1958, *2*, 444–480.

In these two articles, the author reports his investigations of types of latent organizational roles. The two types studied were labeled locals, those "who are identified with and affirm the distinctive ideology of their organization," and cosmopolitans, those who have "relatively little integration in either the formal or informal structure of the organization." The sample for investigating these types came from faculty at "Co-Op College." Differences were found between cosmopolitans and locals with respect to influence, participation, acceptance of organizational rules, and informal relations. The author suggests that "these two identities may reflect the tension between the organization's simultaneous need for both loyalty and expertise." The terms *cosmopolitans* and *locals* have become part of the vocabulary for subsequent typologies of faculty.

509 Gray, William S. *The Preparation and In-Service Training of College Teachers: Proceedings of the Institute for Administrative Officers of Higher Education*. Chicago: University of Chicago Press, 1938. 230 pages.

These chapters are derived from papers given at a meeting of the Institute for Administrative Officers of Higher Education, organized at the University of Chicago in the 1920s. Authors are presidents, deans, and faculty members from institutions throughout the country, the majority being from Chicago. In both this and a similarly titled volume published in 1930 by the same editor, there is concern with the growth of curricular content that students are expected to master and with the growing diversity of students themselves. The most satisfactory programs for preparing college teachers, according to a survey reported in the volume, involve cooperation between academic and professional departments. Such programs should be differentiated from programs that are provided for research specialists and should be continuously available throughout one's career. Individual chapters discuss issues specific to particular institutions or to particular disciplines or families of disciplines.

510 Gross, Ronald. *The Independent Scholar's Handbook.* Reading, Mass.: Addison-Wesley, 1982. 261 pages.

This volume is a unique reference for persons doing serious scholarship outside of academia. Skills needed to survive and be successful as an independent scholar are reviewed in ten chapters, illustrated with lively anecdotes. Topics include resources for the independent scholar's work, intellectual craftsmanship, support for work, and interdependence among independent scholars. Brief essays describe the experience of independent scholars Eric Hoffer, Barbara Tuchman, Betty Friedan, Alvin Toffler, and others. Appendixes include lists of specialized bookstores, locations of the Foundation Center's reference collections and of university presses, and information on tax deductions and copyright procedures. A brief annotated bibliography is included.

511 Herman, Joyce; McArt, Effa; and Belle, Lawrence. "New Beginnings: A Study of Faculty Career Changers." *Improving College and University Teaching,* 1983, *31,* 53–60.

Please see entry no. 565 for the annotation of this work.

512 Houle, Cyril O. *Continuing Learning in the Professions.* San Francisco: Jossey-Bass, 1980. 390 pages.

Continuing education for the professions has become an important service of colleges and universities. Topics covered in this analysis are the design and implementation of programs for professionals, the role of the professions in creating a market, the evaluation of outcomes, and ways to improve existing programs. The adult learner has become a major client for higher education, and continuing education opportunities represent one growth element in otherwise steady-state enrollment projections. Houle's book is a basic source for those involved in continuing education for the professions.

★513 Jencks, Christopher, and Riesman, David. *The Academic Revolution.* Garden City, N.Y.: Doubleday, 1968. 580 pages.

This book gave higher education a rationale for the newly discovered power gained by academic professionals during the last half of the twentieth century. This classic deserves to be read by anyone interested in developments in higher education during a time of momentous change for colleges and universities. According to the authors, the book "attempts a sociological and historical analysis of American higher education." The analysis is in the form of a theory of development for higher education that serves as a prelude to both description and sociological analysis of the revolution still under way in colleges and universities. The book presents a balanced critique of both positive and negative aspects of the changes the authors document. Their comments about academic professionalism, meritocracy, and making technical competency an end rather than a means are as relevant today as when published. Many of the issues discussed, such as social stratification and mass higher education, women in higher education, and the role of religion, are no longer viewed as revolutionary, which shows how quickly the world can change in institutions as close to the core of social change as higher education.

514 Kelley, William F. "Twenty Studies of In-Service Education of College Faculty and the Procedures Most Recommended." *Educational Administration and Supervision,* 1950, *36*, 351–358.

Please see entry no. 180 for the annotation of this work.

515 Ladd, Everett Carl, Jr., and Lipset, Seymour Martin. *The Divided Academy: Professors and Politics.* New York: McGraw-Hill, 1975. 407 pages.

This book for the Carnegie Commission on Higher Education analyzes the politics of academic men and women in the United States. Data for the study came from responses of more than 60,000 professors to the Carnegie Commission's Survey of Student and

Faculty Opinion in 1969 and from a supplementary survey completed by the authors in 1972. One widely reported conclusion of the study is the predominantly liberal political orientation of the professoriate. The contents of the book go far beyond that finding, however, as the authors discuss the politics of intellectuals, identifiable differences in professorial politics, and dominant issues of campus politics including campus protests and unionism. The book's value becomes primarily historical as the data grow older; nevertheless, the authors offer interesting and insightful views of an academic society during a time of rapid change.

516 Lazarfeld, Paul F., and Thielens, Wagner, Jr. *The Academic Mind.* Glencoe, Ill.: Free Press, 1958. 430 pages.

This portrait of the American college professor, taken from more than 2,400 interviews conducted on 165 college campuses throughout the United States, represents one of the most comprehensive attempts to understand the academician and the institution in which he or she teaches. Focusing on the social sciences, the authors give detailed information about social origins, self-image, abilities as scientists, and intellectual and political beliefs. The diversity of undergraduate colleges is illuminated during a time of significant change for higher education. A prominent portion of the book is devoted to insightful commentary by David Riesman about the interviews. Together with the reported data, Riesman's remarks and the contributions of the authors make the book an essential resource for anyone interested in academic careers.

517 Leslie, David W., and Beckham, Joseph C. "Research on Higher Education: Dead End or New Directions." *Review of Higher Education,* 1986, *10* (2), 123-129.

This chapter introduces an issue devoted to articles and commentary about the status of research in higher education. The introduction asks, "Has research on higher education accomplished anything of either intellectual or practical importance in its short history? How do we respond to the charge that we are the wholly derivative orphan of a moribund social science enterprise that had its day twenty or more years ago? Have we developed and are we

developing powerful ideas about the core functions and the
performance of colleges and universities?" The articles addressing
these issues include the following titles and authors: "Free at Last?
Breaking the Chains That Bind Educational Research," George
Keller; "A Future-Oriented Comment on the State of the Profes-
sion," Yvonna S. Lincoln; "Critical Choices: From Adolescence to
Maturity in Higher Education Research," Marvin W. Peterson;
"The Search for Good Research: Looking for 'Science' in All the
Wrong Places," John R. Thelin; "Shipyards in the Desert," Stephen
S. Weiner; "Toward an Integrated Research Agenda," Robert
Zemsky and Michael Tierney; and "Toward a Fifth Generation:
Narrowing the Gap Between Theory and Practice for Community
Colleges," William L. Deegan and Dale Tillery. The message that
this thematic collection brings to scholars and researchers in higher
education is that research about colleges and universities does not
often enough address major issues with research methods that are
broad in scope. Higher education research too frequently lacks a
vision of the future. Real issues involving practitioners and their
constituents are often ignored. Higher education research will
continue to have limited impact until the pressures that impede
valuable and illuminating research are reduced. This focused
collection is a visible reminder that research in higher education has
a long way to go before it becomes the handmaiden of the
practitioner's art. Implications are obvious for training researchers
in higher education and for faculty development approaches.

★**518** Lewis, Darrell R., and Becker, William E., Jr. (eds.).
       Academic Rewards in Higher Education. Cambridge,
       Mass.: Ballinger, 1979. 339 pages.

Academic reward systems for faculty are a primary influence on
productivity in higher education. Their influence on faculty
behavior is taken for granted, yet little is known about interactions
between academic rewards and the outcomes they are thought to
stimulate. These essays were taken from a colloquium series
developed by the editors and appear under five headings: (1) What
motivates academic behavior? (2) academic labor markets in higher
education, (3) academic labor productivity and its measurement in

higher education, (4) reward structures in higher education, and (5) implications for policy. The contributors to Part One are Wilbert J. McKeachie, who develops the theme that financial incentives are not effective for faculty; William E. Becker, Jr., who discusses the economic consequences of changing faculty reward structures, and Sanford M. Dornbusch, who writes about the organizational evaluation of faculty performances. In Part Two, the job market for college faculty is discussed by Richard B. Freeman. Part Three begins with a chapter by Wayne B. Kirschling on conceptual problems and issues in academic labor productivity. Darrell R. Lewis and Theodore E. Kellogg present planning and evaluation criteria for allocating departmental and collegial resources in a university setting. A discussion by Kenneth O. Doyle, Jr., on the use of student evaluations in faculty personnel decisions concludes this section. Part Four begins with a discussion of the academic reward structure in American higher education by Howard P. Tuckman and continues with a chapter on academic compensation in higher education by Howard R. Bowen. Helen S. Astin and Alan E. Bayer present an essay on pervasive sex differences in the academic reward systems, and pecuniary rewards to men and women faculty are discussed by George E. Johnson and Frank P. Stafford. Faculty bargaining and faculty reward systems are the topic of a chapter by James P. Begin. Finally, in Part Five, the editors discuss adaptability to change and academic productivity. This important book includes a comprehensive reference section for readers who wish to pursue these topics further.

519 Lewis, Lionel S. *Scaling the Ivory Tower: Merit and Its Limits in Academic Careers.* Baltimore, Md.: Johns Hopkins University Press, 1975. 238 pages.

Perceptive readers will soon conclude from this book that merit has many meanings in the academic communities. While the data do not go beyond 1975, the content is at least as relevant today as when the book first appeared. Lewis examines such topics as academic freedom, tenure, sexism, merit, and other issues in relation to "getting ahead" in higher education. Two chapters discuss the hidden meanings of letters of recommendation. Discrimination in the academic profession is analyzed, as is the role of bureaucracy as a contributing factor to campus unrest. The author's rhetoric is backed up by sound scholarship that adds a serious note to much of what could be interpreted as a "put-down" of American higher education. Readers are advised not to be misled by this occasional irreverence.

520 McGee, Reece. *Academic Janus: The Private College and Its Faculty*. San Francisco: Jossey-Bass, 1971. 264 pages.

The author views the small private four-year college as a social and educational system that has become the hostage of the multiversity. He argues that judgments determining the course of the private liberal arts college are made elsewhere, and these colleges are not in a position of power to exercise self-determination about their futures. The author studied eleven high-quality liberal arts colleges in the United States, using the behavior of the academic labor market as a frame of reference. Chapters cover the social structure of the private liberal arts college, issues of work and mobility, the process of mobility, and institutional reputation and personal prestige. In conclusion, the author states that "a college must be comprehended as a social system, as a dynamic, shifting (although generally stable) balance of forces and counterforces, adjustments, and accommodations. . . . The second conclusion is that colleges are teaching institutions. . . . The third conclusion is that the most serious problems facing the colleges are financial and qualitative." The perceptive reader may conclude that not much has changed with private liberal arts colleges since the publication of this volume.

521 Mandell, Richard D. *The Professor Game*. New York: Doubleday, 1977. 274 pages.

This discursive, and occasionally digressive, volume attempts to portray academia and academics through some interesting illustrations of the hazards of academic work. Writing during a time when the climate in colleges and universities moved from growth and prosperity to retrenchment and economic retreat, the author mixes history, data, and personal vignettes to create a portrait that both informs and instructs. Each chapter is illustrated with a fictional sketch of a professor in an imagined academic context. The author suggests that these illustrations could be considered an appendix to the book and need not be read in order to understand the more substantive chapters they interrupt. This book is an intriguing example of fact and fiction about higher education, reflecting the era of colleges and universities as labor-intensive declining industries.

★**522** Mathis, B. Claude. "Faculty Development." In Harold E. Mitzel (ed.), *Encyclopedia of Educational Research*. (5th ed.) New York: Free Press, 1982, pp. 646-655.

This is the first time faculty development was given a primary listing in the *Encyclopedia of Educational Research*. The article presents an overview of theory and research about faculty development in colleges and universities through 1981. Projects are identified and described, and the conclusions of major studies are discussed. The central focus of faculty development efforts has been the improvement of teaching. The author traces the emergence of faculty development during the 1970s as one response to the retrenchment then taking place in most institutions, and the dominance of an adult development model for conceptualizing changes in faculty roles through time is discussed. A reference list of seventy-four items is included. Students of faculty development seeking a balanced review of the literature that accompanied the growing of interest in faculty development during the past two decades will find the article a useful summary.

523 Mehrotra, Chandra M. N. (ed.). *Teaching and Aging*. New Directions for Teaching and Learning, no. 19. San Francisco: Jossey-Bass, 1984. 102 pages.

As the aging society begins to express itself in the work force of the United States, there is concern about the effects of an older professoriate on the productivity of higher education. Many faculty intend to continue working as long as their health permits, and the removal of the legal ban for continuation after age seventy seems imminent. This book addresses the issue of an aging faculty for colleges and universities. Chapter One discusses the implications of an aging faculty for the quality of institutions and careers. Chapter Two examines developmental theory as a means of understanding and facilitating vitality for college faculty. Chapter Three deals with developmental needs of an aging college faculty, while Chapter Four examines age and teaching. Chapter Five presents the results of interviews with faculty and administrators who are approaching retirement. Chapter Six discusses the program at Eckerd College designed to utilize the experience of high-achieving older professionals, while Chapter Seven reviews institutional concerns and faculty needs. Those who engage in long-range planning in higher education will find this book an essential reference for examining the issue of age and vitality.

524 Nelsen, William C. "Faculty Development: Prospects and Potential for the 1980s." *Liberal Education,* 1979, *65,* 141–149.

From direct examination of a number of faculty development programs and a review of the literature, Nelsen makes the following recommendations: (1) Programs need to be flexible and sensitive to the individual needs of the faculty; (2) individual approaches should be balanced by attention to the activities and goals of the institution; (3) colleges and universities need to expand their definitions of scholarship in order to acknowledge the wide range of intellectual contributions of faculty on their campuses; (4) personnel management techniques for higher education must be improved; (5) faculty members need to become aware of the literature on student development and its application to the classroom; (6) the administration must be willing to take a leadership role in faculty development.

525 Nelsen, William C. *Renewal of the Teacher-Scholar.* Washington, D.C.: Association of American Colleges, 1981. 110 pages. (ED 215 602)

The Project on Faculty Development of the Association of American Colleges attempted to assess the impact of faculty development projects at twenty liberal arts colleges in the United States. The author was project director, and he has written about much that he learned in his visits and interviews. This publication is a companion to the report published by Nelsen and Siegel that presented details of individual projects at these twenty colleges. In this volume, the author reports on the interviews with faculty and administrators and presents many of the issues associated with the need for renewal programs in higher education. A brief annotated listing of resources is contained in the appendix. Together these reports should interest persons who wish to know more about faculty development in liberal arts colleges.

526 Nelsen, William C., and Siegel, Michael E. (eds.). *Effective Approaches to Faculty Development.* Washington, D.C.: Association of American Colleges, 1980. 149 pages.

This monograph reports on the Project on Faculty Development of the Association of American Colleges, which focused on evaluation of faculty renewal projects at twenty colleges. After an introductory chapter on faculty development by project directors Nelsen and Siegel, brief expository chapters present sample programs under the general classifications of professional development, instructional development, curriculum change, organizational development, and consortium approaches. A section of comments from participants is included. The final section of the monograph contains an assessment of effectiveness and future needs. The findings as presented by the project directors discuss the reasons for assessing some programs as more successful than others. Key factors that the project directors felt were involved in determining success are discussed.

527 "New Research on the Academic Professions." *Sociology of Education,* 1974, *47,* 1-169.

This issue of *Sociology of Education* contains articles about research on the academic professions. The theme is introduced by Charles Bidwell in a preface that discusses the purpose of the issue. This is followed by an article on the structure of the academic professions by Donald W. Light, Jr. Oliver Fulton and Martin Trow discuss research activity in American higher education. "Social-Psychological Accessibility and Faculty-Student Interaction

Beyond the Classroom" is the title of an article by Robert C. Wilson, Lynn Wood, and Jerry G. Gaff. Peter M. Blau discusses recruiting faculty and students, and Robert R. Hind, Sanford M. Dornbusch, and W. Richard Scott present a theory of evaluation for university faculty. Cornelis J. Lammers writes about "Localism, Cosmopolitanism, and Faculty Response." Rodney T. Hartnett and John Centra present a research note on situational versus institutional perspectives of the academic environment. Although this issue is over ten years old, much of the content is quite relevant today and well worth the time of those who are interested in research on professional issues.

528 Olswang, Steven G., and Lee, Barbara A. *Faculty Freedoms and Institutional Accountability.* ASHE-ERIC Higher Education Research Report no. 5. Washington, D.C.: Association for the Study of Higher Education, 1984. 77 pages. (ED 252 170)

Requirements for accountability are increasing at many colleges and universities in the United States. The academic freedom that has traditionally protected faculty from external controls may become eroded by requirements that place limitations on activities heretofore under the control of the individual faculty member. The authors review research on academic freedom and institutional responsibilities and accountability. They discuss the issues that define the present climate of accountability and conclude by offering recommendations designed to help institutions maintain some form of accountability and at the same time minimize the impact on faculty freedoms. A comprehensive reference list is included.

529 Rice, R. Eugene. *Faculty Lives: Vitality and Change.* Saint Paul, Minn.: Northwest Area Foundation, 1985. 80 pages. (ED 261 574)

This study of the Northwest Area Foundation's grants in faculty development for the years 1979 to 1984 contains information about the projects together with interpretive comments by the author, who served as the evaluation consultant for the foundation's initiative to support faculty vitality. Grants were made, for the most part, on a system-wide or consortium basis. The major portion of the monograph discusses methods for maintaining faculty vitality in times of retrenchment and decline. The author feels that new approaches to academic career development, and a reexamination of the academic career, are essential in order to meet the needs of faculty in the years ahead. The monograph provides fresh insights about human resource development and highlights efforts of a major foundation to provide meaningful support for faculty development.

530 Robinson, G. M., and Moulton, J. *Ethical Problems in Higher Education.* Englewood Cliffs, N.J.: Prentice-Hall, 1985. 98 pages.

Every area of higher education deals not only with facts but also with values. By way of showing that academia is not sheltered from moral problems, the authors discuss moral issues and illustrate them through dilemmas related to several topics: the institution, hiring and evaluation of faculty, research, and teaching. Issues are examined in light of the following ethical principles: fairness, maximizing benefits, universalization, and treating others as ends and not merely as means. Distinctions between ethical theories and scientific theories are also explored. The volume is appropriate for prospective and practicing college teachers and administrators concerned about the ethical dimensions of their profession.

531 Rosenzweig, Robert M., with Turlington, Barbara. *The Research Universities and Their Patrons.* Berkeley: University of California Press, 1982. 151 pages.

The Association of American Universities sponsored this report on the role of the research university. Research universities train most of the nation's new scientists and scholars as well as house that part of the basic research enterprise not directly sponsored by industry or government. In addition, these unique institutions educate undergraduates. The authors argue that the health of these universities is vital to the nation's economic well-being. Among the topics discussed are advanced graduate training, research libraries, the eroding research base, international and foreign area studies, and the climate for policymaking. Specific recommendations for government, industry, and the research universities themselves are included. Faculty development programs in research universities need to be aware of the unique environment in which they exist. This book charts that context.

★**532** Sanford, Nevitt (ed.). *The American College: A Psychological and Social Interpretation of the Higher Learning.* New York: Wiley, 1962. 1,084 pages.

Please see entry no. 310 for the annotation of this work.

533 Shils, Edward. *The Academic Ethic.* Chicago: University of Chicago Press, 1983. 104 pages.

This slim volume is the report of the Study Group of the International Council on the Future of the University. Participants in the study group, besides Edward Shils, included Jeanne Hersch, Torsten Husen, Thomas Nipperday, John Passmore, Gerd Roellecke, Bruce Smith, and Charles Townes. This international group addresses the traditional obligations that university teachers have to themselves and their students, reaffirming the ethical and moral attitudes that should guide the academic profession. Of particular interest are discussions of the academic ethic in relation to new patterns of dependence emerging in the governmentally dominated university, the bureaucratized university, and the research university. A chapter on the academic obligations of university teachers provides a refreshing reminder that the fundamental purpose of the university is education, and the role of the professor is anchored to that responsibility. Any professor who is confused about his or her role as an academician will find clear and articulate counsel here. The international perspective reminds us that universities in the Western world share a bond of ethics that is often ignored.

534 Shulman, Carol H. *Old Expectations, New Realities: The Academic Profession Revisited.* AAHE-ERIC Higher Education Research Report no. 2. Washington, D.C.: American Association for Higher Education, 1979. 51 pages. (ED 169 874)

In this monograph the author examines the socialization process in the academic profession. She compares the image of the professoriate that developed during the growth years of higher education with the realities of changing conditions apparent today, pointing out that the use of job mobility as a means of obtaining job satisfaction is rapidly disappearing. Reward systems are incongruent with the realities of academic life, but they do reflect the values of the contemporary academic model. Faculty autonomy is in decline. The need for more efficient management contributes to centralized decision making that depends less on faculty involvement. Many of the changes discussed by the author are accepted realities in higher education today.

535 Smith, Albert B. *Faculty Development and Evaluation in Higher Education.* AAHE-ERIC Higher Education Research Report no. 8. Washington, D.C.: American Association for Higher Education, 1976. 76 pages. (ED 132 891)

This report on the status of faculty development, as of 1976, conceptually links faculty evaluation and development. A valuable section of the monograph contains descriptions of four selected faculty development programs, one in a university, another for a college consortium, the third a statewide program, and the fourth in a regional consortium. Also included are descriptions of selected student and faculty evaluation programs. Linking evaluation and development, as this monograph does, contrasts with the literature of the mid 1980s, which tends to separate these processes. Nevertheless, the major premises undergirding programs of faculty development and evaluation are as relevant today as they were in the mid 1970s, and the author's overview of concepts, models, definitions, and research is inclusive. This monograph is useful for students of higher education who are interested in a competent overview of faculty development and faculty evaluation.

536 Toombs, William. "A Three-Dimensional View of Faculty Development." *Journal of Higher Education*, 1975, *46*, 701–717.

This article argues that faculty development should go beyond a focus on a single issue to address the major conceptual issues of the academic profession. The author discusses the dimensions of professional, curriculum, and institutional need that should be included in a faculty development plan. The relative importance of these three dimensions varies from one faculty member to another and from one college to another, as well as from one discipline to another. Nevertheless, all three are involved to some degree in all phases of professional development. In addition to these central dimensions, faculty development programs should recognize the needs of faculty at different career stages. Five different career stages are identified: preservice, new and inexperienced, new and experienced, established and experienced, and nonteaching academics.

537 Trow, Martin (ed.). *Teachers and Students: Aspects of American Higher Education*. New York: McGraw-Hill, 1975. 419 pages.

Sponsored by the Carnegie Commission on Higher Education, this volume of essays contains articles by members of the research group that designed and administered the commission's National Survey of Faculty and Student Opinion between 1968 and 1972, then the largest ever carried out in higher education. Chapter One, by Oliver Fulton and Martin Trow, presents some of the general findings of the survey. Chapter Two by the same authors discusses research activity in American higher education. Chapter Three by Stephen Steinberg is titled "Religious Involvement and Scholarly Productivity Among American Academics." Judy Roizen discusses the black student in higher education in Chapter Four. Chapter Five by Joseph Zelan presents data about undergraduate students in the field of sociology. Oliver Fulton discusses academic women in Chapter Six, and Chapter Seven by Saul D. Feldman points out some of the external constraints, such as marital status, that inhibit graduate and professional education. Chapter Eight, "The Impact of Peers on Student Orientation to College: A Contextual Analysis," by Ted K. Bradshaw, discusses the nature of college impact and student attitudes about college. Appendixes contain a technical report for the survey. This survey is a rich data set for charting changes in student and faculty opinion. Anyone interested in students, faculty, and their interactions in the context of a curriculum should be familiar with this volume.

538 Wergin, Jon F.; Mason, Elizabeth J.; and Munson, Paul J. "The Practice of Faculty Development: An Experience-Derived Model." *Journal of Higher Education,* 1976, *47,* 289-308.

The authors present a model based on examination of a faculty development program at a large urban university. They discuss the need for staff who can establish credibility and trust with faculty as an essential element of the consulting relationship. Faculty development is viewed as an evolving process that begins with low mutual knowledge and trust with the consultant as expert and, if successful, becomes collaborative as trust is established. Techniques for assessment, planning, intervention, and evaluation are described in relationship to the stages of the process.

539 Williams, George. *Some of My Best Friends Are Professors.* New York: Abelard-Schuman, 1958. 250 pages.

The content of this volume is a commentary by the author on his "long and (in general) dispassionate observation of the university world." His comments are organized into chapters covering the failure of the universities, the natural history of the professor, what universities fail to do, how badly can you teach, how to get into college, and schizophrenia among the departments. The last chapter presents a self-cure for the university. The writing is perceptive and the tone is often irreverent. There is something to irritate almost any reader, but the criticisms of academe and of academics are not without merit. One might conclude, after reading the book, that the ills of higher education could all be solved if the solutions were left to this author; nevertheless, the volume projects valuable attitudes about faculty, students, and higher education generally.

540 Wilson, Logan. *The Academic Man.* New York: Oxford University Press, 1942. 248 pages.

For forty-five years this sociological analysis of the occupational culture of the academic profession has survived, and it stands as an example of the sociologist examining the university as a social organization. The author covers such topics as status and role, recruitment, socialization, the career process, professional ethics, academic freedom, and rewards. One is reminded from reading large segments of the book that the more things change, the more they stay the same, although its frame of reference and sources of data are from a less complex era for higher education. Any student of higher education should read the book, if for no other reason than to establish a baseline for comparing the issues and problems of academic man at the beginning of the 1940s with the issues and problems of the academic person during the 1980s.

541 Wilson, Logan. *American Academics, Then and Now.* New York: Oxford University Press, 1979. 309 pages.

The author of *The Academic Man* returns in this volume to the theme he developed thirty-seven years earlier. He observes that much remains the same in higher education, although the issues have changed. The book deals with such topics as professional recruitment, students and apprentices, staff members, administrators, academic governance, status appraisal, professional status, economic status, academic profiles and social status, university prestige and competition, and individual prestige and competition. This is a comprehensive and authoritative survey of higher education, still relevant despite some dated data. Reading this book following the earlier volume establishes the continuity intended by the author.

542 Young, Robert E. "Faculty Development and the Concept of 'Profession.'" *Academe,* 1987, *73* (3), 12-14.

In this brief essay the author argues that "faculty are not given the autonomy in their instructional role that they have as scholars." The college faculty member, according to the author, is a person divided between professional obligations to a scholarly discipline and obligations as a teacher. Faculty development programs recognize this difference by focusing primarily on the teaching function and leaving research and service to be dealt with in other ways. The author makes the point that "faculty development . . . cannot focus just on teaching—or on research or on service . . . where development programs for teaching and research (and sometimes service) exist separately, they should be merged." The author's call for comprehensive efforts in faculty development that reflect the total professional role of faculty implies a more holistic view of career development for academics than is evident in many current programs.

543 Zanna, Mark P., and Darley, John M. (eds.). *The Compleat Academic: A Practical Guide for the Beginning Social Scientist.* Hillsdale, N.J.: Erlbaum, 1987. 225 pages.

These chapters take a practical approach to the opportunities and problems of everyday faculty life. They deal with the hiring process (the editors), controlling one's career (S. E. Taylor and J. Martin), departmental politics (G. R. Salancik), teaching (W. J. McKeachie), doing research and managing relationships with graduate students (the editors), research grants (R. A. Baron), writing for journals (D. J. Bem), and working in nonacademic settings (W. DeJong and L. Saxe). The volume was sponsored by the Society for the Study of Social Issues and written mostly by psychologists, but chapters address issues common to all academics, and much of the advice is applicable well beyond the first years that academics spend in their profession.

Career Development

544 American Association for Higher Education. "Faculty Career Development." *Current Issues in Higher Education,* *No. 2,* 1979, 1–39.

These articles are taken from papers presented at the annual meeting of the American Association for Higher Education. Everett Carll Ladd, Jr., writes about the work experience of American college professors, utilizing the research he did with Seymour Martin Lipset in 1977. Roger Baldwin outlines faculty career stages in his chapter on adult and career development. B. Claude Mathis deals with institutional intervention at critical career stages in his discussion of academic careers and adult development. Robert T. Blackburn concisely summarizes the factors that affect faculty productivity in his chapter on patterns and possibilities in academic careers. Barbara Lazarus and Martha Tolpin discuss career planning for junior faculty. Finally, Allan O. Pfnister, Jill Solder, and Nina Verroca outline contributions of growth contracts for career management.

545 American Association for Higher Education. *Expanding Faculty Options: Career Development Projects at Colleges and Universities.* Washington, D.C.: American Association for Higher Education, 1981. 107 pages. (ED 217 780)

This monograph reports results of a project carried out by AAHE career development programs for faculty in colleges and universities in the United States. The principal staff work was done by Roger Baldwin, and he contributed the major portion of the content. Russell Edgerton discusses the need to rethink faculty careers, Janet Hagberg comments on the process of reexamining faculty careers, Thomas Maher writes about designing new roles in academe, and Lewis Brakeman discusses new roles in off-campus settings. The list of institutions reporting projects is impressive, and the approaches to career planning are varied.

546 Baldwin, Roger G., and Blackburn, Robert T. "The Academic Career as a Developmental Process." *Journal of Higher Education*, 1981, *52*, 598–614.

The authors present a study of 106 male college faculty members from twelve liberal arts colleges in the Midwest. Based on a 75 percent response rate to a brief questionnaire and on an extensive personal interview, faculty characteristics at five stages of an academic career are reported. These stages are (1) assistant professors in the first three years of full-time college teaching; (2) assistant professors with more than three years of college teaching experience; (3) associate professors; (4) full professors more than five years from retirement; and (5) full professors within five years of formal retirement. While some characteristics remain stable across the five stages, other are principally associated with a particular stage. The authors conclude that greater attention must be paid to the characteristics and concerns of each phase of the academic career. Institutions are advised to maintain the flexibility needed for professional growth. This developmental research underscores the need to view professional development for faculty as unique for each individual faculty member.

547 Blackburn, Robert T.; Behymer, Charles E.; and Hall, David E. "Research Note: Correlates of Faculty Publications." *Sociology of Education*, 1978, *51*, 132–141.

Using a national sample of faculty in four-year colleges and universities, the authors set out to discover correlates of scholarly productivity. The major dependent variables were rate of article production, total articles published, and books published. The large size of the sample (1,216 at four-year colleges and 7,484 at universities) permits comparisons by discipline. The authors found that distinct patterns differentiate the humanities from the sciences as well as four-year colleges from graduate institutions. Predictors of individual productivity include whether or not the faculty member starts producing early, receives his or her degree when young, and engages regularly in publishing. High producers can be identified early in their career. Work environment appears to be a critical factor in productivity: "A favorable one distinctively cultivates scholarship." The data point to the importance of positive interaction between personal motivation and a supportive environment to stimulate scholarly productivity in faculty careers.

548 Blackburn, Robert T.; Chapman, David; and Cameron, Susan. "Cloning in Academe: Mentorship and Academic Careers." *Research in Higher Education*, 1981, *15*, 315-327.

Mentoring has been recognized as an important aspect of career development in several fields. This article focuses on mentoring from the perspective of the mentor: issues of the gender of the person being mentored, the satisfaction of the mentor, scholar productivity, and patterns of influence exerted by mentors in assisting the other person in the relationship during his or her search for employment. The sixty-two mentors studied overwhelmingly nominated as their most successful protege persons whose careers were like their own, and women mentors nominated as successful proteges over twice as many females as men did. The questions raised by the study suggest further research, especially regarding attributes that contribute to success in mentoring and institutional policies that support successful mentoring relationships.

549 Boring, Edwin C. *Psychologist at Large*. New York: Basic Books, 1961. 371 pages.

The author was a central figure in the development of experimental psychology as a specialization in the academic profession. This book constitutes his autobiography and contains selected essays written over the span of his career. It is the source of a wealth of information about an academic career that began in Titchener's psychological laboratory at Cornell and ended as an emeritus professor at Harvard. His autobiographical commentary provides a fascinating view of an academic career during the first half of this century. Autobiography and biography have rarely been used for examining academic careers. This book provides primary data useful for anyone interested in charting the elusive ecology of academic careers.

★550 Bowen, Howard R., and Schuster, Jack H. *American Professors: A National Resource Imperiled.* New York: Oxford University Press, 1986. 322 pages.

The authors believe that the future for faculties of colleges and universities in the United States should be a matter of national concern. If higher education is not able to attract talent needed to maintain the creativity traditionally associated with professional careers, the authors feel that the nation will be the loser. The book is divided into four major sections. Part One discusses attributes of faculty and the tasks faculty perform. Part Two deals with professors at work, the economic status of the profession, and the conditions of work. Part Three discusses the academic labor market, projections of institutional needs for new faculty appointments, and the flow of exceptional talent to higher education. Part Four presents an agenda for maintaining the vitality of the profession and recommendations for the recruitment and retention of faculty. The authors argue that academic talent will be lost to other careers unless higher education can maintain its attraction as a workplace for the best and brightest in society. This book is among the few basic works about higher education that should be read by anyone interested in an academic career. The impact of its message will continue to be felt throughout the next decade.

551 Brookes, Michael C. T., and German, Katherine L. *Meeting the Challenges: Developing Faculty Careers.* ASHE-ERIC Higher Education Research Report no. 3. Washington, D.C.: Association for the Study of Higher Education, 1983. 47 pages. (ED 232 516)

The authors set the stage for a consideration of faculty careers with an overview of the changes confronting higher education. They articulate a stage theory for faculty careers and discuss the changing role of faculty development in helping professionals accommodate to transitions taking place in the professoriate. Anyone studying faculty careers will find the bibliography valuable.

552 Cameron, Susan W., and Blackburn, Robert T. "Sponsorship and Academic Career Success." *Journal of Higher Education*, 1981, *52*, 369–377.

Questionnaires and selected personal interviews were used with 250 faculty members in English, psychology, and sociology departments in nine research universities in Michigan and Illinois. Four measures of career research success were used: (1) rate of publication, (2) grants received over a three-year period, (3) rate of collaboration, and (4) professional association and publishing network involvement. The authors report that several indicators of sponsorship (financial support, publication support, assistance in first-job placement, work on sponsored research, dissertation funding, and early collaboration with senior faculty) correlated significantly with at least one of the outcome measures (publication rate, grants received, collaboration, and involvement in a professional network).

553 Cartter, Allan M. *Ph.D's and the Academic Labor Market.* New York: McGraw-Hill, 1976. 260 pages.

The author of this informative volume was among the first to warn about the overproduction of Ph.D.'s and the inability of traditional markets to absorb the excess. The book begins with two chapters discussing projections of academic demand and describing a context for the examination of academic labor markets since World War II. Chapters Four and Five present enrollment projections for higher education and their implications for institutional size. Chapters Six and Seven examine the issue of estimating the demand for faculty and discuss the use of several models for determining the balance between institutional requirements and available Ph.D's. Chapter Eight discusses the changing composition of faculty in higher education, and Chapter Nine deals with the first job placements of new doctorates. The final chapter presents an overview of conditions in the academic labor market. Although we now project a shortage of faculty for the next century, Cartter's analysis set the stage for examining the academic labor market in terms that placed institutions of higher education within a market economy. The chapters are well worth reading for what they say about academic careers.

554 Chism, Nancy Van Note (ed.). *Institutional Responsibilities and Responses in the Employment and Education of Teaching Assistants: Readings from a National Conference.* Columbus: Center for Teaching Excellence, Ohio State University, 1987. 374 pages.

Based on presentations and workshops at a national conference, this volume is the largest collection to date of materials related to university teaching assistants. It reflects programs inaugurated on many campuses in recent years to prepare and supervise teaching assistants in their work with undergraduates and to provide special support for international teaching assistants. Sections of the volume cover conditions of teaching assistant employment, research reports on teaching assistant development, descriptions of programs aimed at enhancing the work of teaching assistants, and issues peculiar to international teaching assistants.

555 Clark, Burton R. *The Academic Life: Small Worlds, Different Worlds.* Princeton, N.J.: The Carnegie Foundation for the Advancement of Teaching, 1987. 360 pages.

This volume reports a national field study of American academics completed with support from The Carnegie Foundation for the Advancement of Teaching. The author examines the teaching and research functions of faculty in colleges and universities and presents a comprehensive, contemporary assessment of the diverse settings in which faculty practice their profession. The focus is on the many hierarchies found in the general system we call higher education, and the author's insightful analysis of these interlocking systems provides a dimension for analysis of academics and their work not generally found in similar studies. Part One of the book treats the general topic of the foundation of the academic profession. Part Two includes a discussion of the dimensions of academic professionalism, and Part Three deals with the logic of the profession. Academics are again becoming important subjects for study by social scientists. This book takes its place among studies that will provide a guiding framework for our understanding of the academic life.

556 Crane, Diana M. "Social Class Origin and Academic Success: The Influence of Two Stratification Systems on Academic Careers." *Sociology of Education,* 1969, *42,* 1–17.

The relationship between social class origin and academic success was studied in samples of university professors and recent recipients of doctorates in the arts and sciences and selected professional fields. Doctoral recipients classified as lower class are less likely to have received degrees from top-ranking universities and are also less likely, when compared to middle-class recipients, to obtain positions in major universities. Public universities are shown to have a democratizing effect on these relationships when compared with private universities. The author concludes that attendance at a major private university for the doctorate increases the likelihood of obtaining an academic position in a major university.

557 Eble, Kenneth E., and The Conference on Career Development. *Career Development of Effective College Teacher.* Washington, D.C.: American Association of University Professors, 1971. 135 pages.

This report from the Project to Improve College Teaching, sponsored by the American Association of University Professors and the Assocation of American Colleges, presents the results of conferences on career development held throughout the United States during 1970 and 1971, together with data from responses to questionnaires sent to faculty members at 142 institutions. The monograph calls attention to the neglect of teaching in colleges and universities and to the lack of preparation for teaching in graduate schools. The Project to Improve College Teaching stimulated a much-needed reexamination of the teaching function in colleges and universities, especially in undergraduate studies. This report provides a wealth of suggestions and ideas for faculty development efforts that aim at the improvement of teaching in higher education. A bibliography containing many worthwhile sources of information about college teaching is included.

558 Erskine, John. *My Life as a Teacher*. Philadelphia: Lippincott, 1948. 249 pages.

This memoir of significant phases in the career of a distinguished humanist covers his years at Amherst and Columbia, beginning in 1903 with his appointment to the faculty at Amherst. The book provides many insights into the workings of higher education during the first quarter of this century. The author participated in establishing the American Army University at Beaune in France during World War I, and he gives a personal account of this almost forgotten episode related to the development of higher education in the United States. Anyone interested in the history of colleges and universities, and in the evolution of faculty careers, will find this personal account both intriguing and stimulating.

559 Finkelstein, Martin J. "The Status of Academic Women: An Assessment of Five Competing Explanations." *Review of Higher Education*, 1984, 7, 223–246.

The author asks, "How can we account for the differential status of women professors vis-a-vis majority males?" He indicates that two general explanations have been advanced: overt discrimination based on sex or differential performance, with women not as productive as males. From these explanations, the author derives and assesses five reasons to account for status differences. The two theses—overt discrimination and performance differences—are then discussed in relation to research that supports or denies each argument. The author concludes that the status of women faculty in academe is the "resultant of a constellation of forces." The discussion of these forces, and the comprehensive reference list, make this article an important source of information for those interested in the careers of women in academe.

560 Furniss, W. Todd. "New Opportunities for Faculty Members." *Educational Record*, 1981, 62, 8–15.

"Barriers that prevent faculty members from considering career alternatives and testing them must be removed," according to the author. Pressures on faculty, and changes in the academic labor market, make the traditional career in higher education more difficult for faculty members today. An analysis of faculty careers in terms of stages of adult development suggests that both prewar and boom-time careers offered much more to support transitions between career stages than do the careers of today. Older faculty members may find it especially difficult to adjust to new kinds of students and to other changing work conditions. The author argues that it is in the best interest of institutions to provide support programs for faculty who may wish to change emphases in their careers within the same institution or who may want to seek employment outside higher education. A number of useful examples are offered along with recommendations for faculty, institutions, professional associations, and other agencies responsible for the quality of careers in higher education.

561 Furniss, W. Todd. *Reshaping Faculty Careers.* Washington, D.C.: American Council on Education, 1981. 171 pages. (ED 208 769)

The decade of the 1970s witnessed changes in higher education that stimulated parallel changes in faculty careers. Many teacher/ scholars found themselves in careers that differed significantly from those they had originally embraced. The first part of the book describes today's faculty members in terms of their expectations and needs. This is followed by case studies of faculty at different career stages. Institutional approaches to solving the difficulties of faculty are discussed as well as solutions applied by faculty members themselves. The final section of the book describes some actions that may serve to remediate career problems for faculty. Recommendations are enumerated. This book should be read by all academicians contemplating alternatives to a career in progress.

562 Furniss, W. Todd. *The Self-Reliant Academic.* Washington, D.C.: American Council on Education, 1984. 79 pages. (ED 242 241)

The author states in his preface that this book is for and about the successful academic. It presents a pragmatic course of action for faculty who need to help themselves in order to continue being successful in their careers. Chapter One discusses the almost complete dependence of faculty members on their institutions for help in meeting their professional needs. Chapter Two deals with the reluctance of successful faculty to become knowledgeable about sources of help outside their immediate work environment. Chapter Three makes the case for the establishment of a self-help organization for faculty. Part Two of the book discusses difficulties in moving toward self-reliance in managing one's own career. The author presents a refreshing and useful consideration of the faculty career that goes beyond stages and problems. His implicit conclusion is that we all need to become managers of our own careers rather than remain dependent on others to do it for us.

563 Geiger, Roger L. *To Advance Knowledge: The Growth of American Research Universities, 1900-1940.* New York: Oxford University Press, 1986. 325 pages.

In 1900, the Association of American Universities brought together a group of institutions with a common dedication to graduate education and research. These institutions and their faculties have since that time been regarded by the academic community as models for what is now called the research university. The author shows how research became a major function of higher education. He discusses the role of faculty and the careers of faculty members in research universities, as well as the conflict between teaching and research commitments. The author has written a thorough and lucid history of the development of research universities in the United States, and he sheds light on many issues associated with faculty careers in these unique institutions. The book is recommended for anyone interested in faculty careers in research universities.

564 Graham, Patricia A. "Women in Academe." *Science,* 1970, *169,* 1284-1290.

The author reviews the history of women as students in institutions of higher education. She indicates that "by 1920 women constituted 47 percent of the undergraduates in the country and were receiving roughly 15 percent of the Ph.D.'s. In 1930 the proportion remained

about the same. Today [1970] women constitute only 40 percent of
the undergraduate student body and receive about 10 percent of the
doctorates." The author reviews studies that attempt to find
possible explanations for the underrepresentation of women as both
students and faculty. Measures are suggested to support a more
equitable distribution of women in higher education. One wonders
what the author would write today, almost twenty years beyond the
dismal statistics presented in this article. While much of the growth
in some programs can be attributed to increased enrollments of
women and affirmative action has stimulated the hiring of more
women as faculty, many of the problems and issues presented in this
article remain with us today.

565 Herman, Joyce; McArt, Effa; and Belle, Lawrence. "New
      Beginnings: A Study of Faculty Career Changers." *Improv-
      ing College and University Teaching*, 1983, *31*, 53–60.

The authors report results of a study completed at the Rochester
Institute of Technology during 1981. Twenty-five faculty members
completed a questionnaire and participated in an interview in
which career change issues were examined. Fifteen of the participants had made career changes and ten had not. The authors
conclude that institutions should make career development an
institutionally sanctioned and supported activity. These faculty
members felt that increased off-campus opportunities for career
expansion and exploration should be available. Recommendations
to increase on-campus opportunities for expanding choices, to
extend competencies, and to cross disciplines as part of career
change options in higher education are discussed. The article
provides a useful discussion of reasons why the career changers in
the sample decided to alter the directions of their careers.

566 Livesey, Herbert. *The Professors*. New York: Charterhouse,
      1975. 336 pages.

This book resulted from interviews that the author had with a
number of professors during the academic year 1972–73. The first
chapter is a general discussion of academic careers, followed by
chapters presenting vignettes of each of the subjects. Each chapter

is written in a discursive style that holds the attention of the reader. Many of the subjects are identified by name, although several request anonymity and are given pseudonyms. A reader expecting to find biographies in the usual sense will be disappointed. The author covers a wide range of facts and observations about academic careers in reporting the interviews, and the values and attitudes of the subjects are clearly articulated. The writing is informal and chatty, and no overriding polemic is noticeable in the author's style. The book is of interest to those who wonder what professors were like in 1973 and how they viewed their careers at that particular point in time.

567 Mathis, B. Claude. "The Teaching Scholar—An Old Model in a New Context." *Journal of Teacher Education,* 1978, *29* (3), 9-13.

The new three R's for higher education are reexamination, retrenchment, and retirement. The author discusses their relationship to academic careers and faculty development. He presents a list of factors that should be included in faculty development programs if they are to be responsive to the needs of all faculty members. These include opportunities to talk about educational roles as well as about research and scholarship, in-service experiences for new faculty, opportunities for midcareer faculty to maintain their vitality, and invitations for older faculty to end their careers gracefully. He also discusses the issue of evaluation of faculty, the meaning of professionalism in academic careers, and the necessity for active participation in faculty governance activities. A list of suggested references for faculty development is included. Readers interested in an approach to faculty development that recognizes the many roles faculty have in their academic careers will find this article useful.

568 Menges, Robert J. "Career-Span Faculty Development." *College Teaching,* 1985, *33,* 181-184.

The author suggests that a program of faculty development must aid faculty in making decisions about their careers and should support them during the transitions and changes caused by these decisions. Professional development should be viewed in a broad perspective that takes into account life-span variables. The author urges that boundaries be softened so that faculty might cross them more easily and more frequently within institutions and in and out of academia. The article includes a useful schema for career decisions that matches decisions and possible options for faculty.

569 Palmer, David C., and Patton, Carl V. "Mid-Career Change Options in Academe: Experience and Possibilities." *Journal of Higher Education*, 1981, *52*, 378-398.

This article addresses the issue of midcareer change for academics who consider leaving their academic jobs and the prospects these persons have for managing such a change successfully. The authors discuss academic staffing problems in colleges and universities and the limitations of early retirement options as one solution to promoting turnover in the professoriate. They ask, "Is midcareer change the better option?" The authors conclude that more information should be obtained about employment patterns of Ph.D.'s outside of academe. Personal assessment of opportunities should be available to academics who seek placement outside of academe. The authors point out that "experience with midcareer change programs demonstrates they have potential to increase institutional flexibility during periods of declining student enrollments and shrinking budgets." Midcareer change options are a frequently ignored aspect of faculty development programs. This article provides a sound review of pertinent issues and research.

570 Shils, Edward. "The University: A Backward Glance." *American Scholar*, 1982, *51*, 163-179.

This personal reflection was written from the perspective of a fifty-year career in higher education by a distinguished contributor to the literature on the sociology of higher education. He traces many changes in both faculty and students over that time as seen in his own university context, namely, the University of Chicago, where he has been for the major portion of his career. The interplay between research and teaching, departmental loyalty and commitment to the university, and changes in the educational process are discussed in an informal but informing fashion, and the style of writing makes the piece a delight to read.

571 Waggaman, John S. *Faculty Recruitment, Retention, and Fair Employment: Obligations and Opportunities.* ASHE-ERIC Higher Education Research Report no. 2. Washington, D.C.: Association for the Study of Higher Education, 1983. 65 pages. (ED 227 806)

In the foreword, the author points out that the "conditions facing faculty employment make it both a buyer's and a seller's market. . . . In either case, it is now more important than ever for higher education institutions to carefully review their policies and practices concerning faculty employment." This monograph presents a frame of reference for this review by presenting worthwhile information about the availability of positions and vacancies, preliminary planning, organizing recruitment, screening applicants' files, visits to the campus and making final decisions, and retaining faculty. The author emphasizes the role of the department head in making the recruitment process work fairly. The constraints of frugality, open competitiveness for survival, and the fear of unfair evaluations are offered as factors that can stifle openness and equity in the recruitment process. The management of initial entry into the academic profession, and subsequent changes in employment, represent a neglected aspect of faculty development that is explored in this monograph.

Development as Teachers

572 Andrews, John D. W. "Growth of a Teacher." *Journal of Higher Education,* 1978, *49*, 136–150.

The author was both psychotherapist and teaching consultant for the teacher whose growth is described in this article. The teacher moved from a low-structure style of student-centered teaching to one of much greater structure and finally to a more balanced synthesis of the two styles. Relationships between these changes in teaching style and the issues being explored simultaneously in therapy are pointed out. They illustrate "how teaching, and the effort to improve it, involve the whole person."

573 Andrews, John D. W. (ed.). *Strengthening the Teaching Assistant Faculty*. New Directions for Teaching and Learning, no. 22. San Francisco: Jossey-Bass, 1985. 92 pages.

Several aspects of teaching assistant development programs are explored by contributors to this volume. Chapters address the TA's own point of view (John Boehrer and Ellen Sarkisian), issues of institutional structure (Richard Smock and Robert Menges), the teaching assistant's relationship with the professor (Tom Wilson and Jeanie Stearns), and the special situation of foreign TAs (Michele Fischer). Chapters about specific instructional innovations that are appropriate for teaching assistants and about the process of launching a TA development program are contributed by the editor. This volume is a practical and helpful guide for institutions seeking to serve the TA component of their undergraduate teaching force more effectively.

574 Arrowsmith, William. "The Future of Teaching." In Calvin B. T. Lee (ed.), *Improving College Teaching*. Washington, D.C.: American Council on Education, 1967, pp. 57-71.

"I think we have reached the point where slogans like 'scholar-teacher' merely darken counsel," says this classicist. He contends that the functions of research and teaching are reconcilable only at the expense of teaching. By teaching he means "the molding of men rather than the production of knowledge," and he elaborates the meaning of this "high teaching" and suggests how colleges and universities might reform themselves. "At present the universities are as uncongenial to teaching as the Mojave Desert to a clutch of Druid priests. If you want to restore a Druid priesthood, you cannot do it by offering prizes for Druid-of-the-year. If you want Druids, you must grow forests. There is no other way of setting about it."

575 Bennis, Warren. *The Leaning Ivory Tower.* San Francisco: Jossey-Bass, 1973. 154 pages.

Please see entry no. 613 for the annotation of this work.

576 Bess, James L. (ed.). *Motivating Professors to Teach Effectively.* New Directions for Teaching and Learning, no. 10. San Francisco: Jossey-Bass, 1982. 113 pages.

The authors of these chapters examine how faculty members can be motivated to teach more effectively despite reduced mobility in the academic labor market. Chapter One (Wilbert J. McKeachie) deals with the issue of rewards for teaching, and Chapter Two (Mihaly Csikzentmihalyi) discusses effective teaching and intrinsic motivation. Chapter Three (Edward L. Deci and Richard M. Ryan) carries the discussion of intrinsic motivation beyond the individual faculty member and presents some possibilities and obstacles by examining institutional organizations. Chapter Four (Benjamin Schneider and Mary D. Zalesny) approaches faculty motivation through a consideration of human needs. Chapter Five (Walter R. Nord) and Chapter Six (Richard T. Mowday) present some thoughts about the external control of motivation through contingency reinforcement and expectancy theory. Chapters Seven (Douglas T. Hall and Max H. Bayerman) and Eight (Cortlandt Cammann) examine faculty motivation to teach from the perspective of organizational structure, and Chapters Nine (Robert T. Blackburn) and Ten (James L. Bess) summarize the messages of the text and present some research notes about faculty career phases. Each chapter has a relevant list of references. This issue in the *New Directions Series* would be useful reading for anyone interested in the unique problems of faculty motivation and effective teaching as these issues are expressed in the environment of today's colleges and universities.

577 Christ, Frank L., and Coda-Messerle, Margaret (eds.). *Staff Development for Learning Support Systems.* New Directions for College Learning Assistance, no. 4. San Francisco: Jossey-Bass, 1981. 108 pages.

Professionals working with special students in learning centers deserve special training, termed "self-professionalization," and should experience "transdisciplinary" graduate work. Among training approaches for them are on-campus workshops, institutes bringing people together across campuses, and internships. Specialized activities include programs on tutoring, training for student paraprofessionals, and cultivation of trustees' commitment to learning assistance efforts.

578 Cowley, W. H. *Presidents, Professors, and Trustees: The Evolution of American Academic Government.* Edited by Donald T. Williams, Jr. San Francisco: Jossey-Bass, 1980. 260 pages.

Please see entry no. 624 for the annotation of this work.

579 Dressel, Paul L., and Thompson, Mary M. *A Degree for College Teachers: The Doctor of Arts.* Berkeley, Calif.: Carnegie Council on Policy Studies in Education, 1977. 332 pages.

The Doctor of Arts has been presented as an alternative to the Ph.D. for college teachers. The authors recount the history of the Doctor of Arts and its use in more than twenty institutions. At a time when nearly 500 degrees had been awarded and more than 700 candidates were enrolled, they recount exemplary practices in these doctoral programs and make suggestions for strengthening them. Major areas of concern deal with course work in the candidate's subject field and a culminating "thesis, dissertation research, or evaluation effort." Overall, the authors are optimistic about the degree and conclude that the Doctor of Arts "is very much alive and growing." In retrospect, we can see that this was a promise left unfulfilled.

580 Fink, L. Dee. *The First Year of College Teaching*. New Directions for Teaching and Learning, no. 17. San Francisco: Jossey-Bass, 1984. 119 pages.

Nearly a hundred first-year college teachers were surveyed, and thirty of them were also interviewed and observed in their classrooms during their first year of teaching. Students and colleagues provided additional data. They reported very heavy workloads (much teaching and other kinds of productivity were expected), and they desired more institutional support, including feedback about their work. The research is exploratory and descriptively rich, but without much theory to guide it. Nevertheless, the study's findings are worth pondering by administrators and leaders of professional development programs.

581 Gaff, Jerry G. *Toward Faculty Renewal: Advances in Faculty, Instructional, and Organizational Development*. San Francisco: Jossey-Bass, 1975. 244 pages.

Please see entry no. 505 for the annotation of this work.

582 Gaff, Jerry G. (ed.). *Institutional Renewal Through the Improvement of Teaching*. New Directions for Higher Education, no. 24. San Francisco: Jossey-Bass, 1978. 102 pages.

Institutional renewal was a central focus for faculty development during the decade of the 1970s. This collection of articles reflects that concern and represents the major thrust of the faculty development literature during that period. Advice about faculty development programs in large universities, moderate-sized universities, and small colleges is offered from the experiences of specific teaching improvement projects. The editor is an author for four of the chapters, on the subjects of involvement of students in faculty development, overcoming faculty resistance, evaluating outcomes, and the future of faculty development.

583 Gappa, Judith M. *Part-Time Faculty: Higher Education at a Crossroads.* ASHE-ERIC Higher Education Research Report no. 3. Washington, D.C.: Association for the Study of Higher Education, 1984. 112 pages. (ED 284 513)

The increasing use of part-time faculty in colleges and universities calls attention to questions about the relationship of part-time faculty to the quality of academic programs. The author presents a national profile of these academic professionals. Constraints on institutional policies and practices are discussed, and a survey of these policies and practices is reported. One chapter is devoted to part-time faculty in two-year colleges. The author concludes with recommendations designed to preserve the positive aspects of using part-time faculty while minimizing their treatment as second-class citizens in higher education.

★584 The Group for Human Development in Higher Education. *Faculty Development in a Time of Retrenchment.* New Rochelle, N.Y.: *Change* Magazine, 1974. 90 pages.

The authors of this report represent different academic backgrounds in their views of higher education. Their common concern is with the development of all who participate in the community of higher education. Professional development of faculty members as teachers is highlighted. The authors discuss the need for faculty development, reforms advocated to improve the quality of teaching, the training of future professors, the evaluation of teaching, and midcareer transitions for faculty. The report ends with seven recommendations and a discussion of their implementations. This important document has maintained its relevance regarding the major issues and problems in faculty development. It continues to be a basic resource for anyone seeking an introduction to contemporary thinking about faculty development.

★585 Keller, George. *Academic Strategy: The Management Revolution in American Higher Education.* Baltimore, Md.: Johns Hopkins University Press, 1983. 221 pages.

Please see entry no. 631 for the annotation of this work.

586 Mauksch, Hans O., and Howery, Carla B. "Social Change for Teaching: The Case of One Disciplinary Association." *Teaching Sociology,* 1986, *14,* 73-82.

This paper reports the American Sociological Association's Projects on Teaching Undergraduate Sociology, one of the most ambitious discipline-sponsored teaching development programs. Major project activities occurred from about 1974 through 1981 under financial support from several sources. The paper describes varied activities conducted by a small staff and numerous volunteers, activities directed toward three goals: to create a climate in the association that would increase the recognition and worthiness of teaching; to develop, collect, and distribute materials and resources; and to develop workshops, departmental visitations, presentations, conferences, and consultations. The association followed the good sociological principle that to change teaching requires changing the culture of teaching. The report is significant both for its description of activities and for its analysis of those activities as "planned approaches to social change."

587 Munro, William B. "Report of the Committee on College and University Teaching." *Bulletin of the American Association of University Professors,* 1933, *19* (2), 1-122.

With support from The Carnegie Foundation and the Carnegie Corporation, the AAUP set out to determine attitudes of its 12,000 members regarding the chief problems of college teaching and their solutions. "With no intent to disparage research studies of the educationist type" (an apparent allusion to the "abominable questionnaire"), the association chose to employ a field director to gather information by visiting more than seventy institutions, usually meeting with members of the local chapter as well as with others. The committee makes few strong recommendations, often opting for institutional or departmental autonomy in dealing with problems—for example, "the committee believes that the working out of criteria by which effective teaching can be recognized is a matter for local self-determination." The problems identified are significant and well delineated; many of them still exist in pretty much the same form as in the twenties and thirties.

588 Rieff, Philip. *Fellow Teachers.* New York: Dell Publishing, 1972. 243 pages.

Please see entry no. 422 for the annotation of this work.

589 Veblen, Thorstein. *The Higher Learning in America.* New York: B. W. Huebsch, 1918. 286 pages.

Please see entry no. 645 for the annotation of this work.

Development as Individuals

590 Bess, James L. "Patterns of Satisfaction of Organizational Prerequisites and Personal Needs in University Academic Departments." *Sociology of Education,* 1973, *46,* 99–114.

The author studied thirty academic departments in fifteen universities to determine the differences between those of high and low quality. The 1966 Cartter Report provided the criterion measure of quality. Parson's concept of "functional prerequisites" and Maslow's "needs hierarchy" provided a basis for comparing departments of high and low quality. Six of eight organizational prerequisite scales discriminated between high- and low-quality departments. No relationship to Maslow's concept of needs was found. These findings raise questions about the relationship between organizational achievements and personal satisfaction in academic departments. The widespread use of the Cartter ratings is also criticized.

591 Blackburn, Robert T.; Horowitz, Stephen M.; Edington, Dee W.; and Klos, Donald M. "University Faculty and Administrator Responses to Job Strains." *Research in Higher Education,* 1986, *25,* 31–41.

Quality of life indicators (job satisfaction, life satisfaction, and health) were assessed by fifty-seven nonacademic, high-level administrators and forty-six faculty in humanities and natural science departments at the University of Michigan. Results tend to confirm the authors' theoretical model that hypothesizes that job-related stress and job-related strain (independent variables) are mediated by three types of intervening variables (personal, social support, and fitness) in their influence on the dependent variables of health, job strain, and life satisfaction. Thus, persons who have higher self-esteem, higher self-responsibility for health, higher tolerance for overload, higher social support, and more positive health habits and indexes of fitness should have a higher quality of life, given the same level of job stress and strain.

592 Boice, Robert. "Reexamination of Traditional Emphases in Faculty Development." *Research in Higher Education,* 1984, *21,* 195-209.

The author shows how personal and scholarly renewal can be combined usefully. He worked with sixteen faculty who were self-described blocked writers and who also indicated significant dissatisfaction with their teaching. His clinical approach involved a program of contingency management to increase writing productivity and a program of video-mediated self-observation to enhance classroom teaching. The latter focused on such behaviors as appropriate gesturing, vocal relaxation, and classroom explanations. Both treatments had a positive impact on those participating.

593 Boring, Edwin C. *Psychologist at Large.* New York: Basic Books, 1961. 371 pages.

Please see entry no. 549 for the annotation of this work.

594 Braskamp, Larry A.; Fowler, Deborah L.; and Ory, John C. "Faculty Development and Achievement: A Faculty's View." *Review of Higher Education,* 1984, *7,* 205-222.

Please see entry no. 484 for the annotation of this work.

595 Brown, David G., and Hanger, William S. "Pragmatics of Faculty Self-Development." *Educational Record,* 1975, *56,* 201-206.

The authors suggest that academic leaders support the self-development of faculty, and they urge the design of institutional policies that erase barriers to self-growth, the introduction of rewards that stimulate self-development activities, the creation of departmental options for faculty activity, and the dissemination of information about growth opportunities. The authors caution that faculty differ in their needs, abilities, attitudes, and personal circumstances, thus requiring flexibility in self-development policies. Programs of faculty self-development should be designed and implemented by faculty for faculty. Faculty members must perceive a personal gain before they will become motivated to become involved in a development program. Program planning suggestions for faculty and administrators are included.

596 Cares, Robert C., and Blackburn, Robert T. "Faculty Self-Actualization: Factors Affecting Career Success." *Research in Higher Education,* 1978, *9,* 123-136.

Data from the American Council on Education/Carnegie Commission national survey are employed to study relationships between satisfaction and faculty growth and development, environmental factors, and career success. The sample consisted of 7,534 faculty at the rank of assistant professor or above teaching in arts and sciences departments. Trust was the only personal factor consistently related to success and satisfaction. The best predictor of the outcome variables (career success and satisfaction) was control of the environment. The authors point out that, while no causal links were found, the study suggests a strong relationship between factors that can more easily be changed (environmental rather than personal) and feelings about success and achievement. The things faculty can change are perceived as more positively affecting faculty growth and development. Implications for administrative management systems are discussed.

597 Cytrynbaum, Solomon; Lee, Susan; and Wadner, David. "Faculty Development Through the Life Course." *Journal of Instructional Development,* 1982, *5,* 11-22.

Adult development theory is applied to five faculty groups: (1) age-thirty transition faculty, (2) dual-career couple faculty, (3) midlife faculty, (4) late-entry faculty, and (5) senior retiring faculty. The authors discuss each faculty group in terms of development tasks, potentialities, and critical transitions. Specific issues and dilemmas are identified and gender differences are discussed. Appropriate personal, organizational, and policy interventions are proposed. The article contains a comprehensive summary of theory relating to age-specific states of adult development. An extensive, but selective, bibliography is included. This article would be helpful to anyone who needs an introduction to how adult development theory applies to faculty development.

598 Furniss, W. Todd. *The Self-Reliant Academic.* Washington, D.C.: American Council on Education, 1984. 79 pages. (ED 242 241)

Please see entry no. 562 for the annotation of this work.

599 Hodgkinson, Harold L. "Adult Development: Implications for Faculty and Administrators." *Educational Record,* 1974, *55,* 263–274.

Research-based stages of adult development are used to discuss the phases of career development for faculty and administrators. These stages include (1) leaving the family, (2) getting into the adult world, (3) the age-thirty transition, (4) settling down, (5) "middlescence" between the ages of thirty-nine and forty-three, (6) restabilization, and (7) hanging on or "toughing it out." The mental and emotional problems of faculty and administrators at each stage are discussed, and adult development theory is recommended as a diagnostic tool for understanding the personal growth of individual faculty members. The author warns against premature classification.

600 Lawrence, John S. *The Electronic Scholar: A Guide to Academic Microcomputing.* Norwood, N.J.: Ablex, 1984. 181 pages.

This book is a readable, critical guide, illustrating how scholarly work can be served by technology. It includes chapters on word processing, cooperative writing and revision, electronic filing, electronic information searching, electronic publishing, and such "helping" chores as statistical analysis and course record keeping. The information is not limited to any particular microcomputer brand or operating system.

601 McGrath, Earl J. "Fifty Years in Higher Education: Personal Influences on My Professional Development." *Journal of Higher Education*, 1980, *51*, 76-93.

This autobiographical essay illuminates influences on the professional life of one of the major contributors to the study of higher education in the United States. The author traces the forces and persons who shaped a career that culminated in appointment as U.S. Commissioner of Education from 1949 to 1953, and he recounts his directorship of two institutes of higher education (at Teachers College, Columbia University, and at Temple University). McGrath's interest in general education is linked to his graduate student days at the University of Chicago during the tenure of Hutchins. The twelve years spent as director of the Institute of Higher Education at Teachers College, initiated with a grant from the Carnegie Corporation, were exciting times for higher education in America. Many publications of the institute are still important resources. Anyone interested in the history of higher education since World War II will find this personal account of value.

602 Martin, Warren Bryan. "Faculty Development as Human Development." *Liberal Education*, 1975, *61*, 187-196.

Most faculty development programs are faulted by Martin because they do not have adequate theory, they do not employ a comprehensive approach, and they do not show a deep intention. He argues that faculty development has its roots in a theory of human development and calls for a renewal of the basic tasks and responsibilities that faculty have traditionally called their own. Faculty need to prepare to work with new students in new places, to become acquainted with alternative modes of teaching and learning, to be more sophisticated in their knowledge about the institutions in which they work, and to become more aware of competencies their students should acquire as a result of the classes they offer. The author suggests that faculty often hesitate to become involved in faculty development programs because they perceive the programs to be more valuable to their institutions than to themselves. Faculty must be convinced that they will gain personally from participation in faculty development programs before they will commit themselves to these activities.

603 Melendez, Winfred A., and de Guzman, Rafael M. *Burnout: The New Academic Disease.* ASHE-ERIC Higher Education Research Report no. 9. Washington, D.C.: Association for the Study of Higher Education, 1983. 103 pages. (ED 242 255)

Stress in the academic workplace has become a problem of increasing concern. These authors discuss the stresses that occur in an academic setting and relate stress to physical and psychological indicators of the condition known as burnout. A model emphasizing interactions between the person and the environment is articulated, along with other models, to account for the effects of stress in the workplace. Remedial steps are presented, and the authors include a comprehensive bibliography on stress and burnout that would be helpful for any student of this phenomenon.

604 Menges, Robert J. "Intellectual Journeys in Faculty Development." In S. C. Inglis and S. Scholl (eds.), *To Improve the Academy.* Orinda, Calif.: John F. Kennedy University, 1982, pp. 47–90. (ED 216 591)

Professionals in the field of faculty development were asked "to describe and reflect on processes of their intellectual work, in effect to share their intellectual journeys." Ron Smith describes his mathematician's journey "from applying the pure to purifying the applied." Robert Young reflects on influences from students and colleagues on the questions he has attempted to answer through research with faculty and the research methods he has used. Rita Weathersby elaborates the "transformative gestalt" as a powerful way of seeing situations differently and more adequately while teaching and doing research in organizational studies. John Andrews discusses "fertile incongruities" that have made his faculty development and therapeutic work productive. These papers provide an unusual illustration of the interaction of personal dispositions with scholarly pursuits.

605 Near, Janet P., and Sorcinelli, Mary Deane. "Work and Life Away from Work: Predictors of Faculty Satisfaction." *Research in Higher Education,* 1986, *25,* 377-392.

The authors studied 112 faculty members at a large Midwestern university, exploring relationships between work and life away from work. Included in the sample were faculty members from the humanities, the natural sciences, and two professional schools. Data from lengthy interviews and questionnaires indicated a relationship between work satisfaction and life outside of work. Also, work as well as nonwork conditions were related to satisfactions in life away from work. The authors conclude that "unlike the general population, academics appear to experience a high degree of 'spillover' between work and life away from work."

606 Newble, D. I., and Cannon, R. A. "How to Make a Presentation at a Scientific Meeting." *Medical Teacher,* 1984, *6,* 6-10.

Especially for new faculty members, giving a paper is an anxiety-producing experience. This practical discussion covers planning the paper, visual aids, drafting and rehearsal, abstracts and proceedings, handling questions from the audience, and the ever-present problem of timing. Novice and experienced presenters, as well as countless listeners, would benefit if this advice were heeded.

607 Pfaffenberger, Bryan. *The Scholar's Personal Computing Handbook: A Practical Guide.* Boston: Little, Brown, 1986. 359 pages.

Electronic scholarship "involves preserving basic scholarly standards and values in the new world the computer is making for us." This book is a reader-friendly guide to that world. Chapters cover personal computer use for writing, managing information, communications, and crunching numbers. Appendixes discuss data bases that are available on-line, including bibliographic services. The book also contains a glossary.

608 Schrecker, Ellen W. *No Ivory Tower: McCarthyism and the Universities.* New York: Oxford University Press, 1986. 437 pages.

In the 1950s Senator McCarthy's investigations of Communist connections produced a climate of fear in institutions of higher education as has no other event in this century. The effects of McCarthyism on universities in the United States are presented by the author in a thoroughly documented investigation that shows the vulnerability of higher education to a zeitgeist that seized the public conscience with traumatic and devastating results. The book demonstrates that faculty are no more the creatures of logic than anyone else when thrust into value-laden situations buttressed by pressures to conform. Those interested in academic freedom and individual rights should read this book to learn of an interval in the history of higher education in the United States when the academic profession failed to reflect the principles it vigorously defends today. Younger faculty whose careers were started after the McCarthy era will find here a reason to examine their academic obligations from a broader perspective than individual self-interest.

609 Seldin, Peter (ed.). *Coping with Faculty Stress.* New Directions for Teaching and Learning, no. 29. San Francisco: Jossey-Bass, 1987. 98 pages.

In nine chapters these authors discuss a wide range of issues relating to academic stress for faculty. The issues cover academic burnout, research on academic stress, institutional strategies for dealing with stress, part-time faculty and stress, balancing career demands and personal living, short-term coping techniques, long-term stress management, preventive stress management for institutions, and an example of how one university has approached the problem of academic stress. The authors are experts in the areas in which they write, and since recent surveys report that faculty members feel that academic careers are becoming more stressful, the choice of topics is both timely and informative. This volume directs attention to what can become a serious problem in higher education unless institutions become more aware of the loss of productivity that stress produces.

Organizational Development

610 Austin, Ann E., and Gamson, Zelda F. *Academic Workplace: New Demands, Heightened Tensions.* ASHE-ERIC Higher Education Research Report no. 10. Washington: D.C.: Association for the Study of Higher Education, 1983. 122 pages. (ED 243 347)

The nature of academic work has changed dramatically during the last three decades. The authors conclude that external pressures have so altered work environments for faculty in colleges and universities that academic careers may begin to lose their attractiveness as desirable options for professional employment. They discuss the social structure of colleges and universities and the work experience of faculty and administrators. While intrinsic aspects of academic work seem to remain stable, the extrinsic aspects show signs of decline in satisfaction as reported by faculty. More work for the same pay appears to be an increasing problem. The authors recommend that leaders of colleges and universities spend more time articulating the purposes of their institutions. The decision-making structures of institutions need to become more collaborative and less hierarchical and programs for career planning for all employees should be implemented. A comprehensive reference list of items through 1983 is included.

611 Barzun, Jacques. *The American University: How It Runs, Where It Is Going.* New York: Harper & Row, 1968. 319 pages.

Please see entry no. 381 for the annotation of this work.

612 Becker, William H. "A Collegial Approach to Faculty Development." *Liberal Education,* 1981, *67,* 19–35.

This article presents a view of faculty development that is personalistic in its emphasis on the rights and dignity of the faculty member. After an opening section defending the centrality of faculty development, the author presents his collegial approach that emphasizes introducing "new incentives toward collegial concern for teaching into structures and relations that already exist on campus, and by creating new structures designed to foster this concern." A section on implementing collegial faculty development is devoted to a list of two dozen activities and strategies to be used in faculty development programs. While the article draws on the work of others, the concept of collegial faculty development is a practical approach accompanied by specific suggestions for implementation.

613 Bennis, Warren. *The Leaning Ivory Tower.* San Francisco: Jossey-Bass, 1973. 154 pages.

This slim volume presents the author's personal reflections on several years in higher education that bridged the end of the 1960s and the beginning of the 1970s. Bennis was actively involved in the upheavals marking the more public part of this paradigm shift in higher education, and his account of presidential searches by three major universities presents a vivid, action-oriented narrative of higher education searching for stability in a time of turbulence. The major portion of the book discusses the turmoil at the State University of New York, Buffalo, during the author's time there as an administrator. Through the examples of the presidential searches, the organizational life of the university is exposed and examined. Much that the public takes for granted about the process of decision making in higher education is challenged by the author's personal and illuminating account of his participation in decision processes at the highest levels of administration.

614 Bess, James L. "Patterns of Satisfaction of Organizational Prerequisites and Personal Needs in University Academic Departments." *Sociology of Education,* 1973, *46,* 99–114.

Please see entry no. 590 for the annotation of this work.

615 Bess, James L. (ed.). *Motivating Professors to Teach Effectively*. New Directions for Teaching and Learning, no. 10. San Francisco: Jossey-Bass, 1982. 113 pages.

Please see entry no. 576 for the annotation of this work.

616 Bess, James L. *University Organization, A Matrix Analysis of the Professions*. New York: Human Science Press, 1982. 334 pages.

The organization of work for faculty in higher education has become more complex as institutions themselves have grown. This book is based on responses to a questionnaire sent to 2,400 faculty at six universities dealing with the three major faculty roles of research, teaching, and service. The faculty members indicated, on a scale of 1 to 5, whether they would "like to do the activity because of its intrinsic reward." According to the author, results "revealed patterns of faculty preferences for tasks that suggested new and more efficient organizational forms for academic work." A redesign of university organization would reduce many of the interpersonal dilemmas to which faculty are now exposed because of discontinuities between faculty roles and the organizational setting in which those roles are expressed. Other chapters deal with the academic profession and with theoretical perspectives on the division of labor in higher education.

617 Blau, Peter M. *The Organization of Academic Work*. New York: Wiley, 1973. 310 pages.

Data from a sample of 115 American colleges and universities is used to study the relationship between bureaucracy and scholarship, based on an analysis of the influences of administrative structures in higher education on academic work. Differences among American colleges and universities are analyzed at length. Internal differentiation receives particular attention. The author concludes that the size of academic institutions is not related to bureaucratic growth in the same way that size and bureaucracy are linked in other organizations. Large academic institutions tend to be less bureaucratic in most respects than smaller ones. The content of the book is not easily digested at one sitting, and the reader should have a basic knowledge of statistics to follow the analysis. Nevertheless, understanding the conclusions of the study is worth the effort. The book has much to offer students of higher education in particular, and students of organizational structure in general. Also, those who are interested in the use of sophisticated methodology to investigate problems in higher education will find the book to be a creative model.

618 Bok, Derek. *Beyond the Ivory Tower: Social Responsibilities of the Modern University.* Cambridge, Mass.: Harvard University Press, 1982. 318 pages.

Please see entry no. 387 for the annotation of this work.

619 Bowen, Howard R. *The Costs of Higher Education: How Much Do Colleges and Universities Spend Per Student and How Much Should They Spend?* San Francisco: Jossey-Bass, 1980. 287 pages.

This report, issued by the Carnegie Council on Policy Studies in Higher Education, examines factors that determine the cost of higher education in the United States. While the book is essentially a financial report and economic analysis of higher education, chapters on faculty and staff compensation, institutional affluence and resource allocation, institutional affluence and educational outcomes, and the author's discussion of efficiency and equity have implications for curriculum and faculty development. The author points out that decisions about educational programs, curriculum, and faculty research systems are ultimately controlled by economic considerations. The author raises many basic questions about higher education as a growth industry. The basic question that helps to organize the report has to do with how much colleges and universities spend per student and with how much they should spend.

620 Chait, Richard P., and Ford, Andrew T. *Beyond Traditional Tenure: A Guide to Sound Policies and Practices.* San Francisco: Jossey-Bass, 1982. 291 pages.

In their preface the authors indicate that "academic tenure is too prevalent a practice to disappear and too consequential a policy to disregard." The book looks beyond traditional tenure arrangements to a survey, analysis, and evaluation of other options. These options by selected colleges and universities include modifications of traditional policy, alternative policy, and changes in which tenure arrangements are more consistent with personnel policies in general. Case studies illustrate new approaches in force at some institutions. The first chapter discusses the concept of tenure and how the context of higher education supports it. Several subsequent chapters examine institutions without tenure, modification of probationary periods, and the "up-or-out" rule. Tenure quotas are discussed in Chapter Six, and this is followed by four chapters dealing with characteristics of a sound tenure policy, evaluation of faculty who have tenure, and rewards and sanctions in applying tenure policy. The final chapter discusses auditing and improving personnel systems for faculty. As more institutions evaluate their tenure policies in light of changing regulations about retirement, institutions should find ways to preserve the best from what tenure has to offer and to overcome the negative aspects of traditional policies. This book provides an informed context for considering these changes.

621 Chronister, Jay I., and Kepple, Thomas R., Jr. *Incentive Early Retirement Programs for Faculty: Innovative Responses to a Changing Environment.* ASHE-ERIC Higher Education Report no. 1. Washington, D.C.: Association for the Study of Higher Education, 1987. 83 pages. (ED 283 478)

Interest in options to encourage early retirement emerged in the 1970s from institutional responses to steady-state enrollments and inflationary cost escalation. This monograph presents both an overview and an assessment of the arrangement "between an employer and an employee that provides a tangible inducement or reward for early retirement." The authors provide pertinent concepts and definitions, discuss the feasibility of establishing an early retirement program, and review institutional experiences with such programs. The final section of the monograph is devoted to conclusions and recommendations. The authors point out that properly structured early retirement programs can have dramatic effects on the staffing patterns of individual institutions. They caution, however, that these programs need to be planned with federal regulations in mind and with the best interest of the faculty as a goal to be achieved.

622 Clark, Burton R. "Organizational Adaptation to Professionals." In Howard M. Vollmer and Donald L. Mills (eds.), *Professionalization*. Englewood Cliffs, N.J.: Prentice-Hall, 1966, pp. 282-290.

The author points out that the organizational structure of higher education is molded by the needs of professional staff members, as opposed to traditional bureaucracies in which the professional staff is expected to adapt to requirements of the organization. His analysis of this phenomenon in higher education leads to a conclusion that universities are structured more in the form of a "federated professionalism" accompanied by "segmentation" and "individualism." The diverse value systems of faculty and their influence on the organization are discussed together with the role of faculty authority. The entrepreneurial activity of faculty and the increasing importance of expertness have moved power in the university organization to individual professors and away from the faculty as a whole. As a consequence, bureaucratic influence within the organization grows. This analysis is presented in a somewhat obscure fashion that owes more to the discipline of sociology than to the rhetoric of the layman, but the content is useful and interesting for understanding the role of the professional, especially the faculty member, in the organization of the university.

623 Clark, Burton R. *The Higher Education System: Academic Organization in Cross-National Perspectives.* Berkeley: University of California Press, 1983. 315 pages.

This book grew out of the author's interest in the analysis of national systems of higher education. His purpose was "to improve the state of the art by detailing systematically how higher education is organized and governed." Part One presents the elements of organization and discusses such topics as the discipline, the academic profession, the divisions of the several academic systems, academic beliefs, levels of authority, and the academic system as an authority system. Part Two covers integration and change. Part Three presents normative theory in which such issues as basic values, conflict and accommodation, the division of power, and the uniqueness of higher education are discussed. The central theme is the deriving of an approach permitting analysis and comparison of national systems of higher education. The content goes far beyond a simple explicative treatment, and the reader will need some background in social theory and the theory of organizations to appreciate the complexity of the topic. The journey through the book is worth the effort for anyone seeking more than heuristic insights about the organization of higher education from an international perspective.

624 Cowley, W. H. *Presidents, Professors, and Trustees: The Evolution of American Academic Government.* Edited by Donald T. Williams, Jr. San Francisco: Jossey-Bass, 1980. 260 pages.

In an attempt to help presidents, professors, and trustees better understand their roles and responsibilities in governing colleges and universities, the author develops the theme of shared governance. He views the roles of professors, presidents, and trustees as interactive. Several of the chapters are devoted to correcting myths about governance. In one chapter, he attacks the myth of faculty as disenfranchised and powerless employees. This book was completed by the editor after the death of the author, who was David Jacks Professor of Higher Education at Stanford. The editor has adhered closely to the outline of the book as it existed at the author's death in 1978, and references are limited to publications in higher education ending with that date. The book is an insightful and interesting excursion into the complex world of power and governance in higher education.

★**625** Davis, Robert H. "A Behavioral Change Model with Implications for Faculty Development." *Higher Education,* 1979, *8,* 123-140.

Please see entry no. 158 for the annotation of this work.

626 Eble, Kenneth E., and McKeachie, Wilbert J. *Improving Undergraduate Education Through Faculty Development: An Analysis of Effective Programs and Practices.* San Francisco: Jossey-Bass, 1985. 248 pages.

Please see entry no. 162 for the annotation of this work.

627 Floyd, Carol. *Faculty Participation in Decision Making: Necessity or Luxury?* ASHE-ERIC Higher Education Report no. 8. Washington, D.C.: Association for the Study of Higher Education, 1985. 103 pages. (ED 267 694)

While faculty participation in institutional decision making is generally accepted as desirable, no one best way has been found for this process to be most effective. The author presents a rationale for faculty participation in decision making and discusses the types of participation found in institutions today. She analyzes participation by function, such as participation in curriculum design and budgeting. Participation at the system and state levels is discussed, and a brief concluding analysis is offered. The monograph ends with recommendations for increasing faculty satisfaction with participation. An agenda for research and an extensive reference list are included.

628 Geiger, Roger L. *To Advance Knowledge: The Growth of American Research Universities, 1900-1940.* New York: Oxford University Press, 1986. 325 pages.

Please see entry no. 563 for the annotation of this work.

629 Gilley, J. Wade; Fulmer, Kenneth A.; and Reithlingshoefer, Sally J. *Searching for Academic Excellence.* New York: Macmillan, 1986. 210 pages.

This volume presents portraits of twenty colleges and universities and their leaders. Each institution has a story of success during times of national crisis for higher education. The strategies, priorities, programs, and ideas associated with their successes are discussed, and characteristics common to at least three-fourths of the twenty institutions are presented. This casebook on academic excellence has omitted some deserving institutions, and the authors have not attempted to engage in any kind of rankings of success. Insights offered by the book are interesting and provocative, and the relationship between success and leadership is clarified by including vignettes of the educational leaders in these institutions.

630 Hook, Sidney. *Academic Freedom and Academic Anarchy.* New York: Cowles, 1970. 269 pages.

Please see entry no. 283 for the annotation of this work.

★**631** Keller, George. *Academic Strategy: The Management Revolution in American Higher Education.* Baltimore, Md.: John Hopkins University Press, 1983. 221 pages.

The author addresses the resistance of colleges and universities to the use of modern management and planning techniques for controlling changes forced on higher education during the last decade. Declining enrollments, increasing costs, and shifts in academic priorities call for colleges and universities to introduce the latest planning and management strategies for their own survival. The book could be viewed as a beginning blueprint for the "corporation" of higher education. Much that it offers for today's college administrator is useful. Although this book does not deal directly with academic careers, it has enormous implications for the roles and activities of faculty. Implementing what the book advocates would signal changes in some elements of academic career patterns, changes that may be resisted by many faculty members.

632 Kerr, Clark, and Gade, Marian L. *The Many Lives of Academic Presidents: Time, Place and Character.* Washington, D.C.: Association of Governing Boards of Universities and Colleges, 1986. 260 pages.

This collection of quotations, vignettes, and first-person accounts provides a narrative description of the academic presidency. The material is derived from 800 interviews used for an earlier study. The pressures and rewards for academic presidents are clearly articulated by the authors, who draw on their own experiences to illuminate many of the interview comments. The role of the president in relationship to faculty is explored, and the ascendancy of the provost and/or academic vice-president in speaking for the faculty is discussed. While the book does not concern itself with faculty development directly, it places the academic presidency in a context that needs to be understood by faculty.

633 Lindquist, Jack. "Social Learning and Problem-Solving Strategies for Improving Academic Performance." In W. R. Kirschling (ed.), *Evaluating Faculty Performance and Vitality.* New Directions for Institutional Research, no. 20. San Francisco: Jossey-Bass, 1978, pp. 17–30.

Please see entry no. 186 for the annotation of this work.

634 Martin, Warren Bryan. *A College of Character: Renewing the Purpose and Content of College Education.* San Francisco: Jossey-Bass, 1982. 215 pages.

Please see entry no. 413 for the annotation of this work.

635 Mortimer, Kenneth P.; Bagshaw, Marque; and Masland, Andrew T. *Flexibility in Academic Staffing: Effective Policies and Practices.* ASHE-ERIC Higher Education Report no. 1. Washington, D.C.: Association for the Study of Higher Education, 1985. 108 pages. (ED 260 675)

The uncertain environments in which colleges and universities have been operating during the past decade, together with a scarcity of resources, have led higher education to implement management strategies unlike those previously used. Flexibility in academic staffing is one such strategy for managing the effects of change. The authors present a critique of research on the issues involved in flexible staffing. They discuss faculty flow models and the reallocation and reduction strategies used by colleges and universities to control resources. Their recommendations include how to develop an appropriate and comprehensive strategy, managing productive links between personnel policies and fiscal policies, and the exercise of managerial prerogatives in a way that reinforces the explicit values of the institution.

636 Near, Janet P., and Sorcinelli, Mary Deane. "Work and Life Away from Work: Predictors of Faculty Satisfaction." *Research in Higher Education*, 1986, *25*, 377-392.

Please see entry no. 605 for the annotation of this work.

637 Nisbet, Robert. *The Degradation of the Academic Dogma: The University in America, 1945-1970.* New York: Basic Books, 1971. 257 pages.

The author, a distinguished sociologist, accuses the American university of having betrayed itself by opening its doors to academic entrepreneurs whose goal is the profitable sale of knowledge rather than the pursuit of knowledge for its own sake. In Part One the author describes the academic dogma that governed academic communities until World War II. In the second part, he presents a description and analysis of changes that have taken place in universities since World War II. Part Three concludes the book with some proposals for revitalizing the university if it is to continue its tradition as a "setting for the discovery and critical examination of ideas, for the dispassionate and objective study of nature, society, and man, the whole undergirded by the functions of teaching and scholarship." Any student of higher education who feels uncomfortable with the present state of the academic dogma in higher education, but who is in doubt about how the present came to be, will profit from this book.

638 O'Connell, Colman. "College Policies Off-Target in Fostering Faculty Development." *Journal of Higher Education*, 1983, *54*, 662–675.

Please see entry no. 199 for the annotation of this work.

639 Parsons, Talcott, and Platt, Gerald M. *The American University*. Cambridge, Mass.: Harvard University Press, 1973. 463 pages.

Please see entry no. 420 for the annotation of this work.

★**640** Patton, Carl V. *Academia in Transition: Mid-Career Change or Early Retirement*. Cambridge, Mass.: Abt Books, 1979. 212 pages.

Midcareer changes and early retirement options for faculty have become popular with colleges and universities looking for ways to control costs and contain programs. In this sensible discussion, the author presents much evidence and discusses many options for early retirement and midcareer programs. Both human costs and institutional costs are analyzed, and cost-effective alternatives are presented. The book concludes with a discussion of policy implications of such efforts. An evaluation of early retirement schemes is given, and considerations are outlined for institutions considering early retirement and career change options.

641 Rosenzweig, Robert M., with Turlington, Barbara. *The Research Universities and Their Patrons*. Berkeley: University of California Press, 1982. 151 pages.

Please see entry no. 531 for the annotation of this work.

642 Shils, Edward. "The University: A Backward Glance." *American Scholar*, 1982, *51*, 163–179.

Please see entry no. 570 for the annotation of this work.

643 Simerly, Robert. "Ways to View Faculty Development." *Educational Technology*, 1977, *17* (2), 47–49.

This author organizes major faculty development approaches in a hierarchy from those that have the least impact on the organization to those that have the greatest impact. Faculty development practices identified by the author, in the order of their increasing effectiveness, are (1) a "hands-off" attitude, (2) a program of introduction and initiation, (3) career development, (4) curriculum reform, (5) an overall concept that attempts to integrate the individual and the organization, and (6) institutionalizing faculty development as an organizational goal.

644 Tuckman, Howard P. *Publication, Teaching, and the Academic Reward Structure*. Lexington, Mass.: Heath, 1976. 122 pages.

According to Tuckman, "the purpose of this book is to explore the nature of the reward structure at American universities. This involves an analysis of the nature of the marketplace for academic labor and an empirical investigation of the reward structure in several of the different disciplines found at the modern university." In Chapter One, the author provides information about changes in the academic reward structure. A review of the literature is offered in Chapter Two. A conceptual model representing interrelationships between the process of salary determination and reward structure is the theme of Chapter Three, and issues involved in how the reward structure functions are discussed in Chapters Four and Five. Chapter Six examines publications and academic rewards, Chapter Seven discusses faculty time allocations, and Chapter Eight presents the conclusions of an empirical study of selected academic departments. Readers seeking a better understanding of the academic reward structure will find this volume an appropriate source of useful information.

645 Veblen, Thorstein. *The Higher Learning in America*. New York: B. W. Huebsch, 1918. 286 pages.

This book was written at a time of increasing involvement by businessmen in the boards controlling universities. Their management philosophy was beginning to be felt in the decisions influencing the operations of these institutions. With reference to the University of Chicago, where he was a member of the faculty, the author discusses governing boards, the academic administration, academic prestige, academic personnel, science and the scientist, and vocational training. The author observes, in his summary, that "business principles take effect in academic affairs most simply, obviously and avowably in the way of a businesslike administration of the scholastic routine; where they lead immediately to a bureaucratic organization and a system of scholastic accountancy." These words have a familiar ring today as the management revolution in higher education takes hold and accountability becomes a driving force for determining the division of labor for the many tasks of the university. While this essay may appear to have only historic interest for the reader, it deserves to be considered in the context of today's issues.

646 Wolff, Robert Paul. *The Ideal of the University*. Boston: Beacon Press, 1969. 161 pages.

Please see entry no. 435 for the annotation of this work.

647 Yuker, Harold E. *Faculty Workload: Research, Theory, and Interpretation*. ASHE-ERIC Higher Education Research Report no. 10. Washington, D.C.: Association for the Study of Higher Education, 1984. 111 pages. (ED 259 691)

Determining workload for faculty has been a subject of much debate in higher education, and this monograph brings up-to-date earlier summaries of information. It presents the problems of defining workload and of getting and using data from institutional and faculty reports. These problems include developing workload formulas and the difficulties of determining time devoted to the many categories of work of faculty members. Including instructional activities and research, scholarship, and creative activities together with advising, consulting, institutional service, public service, and professional activities in the assessment of workload presents special problems. The author includes recommendations relating to the study of workloads and the validity of data used to estimate faculty workloads.

6

Periodicals and Reference Tools on Teaching Learning, Curriculum, and Faculty Development

Resources listed below take us beyond the items annotated in previous chapters. They include periodicals, bibliographic indexes, bibliographic data bases, and separately published bibliographies. These items can provide the breadth, depth, and currency of knowledge essential for advancing both research and practice.

Periodicals

The following list includes major American and British periodicals that give primary or substantial attention to the topics of this key resources volume. Although many more publications deal with higher education, the items on this list are most likely to cover teaching, learning, curriculum, and faculty development. For an annotated list of journals on two-year colleges, see the companion volume, *Key Resources on Community Colleges* (1986, no. 650). For further information about these periodicals, including publisher, place and dates of publication, and a brief description of contents, see *The Standard Periodicals Directory* (1987) or *Ulrich's International Periodicals Directory* (1987).

AAHE Bulletin
Academe

Adult Education (London)
Adult Education (Washington)
Adult Leadership
American Educational Research Journal
American Journal of Education (formerly *School Review*)
American Journal of Pharmaceutical Education
American Journal of Physics
American Mathematical Monthly
American Scholar
Anthropology and Education
ASHE-ERIC Higher Education Reports
Assessment in Higher Education
AV Communication Review
Behavioral Science Teacher
British Journal of Educational Psychology
Canadian Journal of Higher Education
Change: The Magazine of Higher Learning
Chronicle of Higher Education
College Composition and Communication
College English
College Mathematics Journal
College Student Journal
College Teaching (formerly *Improving College and University Teaching*)
Communication Education
Community-Junior College Research Quarterly
Convergence: International Journal of Adult Education
Counseling Psychology
Current Issues in Higher Education (through 1984)
Database
Database Searcher
Educational Psychologist
Educational Record
Educational Technology
Educational Technology Research and Development (formerly *Journal of Instructional Development*)
Educational Theory
Engineering Education

Exchange: The Organizational Behavior Teaching Journal
For the Learning of Mathematics
Harvard Educational Review
Higher Education
Higher Education: Handbook of Theory and Research
    (Annual)
Higher Education Research and Development
Higher Education Review
History Teacher
Innovative Higher Education (formerly *Alternative Higher*
    Education)
Instructional Science
Issues in Accounting Education
Journal of Adult Education
Journal of Aesthetic Education
Journal of Applied Behavioral Science
Journal of Architectural Education
Journal of Biological Education
Journal of Chemical Education
Journal of Classroom Interaction
Journal of College Science Teaching
Journal of College Student Development
Journal of College Student Psychotherapy
Journal of Cooperative Extension
Journal of Creative Behavior
Journal of Dental Education
Journal of Economic Education
Journal of Education for Library and Information Science
Journal of Education for Social Work
Journal of Education for Teaching (formerly *British Jour-*
    nal of Teacher Education)
Journal of Educational Computing Research
Journal of Educational Psychology
Journal of Educational Research
Journal of Experiential Learning and Simulation (through
    1981)
Journal of Experimental Education
Journal of General Education

Journal of Geography
Journal of Geography in Higher Education
Journal of Geological Education
Journal of Higher Education
Journal of Instructional Psychology
Journal of Legal Education
Journal of Medical Education
Journal of Moral Education
Journal of Negro Education
Journal of Nursing Education
Journal of Personnel Evaluation in Education
Journal of Psychiatric Education
Journal of Research in Music Education
Journal of Research in Science Teaching
Journal of Social Work Education
Journal of Staff, Program, and Organizational Development
Journal of Teacher Education
Journalism Educator
Junior College Journal
Learning and the Law
Liberal Education
Mathematics Teacher
Media and Methods
Medical Education
Medical Teacher
Metaphilosophy
New Directions for College Learning Assistance (through 1983)
New Directions for Community Colleges
New Directions for Continuing Education
New Directions for Experiential Learning (through 1983)
New Directions for Higher Education
New Directions for Program Evaluation
New Directions for Student Services
New Directions for Teaching and Learning
Nurse Educator
Personnel and Guidance Journal
Phi Delta Kappan

Physics Education
Physics Teacher
Religious Education
Research in Higher Education
Research in the Teaching of English
Review of Educational Research
Review of Higher Education
Review of Research in Education (Annual)
Science Education
Simulation & Games
Simulation/Gaming/News
Small Group Behavior
Social Education
Sociology of Education
Studies in Higher Education
Teachers College Record
Teaching and Teacher Education
Teaching History
Teaching of Psychology
Teaching Philosophy
Teaching Political Science
Teaching Professor, The
Teaching Sociology
Teaching Statistics
Theological Education
To Improve the Academy
Training and Development Journal

Indexes

Several helpful indexing resources cover the literature on teaching, learning, curriculum, and faculty development in higher education.

Higher Education Abstracts. A quarterly publication since 1965, *Higher Education Abstracts* monitors more than 300 journals. (Prior to 1984 this publication was called *College Student Personnel Abstracts.*) It lists books and monographs, covers research reports from higher education organizations, and includes conference papers read at meetings of higher education associations. Each issue carries at least 300 abstracts of 100 to 300 words.

Resources in Education. A monthly since 1966, *Resources in Education* lists items from the fugitive literature as they are added to the computerized data base of the Educational Resources Information Center (ERIC). This literature includes institutional and governmental reports, conference papers, aggregates of statistical information, instructional materials, and program and course descriptions. Much of this material is oriented more toward policy and practice than toward research. Citations are accompanied by abstracts of up to 200 words. These items are available on microfiche at approximately 750 libraries or by mail from a central reproduction service.

Current Index to Journals in Education. A monthly since 1969, *Current Index to Journals in Education* cites articles from more than 700 periodicals in the field of education and carries fifty-word annotations of each article. These periodicals are usually found in library collections. Articles are also available by mail from University Microfilms International.

Other Indexes. Several other indexes to the periodicals literature, all of them predating ERIC, can be helpful to scholars of higher education. They cover a broad range of topics, as defined by academic discipline boundaries, and include some items that do not appear in ERIC. The major indexes are *Education Index* (since 1929), *Psychological Abstracts* (since 1927), *Sociological Abstracts* (since 1953), and *Sociology of Education Abstracts* (since 1965).

Dissertation Abstracts International. Doctoral dissertations can be located through *Dissertation Abstracts International,* which has reproduced abstracts and indexed dissertations since 1938. That collection can also be searched by computer using the Dissertation Abstracts Online Service.

Data Bases

Bibliographic Data Bases. Many libraries offer on-line computerized searches of various education bibliographic data bases. Individuals who subscribe to on-line services can search these data bases at home or in their offices, using a personal computer.

Searches result in computer-generated lists of bibliographic citations, often with abstracts. The two ERIC data bases, *Resources in Education* and *Current Index to Journals in Education,* are fully computer searchable, back to their beginning dates of publication. More recent years of *Education Index, Psychological Abstracts,* and *Sociological Abstracts* can be searched by computer. *Resources in Education, Current Index to Journals in Education, Psychological Abstracts,* and *Education Index* can also be searched using the technology of compact disc, read only memory (CD-ROM).

Other Data Bases. In addition to these bibliographic data bases, other collections of data about higher education are stored on computer. Most of these are of greater relevance to administration and governance than to the research about students and faculty. James Ratcliff (1987) describes several of these data bases and notes that the monthly journal *Database* reviews electronic data bases in all fields. One of the most widely used data bases in postsecondary education has been the Higher Education General Information Survey (HEGIS), reorganized in 1987 as the Integrated Postsecondary Education System (IPEDS).

A data base more pertinent to teaching and faculty development is maintained by the Instructional Development and Effectiveness Assessment (IDEA) system at the Center for Faculty Evaluation and Development, Kansas State University. It includes student ratings for thousands of courses. Individual institutions and state or consortium groups have also established data bases that may aid researchers, although there is not yet a convenient, central means for accessing them.

Bibliographies

Many previously published bibliographies touch on teaching, learning, curriculum, and faculty development in postsecondary education. The most significant are annotated below. We also cross-reference items from other chapters that contain particularly comprehensive reference lists.

Some of the earliest essays and empirical investigations in higher education are listed and summarized by Klapper (1920, no. 31) and in Good's (1929, no. 22) eighty-page bibliography. The massive works by Eells (1957–1967, no. 654), totaling more than 7,000 entries, extend coverage through the mid 1960s. Parker and Parker (1980, no. 676) include more than 3,000 works from both the nineteenth and twentieth centuries. For highly selective current coverage, Halstead's (1987, no. 662) annual series is promising.

Recent bibliographies that are international in scope include Leitner (1978, no. 664), Teather (1979, no. 683), and Rochte (1980, no. 680). Several entries are specific to a particular discipline: Goldsmid and Goldsmid (1982, no. 657) on sociology, Fulkerson and Wise (1987, no. 655) on psychology, and Marshall and Durst (1987, no. 670) on English. The volume by Cohen, Palmer, and Zwemer (1986, no. 650) deals specifically with community colleges.

Unusually strong coverage of unpublished reports is provided by Parker and Parker (1980, no. 676). Quay (1980, no. 678) deals exclusively with anthologies, and the bibliographies by Leitner (1978, no. 664) and Quay (1985, no. 679) are devoted solely to listings of other bibliographies.

Many of these bibliographies go beyond lists of citations in order to summarize and sometimes to appraise entries. Most notably, Mayhew (1971, no. 672; 1972, no. 673) provides integrative essays as well as descriptive and often evaluative annotations about individual items. In the bibliographies by Eells (1957–1967, no. 654) and by Cohen, Palmer, and Zwemer (1986, no. 650), asterisks are used to designate entries of special interest.

References

Cohen, A. M.; Palmer, J. C.; and Zwemer, K. D. *Key Resources on Community Colleges: A Guide to the Field and Its Literature.* San Francisco: Jossey-Bass, 1986.

Ratcliff, J. "Telecommunications and Computer Databases." In J. J. Gardiner (ed.), *ASHE Handbook on Teaching and Instructional Resources.* Washington, D.C.: Association for the Study of Higher Education, 1987.

The Standard Periodicals Directory, 1987. (10th ed.) New York: Oxbridge Communications, 1987.

Ulrich's International Periodicals Directory, 1987–88. (26th ed.) New York: Bowker, 1987.

Bibliographies

648 Blackburn, Robert T.; Lawrence, Janet H.; Ross, Steven; Okoloko, Virginia Polk; Bieber, Jeffery P.; Meiland, Rosalie; and Street, Terry. *Faculty as a Key Resource: A Review of the Research Literature.* Ann Arbor: National Center for Research to Improve Postsecondary Teaching and Learning, University of Michigan, 1986. 46 pages.

Please see entry no. 481 for the annotation of this work.

649 Bligh, Donald A. *Methods and Techniques in Postsecondary Education.* Paris: UNESCO, 1980. 138 pages.

Please see entry no. 3 for the annotation of this work.

650 Cohen, Arthur M.; Palmer, James C.; and Zwemer, K. Diane. *Key Resources on Community Colleges: A Guide to the Field and Its Literature.* San Francisco: Jossey-Bass, 1986. 522 pages.

During the past two decades, the community college has taken an essential place in the collection of institutions making up higher education in the United States. During this time of institutional growth, the literature on community colleges has also grown. This volume presents a comprehensive search and careful sample of the literature on the junior and community college from the past twenty years—a time period that also corresponds to the two-decade life of the Educational Resources Information Center (ERIC) Clearinghouse for Junior Colleges. The bibliographic citations and their abstracts are organized around such themes as students, faculty, governance, administration, planning, financing, budgeting, instruction, student support, and educational programs. Each chapter is introduced by a general statement from the authors about the citations in that chapter. This volume brings together for the first time reference to significant sources of information about community and junior colleges, many of them in the ERIC collection. It should be consulted by anyone interested in the role of the junior and community college in providing postsecondary education for a group of learners often ignored by four-year colleges and universities.

651 Conrad, Clifton F. "Undergraduate Instruction." In H. E. Mitzel (ed.), *Encyclopedia of Educational Research.* (5th ed.) New York: Free Press, 1982, pp. 1963–1973.

Please see entry no. 220 for the annotation of this work.

652 Dressel, Paul L., and Pratt, Sally B. *The World of Higher Education: An Annotated Guide to the Major Literature.* San Francisco: Jossey-Bass, 1971. 238 pages.

Not quite as broad as it appears from the title, this volume arose out of an interest in institutional research. It "reviews research relevant to understanding and making decisions about higher education problems." The seven chapters cover such topics as students, faculty and staff, curriculum and instruction, and related bibliographies and other reference materials. Several hundred items are given descriptive and sometimes evaluative annotations. This publication also contains a title and an author index.

★653 Dunkin, Michael J. "Research on Teaching in Higher Education." In M. C. Wittrock (ed.), *Handbook of Research on Teaching.* (3rd ed.) New York: Macmillan, 1986, pp. 754–777.

Please see entry no. 224 for the annotation of this work.

★654 Eells, Walter C. *College Teachers and College Teaching: An Annotated Bibliography on College and University Faculty Members and Instructional Methods* (with Supplements). Atlanta: Southern Regional Education Board, 1957, 1959, 1962, 1967.

The expected growth in the need for college teachers prompted this bibliographic project, which covers literature from approximately the mid 1950s to the mid 1960s. The two major sections cover college teachers (recruitment and selection, instructional status) and college teaching (changing conditions, teaching methods in general, teaching methods in special fields). Books, periodicals, and dissertations are listed with informative three- or four-sentence annotations. Items of exceptional importance are designated. The basic work holds 2,665 entries, and the supplements hold 1,103, 1,888, and 1,364 items, respectively. These well-indexed works are indispensable for researchers wishing to place their own work in historical perspective.

655 Fulkerson, Frank E., and Wise, Paula S. "Annotated Bibliography on the Teaching of Psychology: 1986." *Teaching of Psychology,* 1987, *14,* 250–256.

These annotated bibliographies have appeared periodically over a number of years in this journal. This particular article includes items numbered 2,512 through 2,668, listed alphabetically by author.

656 Gardiner, John J. (ed.). *ASHE Handbook on Teaching and Instructional Resources: An Instructional Resource Handbook for Courses in the Field of Higher Education.* Washington, D.C.: Association for the Study of Higher Education, 1987. 164 pages.

Please see entry no. 19 for the annotation of this work.

657 Goldsmid, Charles A., and Goldsmid, Paula L. "The Teaching of Sociology, 1981: Review and Annotated Bibliography." *Teaching Sociology,* 1982, *9,* 327–352.

The sixth in a series of annual compilations, this bibliography includes more than seventy items, annotated and listed alphabetically by the authors. A ten-page analytical essay precedes the entries.

★658 Good, Carter V. *Teaching in College and University: A Survey of the Problems and Literature in Higher Education.* Baltimore, Md.: Warwick and York, 1929. 557 pages.

Please see entry no. 22 for the annotation of this work.

659 Good, Carter V. "Colleges and Universities: Methods of Teaching." In Walter S. Monroe (ed.), *Encyclopedia of Educational Research*. New York: Macmillan, 1941, pp. 242-248.

Please see entry no. 228 for the annotation of this work.

660 Halstead, D. Kent (ed.). *Higher Education: A Bibliographic Handbook*. Vol. 2. Washington, D.C.: U.S. Government Printing Office, 1981. 641 pages.

Associate editors for each of twenty-two chapters selected items for annotation and discussion. Annotations run about half a page, and each chapter has a brief introduction defining its topic and explaining its organization. In all, there are 631 entries for items published from 1961 to 1981. Pertinent chapters include community colleges (A. Cohen), curriculum (A. Chickering), educational communications and technology (J. Brown), faculty (K. Mortimer and E. Ladd), lifelong learning (R. Peterson), and teaching and learning (W. McKeachie and S. Ericksen). This publication includes author, title, and publisher indexes.

661 Halstead, D. Kent (ed.). *Higher Education: A Bibliographic Handbook*. Vol. 1. Washington, D.C.: U.S. Government Printing Office, 1984. 750 pages.

Although published several years after Volume Two (the preceding entry), this volume was actually planned first. It is similar in format to the second volume and contains eighteen chapters with about 700 entries annotating items originally published from 1960 to approximately 1981. Pertinent chapter topics include educational opportunity (K. P. Cross), history (F. Rudolph), philosophy (K. Benne), and student characteristics and development (A. Astin).

★662 Halstead, Kent (ed.). *Higher Education Bibliography Yearbook, 1987*. Washington, D.C.: Research Associates of Washington, 1987. 416 pages.

The first in a projected annual series, this yearbook notes 215 books and journal articles "of greatest interest and value to the generalist and practitioner" that were published during 1986, with a few from 1985. About 100 scholars, assigned to thirty-four topic areas, prepared one- or two-page summaries of each item. Most relevant to this volume are sections on teaching and learning (five entries), curriculum (three entries), faculty (five entries), student characteristics and development (one entry), community colleges (five entries), and adult and continuing education (four items). Among other major sections are those on institutions and on state and national issues. There is brief descriptive information about other bibliographies, ERIC, and sources for literature review and synthesis. A directory of scholars who contributed to the book and an author index are also included. This series promises to be a valuable, highly selective complement to the broad coverage of *Higher Education Abstracts*.

663 Klapper, Paul (ed.). *College Teaching: Studies in Methods of Teaching in the College*. Yonkers-on-Hudson, N.Y.: World Book, 1920. 583 pages.

Please see entry no. 31 for the annotation of this work.

664 Leitner, Erich. "Selective Bibliographies on Research into Higher Education: An International Inventory." *Higher Education*, 1978, 7, 311–330.

Three hundred bibliographies from all over the world are listed alphabetically by author. English and German titles are most numerous. Japan and Poland are also fairly well covered. All but three items were published between 1956 and 1977.

665 McCord, Michael T. "Methods and Theories of Instruction." In John C. Smart (ed.), *Higher Education: Handbook of Theory and Research*. Vol. 1. New York: Agathon Press, 1985, pp. 97–131.

Please see entry no. 233 for the annotation of this work.

666 McKeachie, Wilbert J. "Research on Teaching at the College and University Level." In N. L. Gage (ed.), *Handbook of Research on Teaching.* Skokie, Ill.: Rand-McNally, 1963, pp. 1118–1172.

Please see entry no. 234 for the annotation of this work.

667 McKeachie, Wilbert J., and Kulik, James A. "Effective College Teaching." *Review of Research in Education,* 1975, *3,* 165–209.

Please see entry no. 236 for the annotation of this work.

★668 McKeachie, Wilbert J.; Pintrich, Paul R.; Lin, Y.; and Smith, D. *Teaching and Learning in the College Classroom: A Review of the Research Literature.* Ann Arbor: National Center for Research on Improving Postsecondary Teaching and Learning, University of Michigan, 1986. 106 pages.

Please see entry no. 237 for the annotation of this work.

669 MacKenzie, Norman I.; Eraut, Michael; and Jones, Hywel C. *Teaching and Learning: An Introduction to New Methods and Resources in Higher Education.* (2nd ed.) Paris: UNESCO, 1976. 224 pages.

Please see entry no. 37 for the annotation of this work.

670 Marshall, James D., and Durst, Russel K. "Annotated Bibliography of Research in the Teaching of English." *Research in the Teaching of English,* 1987, *21,* 202–221.

This annual bibliography presents items in four categories: writing, language, literature, and teacher education. Each entry includes a one-sentence annotation. The 1987 bibliography consists of 169 items covering all levels of education.

★671 Mathis, B. Claude. "Faculty Development." In Harold E. Mitzel (ed.), *Encyclopedia of Educational Research.* (5th ed.) New York: Free Press, 1982, pp. 646–655.

Please see entry no. 522 for the annotation of this work.

672 Mayhew, Lewis B. *The Literature of Higher Education, 1971.* San Francisco: Jossey-Bass, 1971. 162 pages.

This is the first of two hardcover annual "reflections on the higher education literature." The author begins with a thirty-page essay covering literature from 1965 through 1970. Each of nine other chapters critically annotates pertinent items on selected topics: campus unrest, teaching, curriculum, history, and so on. The volume catches the highlights of then-current higher education literature in a convenient and readable format. It includes a title and an author index.

673 Mayhew, Lewis B. *The Literature of Higher Education, 1972.* San Francisco: Jossey-Bass, 1972. 184 pages.

In this second of two annual volumes, critically annotated entries are gathered under such chapter titles as "Students and Their Affairs," "Faculty and Their Affairs," "Curricular and Instructional Concerns," "Bibliographies," and "Student Protest: End of an Era?" While not claiming to contain everything that appeared during that year, the author's selection appears to be representative and the annotations are lucid. A title and an author index are included.

674 Meeth, L. Richard (ed.). *Selected Issues in Higher Education: An Annotated Bibliography.* New York: Teachers College Press, 1965. 212 pages.

More than 1,200 entries are listed and briefly annotated, covering all areas of higher education. A few items concern precollege education, and some project reports and dissertations are included. The thirty-nine sections touch on several aspects of administration, governance, and finance and on faculty development (twenty-two items), curriculum development (twenty-five), evaluation of a college education (eighteen), improvement of instruction (fifty-four), and class size (twenty-eight). An author index is included.

675 Miller, Richard I. *Developing Programs for Faculty Evaluation: A Sourcebook for Higher Education*. San Francisco: Jossey-Bass, 1974. 248 pages.

Please see entry no. 194 for the annotation of this work.

676 Parker, Franklin, and Parker, Betty J. *U.S. Higher Education: A Guide to Information Sources*. Education Information Guide Series, vol. 9. Detroit, Mich.: Gale Research Company, 1980. 675 pages.

This alphabetical listing of 3,194 books and reports on higher education in the United States seeks to include "the most important 19th-century works and to approach comprehensive inclusion of 20th-century works, particularly those published since World War II." An author index of thirty pages, a title index of fifty-four pages, and a subject index of seventy-five pages lead the user to entries of interest. For example, twenty-five items are listed under "curriculum," twenty-two under "teaching methods," forty-six under "college teachers, fiction about," and twenty-nine under "college teaching, improvement of." The volume is especially valuable because it includes reports not commercially published.

677 Payne, Fernandus, and Spieth, Evelyn W. *An Open Letter to College Teachers*. Bloomington, Ind.: Principia Press, 1935. 380 pages.

Please see entry no. 43 for the annotation of this work.

678 Quay, Richard H. *Index to Anthologies on Postsecondary Education, 1960–1978*. Westport, Conn.: Greenwood Press, 1980. 342 pages.

Two hundred and eighteen anthologies are listed, and each chapter in them is cited under appropriate headings. These thirty-one headings include philosophy of postsecondary education, faculty, planning and policy development, minorities and women, legal issues, and so on. Only 13 percent of the chapters in the anthologies listed here are reprinted essays, so most of them would not be found in standard sources. Coverage of anthologies is comprehensive, although two deliberate exclusions should be noted: Several anthologies on student activism are omitted, as are the Jossey-Bass sourcebooks.

679 Quay, Richard H. *Research in Higher Education: A Guide to Source Bibliographies.* (2nd ed.) Phoenix, Ariz.: Oryx Press, 1985. 133 pages.

This second edition of Quay's bibliography contains all but twenty of the original items and adds many new ones, most of them institutional publications or ERIC documents. The 932 items are classified into fifteen sections. Most pertinent to this volume are the following: comprehensive sources, students, faculty, curriculum and instruction, an appendix on higher education as a field of study, and a directory of higher education research centers and advanced study programs. Author and subject indexes are included.

680 Rochte, Newton C. "Recurrent Education." *Educational Documentation and Information,* 1980, *54* (215), 1–107.

This issue of the UNESCO journal is devoted to a bibliography on the topic of recurrent education. Recurrent education is defined to include education and training at various levels, formal and informal, distributed over the life span in a recurring way. Most of the nearly 400 annotated entries are listed by the region of the world in which they were published. An author index is included.

681 Schuster, Marilyn R., and Van Dyne, Susan R. *Women's Place in the Academy: Transforming the Liberal Arts Curriculum.* Totowa, N.J.: Rowman & Allanheld, 1985. 328 pages.

Please see entry no. 452 for the annotation of this work.

★**682** Stark, Joan S., and Lowther, Malcolm A. *Designing the Learning Plan: A Review of Research and Theory Related to College Curricula.* Ann Arbor: National Center for Research to Improve Postsecondary Teaching and Learning, University of Michigan, 1987. 88 pages.

Please see entry no. 430 for the annotation of this work.

683 Teather, David C. B. *Staff Development in Higher Education: An International Review and Bibliography.* New York: Nichols, 1979. 336 pages.

For purposes of this bibliography, the term *staff development* covers faculty competence in "teaching and examining, research and research supervision, consultancy and administration; it also applies to administrative, technical, and clerical staff." The review is organized by country; each chapter covers one of twelve countries, accounting for about 250 pages. Approximately thirty pages are devoted to references. There are also a list of centers and associations, a subject index, and an author index.

684 Thielens, Wagner, Jr. "Teacher-Student Interaction, Higher Education: Student Viewpoint." In L. C. Deighton (ed.), *The Encyclopedia of Education.* Vol. 9. New York: Macmillan, 1971, pp. 54–63.

Please see entry no. 244 for the annotation of this work.

685 Trent, James W., and Cohen, Arthur M. "Research on Teaching in Higher Education." In R.M.W. Travers (ed.), *Second Handbook of Research on Teaching.* Skokie, Ill.: Rand McNally, 1973, pp. 997–1071.

Please see entry no. 246 for the annotation of this work.

686 White, Jane N., and Burnett, Collins W. (eds.). *Higher Education Literature: An Annotated Bibliography.* Phoenix, Ariz.: Oryx Press, 1981. 177 pages.

Of the six major sections of this 1,618-item bibliography, two are of special interest for this key resources volume. The section on teaching-learning environments contains 442 items, and the section on higher education as a field of study consists of 8 items. Each item is descriptively annotated in a sentence or two. Periodicals are not included. The ten appendixes include lists of reference sources, journals, higher education programs of study, associations, and publisher. Author and subject indexes complete the book.

7

Key Trends and Issues
for Research and Practice

If visitors from a hundred years ago were to appear at our colleges and universities, they would be truly astonished. Facilities today are spacious, and much campus architecture is grandly conceived and dramatically executed. There has been an impressive increase in the number of persons who teach and administer these institutions, in their knowledge of academic specialties, and in their familiarity with management practices. The proportion of our citizens taking courses and seeking degrees is higher than ever before. Offerings are diversified; something is available for nearly everyone. Students pursue their learning in a variety of ways, both inside and outside the classroom.

Discerning visitors would also find reasons for concern. Facilities are rarely fully utilized and sometimes poorly maintained. Not infrequently, bureaucratic management impedes rather than facilitates teaching and learning. Few professors are trained as teachers, and at many institutions they spend much of their time in activities that have little to do with students. Nearly all learning is teacher-directed rather than self-initiated or collaborative. Typical students are less well prepared for higher learning. Their career values are inconsistent with the intellectual reflection they are expected to pursue. Despite considerable diversity in curriculum, little attention is given to non-Western cultures and to modes of knowing other than narrow cognitive rationality. The curriculum lacks logic and coherence, even in the opinions of those who have created it.

Researching this book has exposed us to provocative ideas, stimulating proposals, and exciting experiments. Although much

360

more needs to be learned, there already exists an impressive base of knowledge for improving practices. In this chapter, we comment on some of the trends apparent in the literature, and we identify some areas for scholarly attention in the future.

Diversity and Fragmentation

The literature on teaching, learning, curriculum, and faculty development leaves an indelible impression of enormous diversity, even of fragmentation. This literature is often unwieldy; it needs middle-range theoretical constructs to unify themes emerging from the individual pieces. Many of these research reports, summaries of studies, commentaries, and personal opinions seem to be independent of scholarship in other areas. Thus, teaching stands alone, as do learning, the curriculum, and the faculty. In our view, teaching, learning, curriculum, and faculty must be seen as interacting elements in the broader universe of higher education.

We contend that these areas are best studied when their impact is viewed as multiplicative rather than additive. No single area is sufficient; without each of them, there is nothing. One might concentrate research and scholarship on a single area, but implications should be viewed in the context of other areas of study, rather than within discrete and independent subsystems. The scholar who studies teaching should view results in terms of relationships: teaching as an influence on learning, the meaning of teaching in the context of a curriculum, and the role of the faculty member as teacher. Such scholarship is hard to sustain in a society that prizes fragmented specializations with their independent information systems.

Networks and Organizations

The study of higher education has not yet diversified organizationally in ways characteristic of more mature fields of study. Although the number of persons publishing in the field is increasing, the two major research networks, the Division on Postsecondary Education of the American Educational Research

Association (AERA) and the Association for the Study of Higher Education (ASHE), are still small enough to permit rewarding interchange.

National centers supported by the federal government provide another context for diffusion and communication. The National Center for Research to Improve Postsecondary Teaching and Learning at the University of Michigan, for example, has brought together scholars interested in issues and problems about teaching, learning, curriculum, and faculty in an environment that recognizes the interactive nature of these educational processes. Such centers and their dissemination functions are vulnerable, however, because of uncertain support from external funding agencies.

Membership in AERA's Division on Postsecondary Education and in the Association for the Study of Higher Education is increasing. The number of persons viewing themselves as specialists in higher education will continue to increase as will the number of doctoral programs in higher education. Expansion can be positive when scholars and researchers are linked across institutional and disciplinary boundaries. On the other hand, specialization may produce smaller programs with researchers whose interests do not span the spectrum of problems and issues found in larger and more eclectic graduate programs. Expansion in numbers would then exacerbate compartmentalization.

Graduate Training

Growth in the number of doctoral programs implies that higher education as a field of study has found some independence from the disciplines that traditionally nurture research about colleges and universities. These historic disciplinary links are apparent in the literature, with sociology and sociologists having a claim to owning research about the faculty. Psychology has influenced research about teaching and learning, and the study of curriculum has been in the hands of a wide range of disciplinarians, particularly those in the humanities.

These links with the social sciences are beginning to loosen as the field of higher education develops its own identity. The field continues to be concerned about rigor and sophistication of training in research, and many research skills are derived from the basic disciplines. One distinctive aspect of the field is the problem of the relationship between knowledge and practice. Because persons who seek graduate degrees in higher education do so for many reasons other than to become research scholars in academic settings, the issue of knowledge as a basis for practice will continue to be of widespread concern.

To accompany the greater sophistication of research in higher education, the field may well see less independent scholarship and more collaborative efforts involving scholars with different training, bringing multiple perspectives to the problems being studied. Studies of curriculum, for example, could examine issues of emergence, application, and outcome as parts of a single process rather than as discrete elements. Training programs should be interdisciplinary in scope, involving a wide range of scholars who can serve as models for those entering the profession.

Program models should require scholars to interact and collaborate frequently and informally. Professional associations provide these opportunities, but only infrequently. One approach is to pool talent in appropriate geographical regions. Cooperative efforts among institutions, especially those in urban areas, would do much to provide a broader base of scholarship for graduate students in higher education than is possible in individual institutions.

Topics for Further Research

Many problems and issues stand out from this literature as beacons to guide further research. Some light the path to the future more brightly than others. For example, the balance between vocationalism and the liberal arts continues to stimulate controversy and to require illumination. Tensions between the vocational demands of students and the economic needs of colleges and universities could keep scholars busy for some time. The question of what constitutes liberal education in an environment where economic motives dominate both those who are served and those who provide the service calls for, at best, a revision of definitions and objectives. Recent literature on this topic raises more questions than it answers; research is sparse and sometimes irrelevant.

The changing nature of the academic workplace has already led to ambivalence about academic careers. This includes both those who are practicing scholars and those who contemplate the academic life. If present trends continue, the faculty role will be quite different in the next century from what it has been in the past. What were first seen as irritants in academic careers have now become common in our workplace. For an example, consider the conflict between merit and market in determining a faculty member's worth. As average salaries increase, the differences in averages between fields also increase. How to maintain equity among the disciplines and professional fields and at the same time compete for the best talent available becomes a problem of Solomon-like proportions. Rather than addressing merely the symptoms of changes in career patterns for faculty, research needs to delve into the causes of discontent in academe and to assess potential solutions. Rewards for faculty, other than salary, for supporting morale and stimulating productivity is a topic especially worthy of further study.

Studies tell us that the need for new faculty in the next twenty-five years will be greater than at any time in the history of higher education in this country. These persons will enter a very different work environment than did the academics whose retirements have created the openings. For one thing, they face a different mix of learners. Faculty who started their careers during the growth years of the 1950s and 1960s learned to teach undergraduates who had little experience in the "real" world, but by 1992 it is estimated that half of all college students will be over twenty-five years of age (Hodgkinson, 1985). How teaching methods and grading practices are best adapted to serve these new learners is not yet clear.

College campuses may become even less collegial, in terms of professional interactions between scholars in disparate disciplines, and economic issues relating to outside funding may intensify. The economics of higher education and the marketplace, together with consumerism and vocationalism in students, have eroded opportunities for the freedom and self-determination that were implicit in academic careers. These and other issues challenge researchers to engage in inquiries that are increasingly interdisciplinary, that consider the problems under study within defensible theoretical frameworks, and that bring multivariate analyses to the processing of data.

Studies relating management techniques to the quality of education in colleges and universities are also needed. The increasing influence of corporate management approaches on decision making and the patterns of allocation of resources are often defended in terms of balanced budgets and stable tuition costs. More investigation is needed to find the best balance between effectiveness and efficiency in maintaining and improving quality in educational programs. Future researchers in higher education must be able to relate the several domains of study that impinge on this issue of quality.

Regarding teaching and learning, one topic deserving study is the subtlety of roles that students and teachers play. Among the counterproductive roles sometimes taken are faculty assuming responsibility for students' learning and students attempting to convey an appearance of interest and motivation that is insincere. These roles change with circumstances and with external pressures in ways that are little understood but are critical for effective teaching and learning. Multivariate research in naturalistic settings is essential for understanding such roles, for investigating the circumstances that influence them, and for discovering how they might be modified.

We also need close study of assumptions faculty make about processes of teaching and learning in light of findings from cognitive science and philosophical analysis. It seems probable, for example, that most professors assume a causal relationship between their teaching and student learning. But, as Fenstermacher (1986) points out, the relationship is ontological rather than causal. The student's role, he says, is to perform the tasks of learning and the teacher's role is to help students better perform those tasks. How might our research and practice change if we took seriously implications of the notion that, as he puts it, "a critical task of teaching is to enable the student to perform the tasks of learning" (Fenstermacher, 1986, p. 39)?

A greater variety of settings for teaching and learning

deserves investigation. Most research takes place in the lecture hall and in lecture classes. How similar are the educational processes occurring in peer study groups, at tutorials, around laboratory tables, in studios and practice rooms, at the computer keyboard, and so on? These settings are worthy of study in order to contrast them with more frequently studied classroom settings and to determine how learners and teachers can make optimal use of them.

Methods for Future Research

Methods appropriate for investigating these issues are not the methods typically used by laboratory investigators. Methods must fit the natural environment of academic workplaces and study places. Research procedures must be sufficiently flexible to accommodate frames of reference possibly quite different from those initially held by researchers. Data should be collected from dialogue, since inquiry is itself an interactive teaching-learning encounter. Discussion of results from such research may well be more elaborative than reductive, and conclusions are likely to be more suggestive than definitive.

Much of the literature covered by this volume reflects early applications of experimental methods to classroom research as part of the positivist's search for generalizable laws of behavior as well as the scientists' search for prediction and control. This positivist paradigm is now in disrepute, and there is no agreement at this time on a paradigm with which to replace it. There is no need to delay, however, in exploring complementary approaches.

The Interpretive Approach. We find compelling what has been called the interpretive approach (Rabinow and Sullivan, 1979). To use an interpretive approach is to emphasize multiple meanings rather than fixed findings, in particular to seek meanings for events that are held by the persons being studied; to search for understanding and insight rather than for prediction and control; to explicate particular contexts rather than to discover universal generalizations; and to attend to the intentional and value-laden aspects of human action and interaction.

The interpretive approach is characterized by Neugarten in this way: "The study of the human world can never be context-free;

the observer can never stand outside his subject-matter but must always share the context of cultures, languages, and symbols that constitute that world. In this view the observer stands within the same circles of human meaning as do the objects of his studies, and there is no outside, detached standpoint from which to gather observations. . . . Social scientists are all caught in a hermeneutic circle: Ultimately a good explanation is one that makes sense of the behavior we see, but what makes sense is itself based on the kinds of sense we can make. In different words, there is no 'objective' nor absolute verification procedure to fall back on. We can only continue to offer interpretations" (1985, p. 292).

Studies of professors' assumptions about teaching and learning, for example, become radically transformed under this approach. When viewed through the interpretive lens, what do we make of faculty declarations about "objective standards of grading" and how do we react when faculty offer apologies for "making a value judgment"?

One suitable way to exercise the interpretive approach, to capture meanings that people give to events, is through analysis of their verbal reports. Conversations and relatively unstructured interviews can retain the spontaneity of improvised communication. Responses to fixed, written questions may also be useful; they can take the form of short essays or be spoken and later transcribed. Once entered for computer analysis, verbal reports may be examined in a variety of ways.

When respondents formulate these reports, they are constructing narratives about their experience. It appears that even complex experiences and sequences of experiences can be captured coherently in this way. Bruner (1987), for example, has been studying a topic that is literally as large as life itself by asking people to tell the stories of their lives, constrained by a thirty-minute time limit. His research is actually less about lives as such than about how people view, construe, and even guide their lives. "I believe that the ways of telling and the ways of conceptualizing that go with them become so habitual that they finally become recipes for structuring experience itself, for laying down roots into memory, for not only guiding the life narrative up to the present but directing it into the future" (p. 31).

A narrative study about faculty life or about classroom experiences is likewise less about what actually occurs than about how the actors perceive events and relationships. For example, in one study (Menges and Kulieke, 1984) we asked students to describe classroom incidents they found satisfying and others they found dissatisfying. When these accounts were examined, there seemed to be few differences between the two categories and little similarity within them, until particular features of the course were examined. Then it became clear that satisfying incidents tended to occur in courses where there was greater consistency in such features as teaching method, class size, and instructional objectives. (A simple example of consistency would be using the lecture method in a large class where the teacher's goal is information transmission.) In classes where unsatisfactory incidents occurred, consistency was less likely. A study not incorporating narratives would probably have missed these relationships, since they were not part of the framework from which the study was originally designed.

The interpretive approach can employ a variety of techniques. Students may be asked to construct problems or to solve them (intellectual tasks), or they may be presented with tasks calling for communication or interaction with others (social tasks). Faculty may be asked to recount the decisions they make while designing instruction or while engaged in teaching. The resulting records take narrative form: commentaries about events as the events unfold or as stimulated by playing a recording. Alternatively, the narrative may be in response to structured but ambiguous stimuli, such as drawings and photographs used in Thematic Apperception and Rorschach Tests.

At other times, investigators themselves may stimulate events of interest deliberately and openly. For example, it is important to know how people go about increasing the quality and quantity of student contributions to class discussions. To study that problem, a researcher would work with other teachers and students who share the goal. Thoughts and behaviors of each of them, including the investigator, would be documented, circumstances facilitating or inhibiting change would be noted, and consequences would be ascertained. For these studies, the researcher participates in events that are intended to induce change. Such research is an important counter to approaches where investigators keep their distance, merely documenting the status quo.

When there is reason to think that verbal reports are less than complete or candid or when more extensive contextual information is desired, data from other sources should be added to verbal reports. Detailed descriptions of behavior and of the context in which behavior occurs are appropriate for this purpose. The family of research methods known as participant observation is consistent with the interpretive approach. Erickson characterizes these methods as being most interested "in human meaning in social life and in its elucidation and exposition by the researcher" (1986, p. 119).

Decision-Oriented Studies. Much of the literature in areas covered by this volume is oriented toward decision making. Data are gathered about learners, courses, programs, and teachers in order to inform decisions about grading them, revising them, continuing or terminating them, and so on. Findings are used proactively to bring about improvement and retroactively to judge the worth of contributions made by people and programs.

Decision-oriented studies can reveal antecedent and consequent conditions and seek evidence about relationships between them, although attempts to establish causal relationships are misguided. The conclusions to be regarded with greatest confidence are more likely to emerge from patterns suggested by the data than from statistical tests of hypotheses.

A widely known approach to evaluation studies, naturalistic inquiry, is consistent with this view. This approach "focuses upon the multiple realities that, like layers of an onion, nest within or complement one another. Each layer provides a different perspective of reality, and none can be considered more 'true' than any other. Phenomena do not converge into a single form, a single 'truth,' but diverge into many forms, multiple 'truths.' Moreover, the layers cannot be described or understood in terms of separate independent and dependent variables; rather, they are intricately interrelated to form a pattern of 'truth.' It is these patterns that must be searched out, less for the sake of prediction and control than for the sake of *verstehen* or understanding" (Guba and Lincoln, 1981, p. 57).

The naturalistic approach requires that information be gathered in a variety of forms from a variety of sources. An aggregate pool of information does not lead to one inevitable conclusion or decision. Instead it leads to understanding and perhaps to more enlightened decisions. The decisions are also likely to be more credible since the parties in the activity being studied will have participated in the process of determining its future.

Regardless of labels used, we affirm the guiding principle that the method be regarded as the servant of the question being asked. No approach is proscribed. It is no more correct to say that all inquiry is fully served by ethnographic methods than it is to say that all inquiry is fully served by methods of positivist science. We encourage productive variety so that research approaches are properly matched with the issues under study.

The Double-Edged Conservatism of Higher Education

Like other institutions, colleges and universities reflect social conditions and trends of their times. They are essentially conservative institutions.

Clark Kerr places this observation within the stream of history. "About eighty-five institutions in the Western world established by 1500 still exist in recognizable forms, with similar functions and with unbroken histories, including the Catholic church, the Parliaments of the Isle of Man, of Iceland, and of Great Britain, several Swiss cantons, and seventy universities. Kings that rule, feudal lords with vassals, and guilds with monopolies are all gone. These seventy universities, however, are still in the same locations with some of the same buildings, with professors and students doing much the same things, and with governance carried on in much the same ways" (1982, p. 24).

The remarkable stability of institutions of higher education, especially the research universities of which Kerr writes, has two edges. One is higher education's glory: the capacity to transmit from generation to generation the best and most enduring aspects of society and culture. The other edge, less welcome, resists adapting to the changing circumstances of students, faculty, and institutional life and hesitates to modify the substance and skills being transmitted, even when there exists knowledge to guide such change.

Our plea is for greater diversity of theoretical assumptions and of research approaches and greater tolerance for innovative practices, so that an analysis of higher education literature twenty years hence will reveal key resources both more defensible in substance and more effective in application than those we identified for this volume.

References

Bruner, J. "Life as Narrative." *Social Research*, 1987, *54*, 11-32.

Erickson, F. "Qualitative Methods in Research on Teaching." In M. C. Wittrock (ed.), *Handbook of Research on Teaching*. (3rd ed.) New York: Macmillan, 1986.

Fenstermacher, G. D. "Philosophy of Research on Teaching: Three Aspects." In M. C. Wittrock (ed.), *Handbook of Research on Teaching*. (3rd ed.) New York: Macmillan, 1986.

Guba, E. G., and Lincoln, Y. S. *Effective Evaluation: Improving the Usefulness of Evaluation Results Through Responsive and Naturalistic Approaches*. San Francisco: Jossey-Bass, 1981.

Hodgkinson, H. L. *All One System: Demographics of Education-Kindergarten Through Graduate School*. Washington, D.C.: Institute for Educational Leadership, 1985.

Kerr, C. "Postscript 1982." *Change*, 1982, *14* (7), 23-31.

Menges, R. J., and Kulieke, M. J. "Satisfaction and Dissatisfaction in the College Classroom." *Higher Education*, 1984, *13*, 255-264.

Neugarten, B. L. "Interpretive Social Science and Research on Aging." In A. S. Rossi (ed.), *Gender and the Life Course*. Hawthorne, N.Y.: Aldine, 1985.

Rabinow, P., and Sullivan, W. M. (eds.). *Interpretive Social Science: A Reader*. Berkeley: University of California Press, 1979.

Name Index

Subject Index

A

AAHE Bulletin, 9, 24, 26, 61, 106, 110, 341

AAHE-ERIC Reports: on curriculum, 217, 226, 227; on faculty development, 293; on learning, 153, 170, 174; on teaching, 80, 82, 87, 116

AAUP Bulletin, 86, 139, 317

Aberdeen University, learning processes at, 177

Abt Books, classic work from, 337

Academe, 101, 297, 341

Academic achievement game, 177

Academic freedom: and faculty development, 290, 296; and learners, 139, 154-155; and McCarthyism, 325

Accent on Developing Abstract Processes of Thought (ADAPT), 66

Accountability, and faculty development, 290

Action science, and faculty evaluation, 98

Active learning: guidelines for, 24-25, 26, 34-35, 43-44; research on, 125-126; and student involvement, 207-208; teaching methods for, 55, 73

Administrative Science Quarterly, 280

Adult development: and career development, 298; and faculty de-velopment, 266, 269; and faculty development as individual, 260, 320, 321; and older students, 148, 149, 151-152, 165, 170-171

Adult Education (UK), 342

Adult Education (US), 342

Adult Leadership, 342

Adult students: development of, 148, 149, 151-152, 165, 170-171; and faculty development, 281; learning processes of, 136, 175-176, 178, 179, 184, 187-188; and self-directed learning, 82, 178; teaching methods for, 82. *See also* Continuing education

Adults, success of, and learner evaluation, 188-189

Aging, and faculty development, 267, 272, 287-288

Alternative Higher Education, 343

Alverno College, competency-based education at, 106

American Academy of Arts and Sciences, 206-207, 262-263

American Academy of Political and Social Sciences, 262

American Army University (France), 305

American Association for Higher Education (AAHE), 4, 206, 257, 298. *See also AAHE Bulletin; AAHE-ERIC Reports*

American Association of Colleges for Teacher Education, 86

for, 52, 54-55, 64, 69, 70, 71. *See also* Small group interaction
Dissertation Abstracts International, 346
Dissertation Abstracts Online Service, 346
Distance education: and curriculum innovation, 242; teaching methods for, 63, 69
Division on Postsecondary Education, 361-362
Dr. Fox effect, in student ratings, 17, 85, 92, 105, 108
Doctor of Arts, 116, 314
Doubleday, classic work from, 282
Dublin University, learning evaluation at, 190

E

Earlham College, student development at, 148
EARTHNET, 79
Eckerd College, and aging faculty, 288
Economics: learning evaluation in, 193; simulations for, 81
Education Commission of the States, 242
Education Index, 346, 347
Educational Psychologist, 185
Educational Administration and Supervision, 100, 282
Educational Documentation and Information, 357
Educational Forum, 157
Educational Psychologist, 54, 342
Educational Record, 31, 87, 228, 269, 277, 305, 319, 321, 342
Educational seduction, evaluation of, 17, 85, 92, 105, 108. *See also* Student ratings; Teaching evaluation systems
Educational Technology, 115, 338, 342
Educational Theory, 342
EDUCOM Bulletin, 53, 55, 81
Effort: faculty, 263; of students, and curriculum evaluation, 250-251

Engineering: innovative curricula for, 245; teaching guidelines for, 37; teaching methods for, 72-73
Engineering Education, 342
English courses: bibliography on teaching, 354; learning evaluation in, 195; personal accounts of teaching, 50; sponsorship in, 302. *See also* Composition
Environmental press, and student development, 169
ERIC Clearinghouse for Junior Colleges, 349
ERIC Clearinghouse on Higher Education, 4, 206, 346, 347, 353, 357. *See also* *AAHE-ERIC Reports*; *ASHE-ERIC Reports*
Ethical issues, and faculty development, 291, 292, 296. *See also* Moral development
Ethnography: and curriculum evaluation, 251; and faculty development, 276; and learning process, 181; and research on teaching, 118
Evaluation: bibliographies on, 110, 189, 356; and competence-based programs for faculty, 97; of continuing education, 85, 114; of critical thinking, 92; of curriculum, 204-205, 246-253; and faculty development, 293; and grading, 93, 137, 188-189, 191-192, 194; guides for, 138, 189, 190, 191; and innovation, 19, 89, 91-92, 97-98, 100-101, 104, 116; of learners and learning, 137-138, 188-195; of learning, classic works on, 191-192; mutual benefit, 97; by peers, 46-47; posttenure, 18, 87, 99, 101, 102, 111; reforming, 191-192; self-, 86, 90; settings for, 138, 188, 189, 190, 191, 193, 194, 195; of teaching, 16-19, 85-117; and teaching improvement, 18, 85, 86, 87-88, 89-90, 92, 93, 98, 101, 102, 103, 106, 109, 110, 114, 115-116; and teaching methods, 88. *See also* Student